Truth
Of A
Lost Soul

MATTHEW SANDERS

Truth of a Lost Soul
Matthew Sanders

Published by:
Anointed Words Publishing Company

Email: mail@awpubco.com www.awpubco.com

ISBN: 9781947558045
Printed in the United States of America

Table of Contents

Chapter 1: An Innocent Understanding

As long as I could remember life has always been hard. The constant struggle to submerge above water and breathe carelessly as life is intended has not been easy. Growing up in the city of Oxnard, California, you can learn a lot of things at a young age. At the early stage of life, I quickly learned the value of a dollar, racism, stress, and life choices.

2321 Earhart court was the address I was raised in until I was about eight years old. My grandmother, granddaddy, mother, uncle, three aunts, and two cousins all lived together in a three-bedroom house. At this point in time, this was one of my favorite moments in life. Things were so simple all I had to do was be a kid. The values and morals that were taught to me in this environment would stick with me through life. Little things that my grandmother would say like; "keep your elbows off the table while you eat" or "say your prayers before you sleep," stick out to me like it was yesterday.

My grandmother was a nurse and worked full time at the hospital. In my eyes she's an angel of some kind; her unselfish ways and kindness are extremely rare. My grandfather worked full time as well. To this day, I'm still unsure what type of employment he worked. I was told he worked for the California Highway Patrol station but was not a trooper. Mr. Lee was a man's man, very short tempered but a fair and a logical person.

My mother, Sherry, the oldest of five children was a lot like my grandfather but, secretly, she has the heart of my grandmother. I would call her a jelly bean because she was hard on the outside but soft on the inside. Mom wasn't too young when I was born but still was the tender age of nineteen. But in 1984, times were different than they are today, so she still was very young. It would be obvious that mom was attracted to the sailors since my father, Marvin, was military. Things didn't work out between them, so he sailed away, like the visions of painted dreams hung upon a wall just four months after my birth.

When nine people are living in a three-bedroom house it can be a bit clustered and crazy. For the longest time, it was me, my mom, my aunts Lisa, Natasha, and Trina in the same room. Then my cousin Roshawn was born and I moved into my Uncle Richard's room. Lucky for me my uncle was around eighteen, so he had a job and would be gone most of the time, so it was like I had my own room for the most part. Richard and I are about twelve years apart so when he was around, I would just annoy him and try to be underneath him a lot. My auntie Trina and Uncle Richard are more like brother and sister to me. I think because they were more interactive with me was the reason for the connection that we had.

Earhart court was located in a small area in Oxnard that was called Lemonwood. I went to Lemonwood elementary school which was across the street. It was predominately an all Mexican school. Oxnard city was predominately a Mexican city, so I quickly was aware of race and racism at a young age. I could remember one time in elementary school, I was playing basketball with all the kids at recess and I was doing really well. But because I was a minority, the majority of the kids started to beat me up until I started running. About a third of the playground was chasing me. They eventually caught me and jumped me just because I was black. I quickly learned and thought from that experience that if I was good at something not to stand out at it because it can be trouble waiting for me.

Some of the advantages of growing up around Mexican heritage were learning somewhat of a second language young. I'm not fluent but could hold a small conversation with someone. I came to appreciate the Mexican cuisine and culture. Seeing Mexican people struggle in many ways that black people struggle showed me that we were similar. A lot of Hispanic people in Lemonwood worked in the strawberry field doing hard labor for peanut money. Yet young, I still was very aware of how hard they worked to survive. Some Hispanics would have their own ice cream truck or even walking carts. Their type of ambition to make money would vary from standing on the corner selling flowers and oranges to being the corn man. The corn man was a person who walked around with a shopping cart filled with corn on the cob, mayonnaise, parmesan cheese, and Mexican spices. I think it's called an elote. I have no idea what that combination was called but it was extremely good. Jobs like those have been taken because a fair amount of the Hispanics were illegal immigrants, so they could not provide proper identification to have a tax documented job.

Working for a tax documented job must not have been too great. My uncle would always come home with things from his store that he said he took out the back door. Any type of electronics; you name it he had it. One day he came home with a big stereo system and I asked him how much it cost, and he said more than what my job could pay me so I ganked it.

Uncle Rich taught me if I want something then take it. I'm sure that wasn't his intent but that is what I got from it. When you're young, you see and learn a lot of stuff, your mind is like a sponge and it soaks everything up. I was already very observant and curious in the early stages in life. I was about eight when I saw my first pound of marijuana. Of course, Rich was the person who I saw with it. Richard was watching me and nobody was home but us, and for some odd reason, I walked into our room and I saw him weighing amounts on a scale. I asked him what's that and he told me, Buddha! I didn't think much of it, so I continued to go play but eventually, I would find out what Buddha was.

Being eight years old in the second grade I had the curiosity to find out what this Buddha was with a sense of urgency. The next day on the playground at recess I'm asking kids what's this Buddha stuff that looks like a plant. After several, "I don't knows", I stumbled upon a "my stepdad has some". Shannon, one of the few black kids that went to Lemonwood replies, *my stepdad has some, he keeps it in his drawer. Can you get some?* I asked, and he said, *yeah, I'll bring it tomorrow.*

Shannon was a child that had it bad through life early. His father was killed when he was younger over a drug deal from what I was told. Shannon had Attention Deficit Hyperactivity Disorder (A.D.H.D) way before it was even a popular diagnosed. Short tempered, bad attitude, punch you in the mouth for no reason was Shannon's reputation. So, I quickly became friends with him, so I wouldn't have to know that side.

Tomorrow came and Shannon brings his stepfather's Buddha joints. After school, we walk across the way to the park beside the school and climb up a tree. He lights one joint up and we commence to smoke it. The first time I hit it, my poor little lungs felt like they were going to explode. Shannon took his turns like a champ, so it was obvious that he has done this before. I didn't know what to expect or what to do after smoking. So, I asked him why do people smoke this Buddha? He told me that he guessed it's supposed to make you feel funny or something, but it just makes him mad.

Five minutes elapsed, and I didn't feel any effect, so we sparked the other joint up. Of course, Shannon still taking hits like a champ and little curious me just trying to hang with the big bad wolf. After that last joint, I started to feel really sick and I vomited. I'm glad we weren't up too high in the tree because I fell out vomiting. I landed right on my wrist and I immediately knew it was broken. So, I go home and check in like usual by 2:30pm.

My granddaddy was home and he asked if I wanted to watch the Woody Wood Pecker cartoon, like I do every day at 2:30pm. I said, *no, but can I go outside? I don't have any homework.* Remember this was a time and era where a kid going outside was pretty much mandatory. I proceeded to go play in the front yard but I'm really thinking of an alibi. *I got it.* I will play with my Frisbee and dive for it like a dog. I just came down the wrong way is what I'd say to granddaddy.

I waited about twenty minutes and then I go in and tell him my master plan. Whew, he believed me, I stay in the house until my mom gets home. My mom gets home and takes me to the hospital. I come out with a broken wrist and cast. My mom never did find out what really happened. That was the last encounter I had with marijuana for a few years.

A couple of summers go by and my mom and I move out into our own apartment. Now I'm located in the south side of Oxnard a small area called Port Hueneme. The Dolphin Bay apartment complex was my new home. Dolphin Bay was where I started to gain knowledge of gang members and which gangs were enemies. I liked to think the heart of Oxnard was out south. That was where I learned about the Black Mafia Gangsters (BMG), Colonia Chiques (COXCH), El Rio Chiques (ERXCH), Neighborhood Crips (NHC), Piru Bloods, Lemon Wood Chiques (LWXCH), and South Side Chiques (SSXCH).

I quickly got introduced to the South Side Chiques and Piru Bloods from the relocation of schools. Not only was I a minority to the area which I lived in, but I was a new minority. That means I had to establish myself quickly because I was definitely a target. Day one at the new school I had on some brand new white British Knight shoes. My teacher introduces me to the class and one kid asked *why you wearing those shoes around here?* I said *because I can*; I'm unknowing that these shoes represent something. Recess time rolls around and I'm at the swings, so a couple of kids ask me where I'm from. I say my address where I live; I'm thinking that since these kids were black that they wanted to hang out. Wrong move. The kids thought I was being funny and told me that my shoes represent blood killer and they were Piru Bloods. When they asked where I was from they were hitting me up to find out what gang I banged, not my address. In my reply, it made things worse, so no matter what I said they did not believe me.

These kids took me as a Neighborhood Crip and started to beat me down. My new white shoes were taken off my feet and covered in dirt. I was beaten up, humiliated, and embarrassed on the first day of school. I came home looking like a Vietnam Prisoner of War. My mom asked what happened, but I was so embarrassed that I lied and told her I was playing soccer with the rest of the kids. Lucky for me, I had no bruises on my face, so she believed me. But on the other end of the stick, I messed up my new shoes carelessly, so I had to pay the piper. Of course, my mother whooped me, and it was a good one. You're talking about a first day of school you will never forget.

The next day I go back to school and its recess. I'm playing by the swings again and somehow when I was swinging, a Mexican girl didn't see me, and I kicked her down on accident. She starts crying and some kids come up to me and start the whole hitting me up process again. I tell them I don't bang but they tell me they bang South Side Chiques. Richard, the leader of this little posse, was the spokesman for them and he tells me *I hate black people,* then punches me. I attempted to fight him, but his friends jumped in, so the outcome was nothing pretty. Day two wasn't any better than day one.

Thank the lord for a man named Rodney who happened to get brutally beaten by Los Angeles police that same night. Due to this event, there was the Los Angeles Riots and pure madness was going on. My mom told me *you're not going to school tomorrow,* because of how she explained it, there was pretty much a race war going on. *When you do go back, you don't speak about it at all. If someone asks you what you think, you don't say anything. I mean this Matt, you don't say a damn word even if your teacher asks why you weren't in school, you just say talk to my mom.* My mom said this with so much seriousness and concern you would have thought it was her that got beat down.

I didn't care why I had to stay home, all I knew was, it's one more day to not be a punching bag. When I did go back to school events like those prior ass kicking carried on for a couple of months every three or four days. Eventually, I had to tell my mom what was going on because I couldn't keep going to a school where I was a target like that. I couldn't focus on my school work; I was more concerned with watching my back than learning. Plus, my grades went all the way down, so I had to explain why. The dark came to light and I told my mom everything.

I transferred back to Lemonwood after the summer vacation. I came back with a lot more experience in fighting and gangs. It's been probably half a year since I've seen anybody from this area, so I was more alert to my surrounding and who was next to me. Fortunately, I have no problems like at the other school. As time goes on I start enjoying school again and develop a love for basketball. The kids from school tell me that I should try out for the basketball team. I take their advice and try out. I make the team and I finally start to have friends for the first time. Javier, Shannon, Eric, Ryan, and I were close friends on and off the basketball court. Javier was super athletic, he played sports year-round. Eric was the hotdog on the court, Shannon was the enforcer, Ryan was just an average player, and I was the team captain.

Coach Hammond was my first basketball coach. He reminds me of a country old man who always wore overalls from the south. If I had to guess I would say he was originally from Alabama. His grandson, Henry, who we called "Carnell", was in 7th grade and helped coach the team. Henry was known for being a good shooter, so we listened to him when he tried to teach us the game. As the season came to an end, we all remained close. Shannon, Eric, and I hung out together more than the others. We ended up staying close until we all went to junior high school.

Chapter 2: The Never Ending Start

I moved from Dolphin Bay Apartments to around the corner on Campbell Street, still remaining in the Hueneme area. I went to Black Stock Distinguished Junior High School, home of the Panthers. By this time, my mom had met a man name Joey, who would be my stepfather down the road. It didn't take long for my brother, Jared, to be born in 1994 after they met. Joey had two sides to him, one side he was a man with a good heart and always meant to do right regardless of what the outcome was. He had a special way to show his love and abnormal life wisdom stories, which made him very unique. Joey's other side was dark, selfish, embarrassing, and coldblooded. Joey was a full-blown alcoholic who hid his ways well the first couple of years into our new blended family. My mother would find mini bottles of liquor shots stashed around the apartment often. But she would think nothing of it, she just figured he likes to drink and forgets to throw them away. But eventually, his problem would come to light just like everything else he would do in the dark.

My mother worked two jobs for the majority of my life, so I hardly got to see her growing up. My brother Jared and I were left to be under the supervision of an alcoholic daily. So, as you can imagine, I grew up a lot quicker than the average kid. Having an irresponsible, alcoholic stepfather as my positive male figure was simply a recipe for disaster. Since my brother and I weren't in the best care, it made us really close. I had to learn how to take care of a toddler as if he was my child.

My childhood went completely out the window and adulthood came faster than a wind breeze through the window. Routine feeding schedules, daily operations like getting him dressed, changing diapers, bathing or just playing with him were added to my daily tasks besides school work. Don't get me wrong, my stepfather would attempt to do all he could, but it wouldn't be done right or at the time it was needed. Since I was spending a ridiculous amount of time caring for my little brother at this level, I developed an unconditional type of love for him. Even now in my life it's more of a fatherly love than a brother's love that I have for him.

During the day my mom would take care of my brother, then when I got out of school, it was basically my shift because she would go to work. Going to school would be my time to be a kid and I took full advantage of that. Junior high school is a time and stage in an adolescent's life where you start to notice the world. When noticing the world, curiosity about certain things in the world or about the world can, and usually does, steer a path of who you're becoming or will become. Some of the curiosity that I had was drugs, alcohol, girls, gangs, and money.

Girls were the first thing I got curious about. I started noticing that the girls in my seventh-grade class were starting to have breasts. I immediately knew junior high school was very different from elementary school. I thought, man, this is going to be the best school ever. It seemed like every girl was trying to be older than what they actually were. Girls in junior high would wear too much makeup and the tightest clothes that they could fit themselves into. The Hispanic girls would draw eyebrows on their face, but it wouldn't look like an eyebrow. Usually, the ones that did that wanted to be gang affiliated. The few black girls that my school had would wear "Daisy Dukes", which are a very small pair of shorts that make your booty look bigger. The white girls wore either "Gothic" attire, which was usually all black with safety pins all over the outfit, or they wore spaghetti strap shirts and showed their breast off. Being as curious as I was, I did not discriminate on any of the girls for any reason.

I would attempt to have as many girlfriends as I could at one time. It's safe to say curiosity got the best of me. Since I first started noticing all the different type of girls in the world, I haven't stopped since. At this early adolescent stage in life, I knew that I wanted to be a "Player", which is nothing more than a ladies' man. About the same time that I figured out that I wanted to be a player, a movie called "How to Be a Player" came out. I used to watch this movie all day and night. I would study and practice lines to say and how to say it. As I watch this movie these days, it has no knowledge of how to be a player or give you skills. Back in junior high, I sure thought it did and I would re-enact everything I saw in the movie. The movie was very helpful; it gave me the motivation to talk to girls and what to tell them. I thought I learned to be smooth, how I should dress, and when or what to compliment the girls on.

In seventh grade, I weighed 170 pounds and was approximately 5'9. Since I was really fat as a child, I had to be very tricky at the mouth with my words on the girls. My appearance was not what young girls wanted. It wasn't too hard to manipulate or even be clever with my words on the ladies because I already had to use my mouth as a tool. Being an overweight kid, children can say a lot of cruel things to you especially in junior high. Junior high is when you just start to find out who you are in your peer group. So, I quickly figured out how to change the topic about me and my weight to someone else or something else. Laughing has always been the option because it's a neutral feeling that everyone shares and besides, who doesn't like to laugh? By attacking someone else first or even making fun of me before other kids did so, was a sure way to be out of sight out of mind.

I developed a technique to spare my emotions, feelings, and pride by placing the spotlight on another kid. But before I was this mean kid who would make people cry, I had my share of being picked on just like all the people that I would soon torment. Kids were very heartless on other children's feelings and emotions at school. I was called some of the nastiest of the nasty names before I developed this projection of displacement. I was called a "fat black ashy nigger, fat ass boy with breast, fat Matt, oily crunchy black, Matthew Lamar the black tar," and these are just some of the embarrassing cruel names I've been called as a young overweight child. Children would take turns laughing at me and calling me names. I would stand up for myself as much as a could with the infamous "Yo Momma" jokes. But of course, being a minority and fat, my attempt to protect my pride would fail quickly because I would get into a fight that turned into me versus three other kids.

The day I decided to do something different was the day I became a bully; more like student becomes the teacher. It was lunch time and I was at Lemonwood in the sixth grade, and just like any other day, it's about time for the regular bullies to make their rounds at recess. Ricky and his cousins, Chewy and Nacho, come around and they start making fun of a girl name Maritza. Poor Maritza didn't have a chance. As soon as they start clowning on her, I immediately jump in with them. Maritza was pale, ugly, and stinky and built like an N.F.L. linebacker, so when it was my turn to get on her, I ate her up. The last thing I can remember was that I told her that she looked like the hunchback of Norte Dame.

All the bullies were laughing at her and other kids as well. It was like once I saw the kids giving me hi-fives and telling me I was funny, I knew that I wouldn't go back to being the fat, black, crunchy kid again. If I wanted to stay cool in their eyes and not be the joke, I had to become like them. I started making fun of people on the regular, it was like it was my job or something. It was an adrenaline rush hearing other kids laughing at someone else that wasn't me for the first time.

I started joking and bullying people to keep bullies off of me, but it soon turned into the adrenaline rush of being cool and funny. Every day I wanted to be funnier and meaner than the day before to get a bigger reaction from my crowd and fans that I suddenly had. The name fat Matt quickly went to funny Matt in a matter of two weeks and I loved it. It all seemed so crazy that all those years of being called names and jokes went away in fourteen days. I got good at manipulating people and putting words together in a way that it was smooth, and you didn't even know I was getting over on you or making fun of you. This skill that I developed would stick with me throughout my life and it got me through junior high school better than it probably would have been as an overweight kid.

Having this appearance and weight that I carried in junior high school was a gift and a curse for me with the ladies. The curse was I learned how to be deviant by manipulating people to do things that I wanted them to do by just using my words. By developing tricky or clever wordplay it also taught me how to be cruel to others for my personal benefit. The gift was my smoothness with the girls to hold a conversation and build the trust needed to proceed into sexual contact or conduct.

Chapter 3: The Scientific Method of Manipulation

Girls in junior high school were mostly the same when it came to manipulating them. They all wanted to hear they were pretty, smart, funny, and dressed nice. I would do my best work when I was on the phone with the girls. When being on the phone, I got their full attention and they wouldn't see the image of the fat, black boy. By not having that image of what they didn't want, the girls would get to know me, or in my case, whoever I wanted them to know. By isolating their minds to a vivid picture that I created for them by just wordplay, it gave me the upper hand on this game I was playing.

I learned that girls like boys for different reasons than boys like girls. Boys are more physically attracted than mentally or intellectually. Girls like a boy for his character, feelings, emotions, and all the other stuff that boys don't like girls for. Since I learned that so fast, I developed certain stages to completely take over a girl's mind.

There are three stages that I used to get what I wanted from these girls in junior high school. Stage one was, you always have to come off as just a normal good guy. In the good guy stage, you say nice things and compliment the girls without knowing you're doing it, supposedly. A perfect example would be "hey, how are you doing today gorgeous?" Acknowledging her beauty and being concerned and thoughtful about what's going on with her day, shows that you care about her and you want to get to know her not just because she's pretty. Girls need compliments all the time in junior high school just to feel good about themselves. I always made sure I opened the conversation with a compliment and ended the conversation with one. This gave them the reassurance they needed. Eventually, I would figure out that girls needing compliments just weren't a junior high thing.

Stage two was the dream seller stage. When selling dreams, you always have to make the dreams reachable where you can see yourself doing it and they could see you doing it as well. When selling a dream, I would start with minor things like; when I go to college I want to study zoology. I always picked zoology because girls like animals so that was a winner and it could show a softer side of me. Girls like boys who are not too tough but still can protect them and make them feel safe. Creating a figment of their imagination of a soft but tough boy showed the girls that I had dreams. Having dreams to do better than what's around us in our lives gave me character. Using an achievable goal that's very reachable is something that she can relate to as well. This choice is a win, win topic where you can build something together because now that I said I want to go to college she'll express that she wants to as well. She'll tell you her goals then you can find something in common that she likes and finds interesting. Now she can start to see how different you are compared to other boys. Slowly she'll start to see her made-up boyfriend in her head and that will be this image that I created.

Stage three is the deal sealer stage. When sealing the deal, I already proved to her that I like her for who she is, not for what she looks like, but I still acknowledged her beauty. I painted a vivid picture of what she would like out of her man and who her man should be. Then I'm telling her, as well as showing her, I'm not the average boy in junior high. All of the other boys in junior high were trying to fit in, but me, I always wanted to stand out and now that she sees that I stand out, she wants to stand out with me. Stage three is signed, sealed, and delivered. When using these steps, I would create a different image every time, but as long as I did these three stages, eight out of ten girls would fall for it every time.

Chapter 4: Who Am I?

Gangs were the second thing I started to notice while having these adolescent curiosities about the world. Being raised in California where gangs formed and originated, I've had my encounters with gangsters and want to be gangsters very early in life. The acknowledgment of gangs came three or four years prior to junior high. Now I was in the time of my life where I thought I needed to belong to a gang for safety and just for some good old juvenile delinquency. There were numerous times at school when rival gangs like the South Side Chiques and the Colonial Chiques would fight. I know you're thinking kids fighting couldn't have been that bad, but yes it was. When these rival gangs fought, there would be jimmy bats, bricks, and even sometimes knives. When watching these gangs go at it, I would think, "Damn, I need to get a clique and I need one fast." Well, me being me, I never wanted to fit in, so of course, I had to stand out, this was my motto. Fitting in would be just joining a gang that already existed. That wasn't good enough for me, so I decided to start my own clique, which would eventually turn into somewhat of a gang later on down the road.

Knowing that I needed to start this clique, I was on the hunt for recruitment. I had friends that I would play with at school but not a homie. A homie is a big difference from your ordinary friend; they're above a best friend. A friend is someone you're cool with and hang out with every now and then. A homie is someone you can ride with and do dirt together. It was a mutual loyalty and respect thing. Doing dirt consist of anything that is forbidden by parents and the law. Riding with someone is just being loyal to one another. When you put those two components together you get a homie and a homie is exactly what I needed.

Chapter 5: The Homies

They say good friends don't come around the corner but, in my situation, my first homie was around the shower stall. At Black Stock Junior High School, you had to take a shower after physical education class and they were serious about it. You had to put your towel in the basket next to the gym teacher before you could leave, or you wouldn't make it to your next class. As I finished taking my shower so I could leave for my next class, I heard somebody yelling, *you dumb chink eye, water head motherfucker! If you don't give me my towel so I can get the fuck up out of here I'm going to beat your ass, dog.* I looked over and I saw a long, lanky, six-foot, nappy headed, crusty lip having, ashy motherfucker, fresh out the shower talking big shit to the towel boy, Dindo, who was Asian and didn't speak well. Apparently, this dude didn't get in the shower and Dindo wasn't trying to give him a towel or he would get in trouble from the gym teacher. Dindo kept telling him no towel unless you shower. The tall lanky dude was acting like he couldn't hear him and told Dindo to get closer to the fence. Poor Dindo did so and this guy just set him up to get socked through the fence. I saw what was about to happen, so I watched and sure enough he popped him in the nose then Dindo gave up the towel as I laughed.

I approached this dude and told him, *I like your style what's your name?* He said, *Robert, why nigga?* I told him my name and said, *I have never seen you around before where you from?* He said, *I don't bang, I ball.* I said *me too.* I asked what class he had next and he told me it was Mr. Powers' class. That class was only for eighth graders, then it made sense why I never saw him before. Physical education was the only class that eighth graders, or eight balls are what we called them, could have with seventh graders, or sevies is what they called us. All through the day, the different grades wouldn't see each other because they took their lunch after ours. I told Robert where I lived and to come over after school *since you claim you ball and we could play basketball.*

Kris was a friend that I hung out with from time to time before he became the homie. I knew Kris through these kids that lived down the street from me named Brandon, Darrel, and Ty. These three were brothers and went to the same junior high school that I did but they were eight balls, so I didn't see them at school much. Ty and Darrel were blood brothers, but Brandon was their brother through marriage. The three brothers were dirty, nasty, white boys who lived two apartment complexes down from me. Tonya was Brandon's mother who married Jeff, which was Ty and Darrel's dad. Jeff did work occasionally, but Tonya was just lazy, fat, stinky, and didn't care. She had the attitude and brains of Peggy Bundy from the TV show "Married with Children." I would go over to their house occasionally with my little brother, Jared. Kris was originally their friend first and then I met him through the brothers. Kris was the only black person I knew that played hockey and played for a team. I believe this was how the three brothers met Kris. There was a local skating arena called the Skating Palace where Kris played hockey and the brothers said they played in a league there too.

Kris came from a better background than us, from what we could tell by looking at him. His mother was a mail carrier and they lived in a better-looking area than what we did. He didn't talk about his father much at all until later in life, but it didn't matter because we saw that he lived in a condo, so his mom was doing alright. Kris always had the good things in life and he always had it first. He would have the best bikes, the best clothes, the best shoes, just simply the best of everything and he always had money in his pockets. So, to us, it was obvious that he didn't live the same type of lifestyle or struggles like the rest of us. Little did we know looks can be deceiving! Kris was a freshman in high school who stood five feet ten with hazel eyes and had light skin with the good hair. The good hair is when you don't have to put much effort into brushing your hair for it to look silky with waves in it. As you can imagine he was a pretty boy, the total opposite of what Robert and I looked like. So yes, we would eventually pick on him down the road for all the luxuries he had. But it was really just jealousy.

Robert came over after school to hang out with me like he said he would. Even though my mom was not at work on this particular day, I still had to stay in the courtyard area. Those restrictions eliminated us from playing basketball at the high school down the street. So, we just hung out talking on the stairs getting to know each other for a while. Kris would show up on his fancy Mongoose bike and I would introduce him to Robert. The first thing Robert said was, *damn nigga, you must be living large. I see you got the Jason Kidd zoom shoes on and you got this fresh ass bike,* Kris said, *yeah just a little bit.* Before they had a chance to get anything else out, you could hear my mom and Joey arguing over his drinking problem like always. *You drink too damn much, nigga, that's your damn problem,* my mom yells out as she slams the door on him. Joey replies with some drunken mush mouth that none of us can make out. We all look at each other and laugh.

Robert said, *my mom and Claude do this shit all the time too; they crazy!* Robert saying that made me feel better, it made me feel like it's more normal than I thought it was. Kris couldn't relate to what was going on, so he couldn't comment on the situation. The three brothers had somewhat similar problems, but we all know that white people problems are different from black people problems. The brothers have seen my parents at it before and they would try to relate but it was in a different way, kind of far but near.

I catch up to Joey and ask him if we could sit in the back of his truck because it had a camper and it was hot outside. Shockingly, Joey said it was cool, so we all located to the back of the truck. It's approximately eighty-five degrees outside so when it's hot in a small confined area if something has a smell, it will be smelled fast. On this day, Robert had a smell to him and the heat in the back of the camper exposed him to the extreme. We're all sitting around talking and out of nowhere, I smell Frito lay chips and ass. Being the comedian and bully that I am now; I express my feelings about this awful smell that's floating around in the air. I asked Kris if he smelled that and he said, *yeah,* with an unforgettable expression on his face. His eyebrows were scrunched up; his face looked like he took a bite out of a lemon and his nose flared up as wide as a golf ball. I said *Robert do you smell that,* he said, *no what do you smell?* I said, *foot and ass, you can't smell that! It's you smelling like foot and ass up in here.* Kris and I started laughing at the top of our lungs, the loudest we could possibly laugh. Robert was sitting there looking very embarrassed, but of course, we don't stop, we're kids, we just keep going. Kris starts joking on him, then I do. Kris and I go back and forward for about five to ten minutes joking on him. Robert was a good sport about it all. His actions made me respect him more because he could of went another route obviously after seeing what he did to Dindo earlier in the day. Robert showed me that there was no exception to being clowned, even if you are cool. I knew there was only so much he was going to take so we stopped at an appropriate time. It was clear as day to me and Kris that he either didn't have many clothes to wear or just didn't have clean clothes on the regular. The expression on Robert's face that he made that day let me know that he knew that we knew what was going on in his personal life. It was that moment right there that I knew he was going to be my first homie.

My mom and Joey came outside arguing again. I hear my brother in the house crying his eyes out. I tell the guys, let's go in the courtyard area so I can get him. I bring Jared outside so he can chill with us and ride his tricycle. Not more than five minutes after we go into the courtyard, Joey and my mom started getting outrageously louder than usual. We all go to the front to see what's going on because it was sounding like World War II out there. We get to the front and all we saw was the truck rocking side to side. It wasn't just a regular rock either it was more like an earthquake happening. We walked up on the back of the camper's tinted window and try to look in. When we look we see my mom on top of Joey punching him and throwing dominoes at him. I asked, *are you okay?* My mom said, *get in the house, I'm fine boy.* We go back to the courtyard area and keep a lookout in case he tries to get bold with my mom. Joey didn't do anything, but as I think about it now, he probably should have. My mom was beating his head like a set of drums and I felt bad for him. Situations like this would occur often but it wouldn't get to this level outside the household much. I tell the guys I'll catch them tomorrow that it's time for me to go in and knock out some homework.

Kris, Robert, and I would hang out every day after that first day that we all chilled together. Sometimes we would go to Brandon, Ty, and Darrel's house to chill. Since they only lived around the way, it was good for me because I had my brother to take care of. I got a chance to have fun and keep my brother safe from whatever could possibly happen while in the care of Joey. The three brother's house was dirty half the time we went over to hang out. It was like their parents didn't care about keeping it clean. There would be pizza boxes on the floor, dirty laundry on the couch and floors, cats running around everywhere, and there would often be a smell. The only reason why we went over to their home was to play the play station game system. This system was brand new and had the best game effects that had ever been made at this time in life. People would pre-order this system one year in advance from Japan just to make sure they had one when it came to the United States. This system was the ultimate kid's dream game and it only cost five hundred dollars when it first came out. It surprisingly shocked me that they had one in the condition they lived in.

I wouldn't dare ask my mother for something like this for any reason, including Christmas. I was used to getting puzzles every year with a two-hundred-dollar limit for gifts. Going to Brandon's house, I got to play and enjoy all the graphics for free and as much as I wanted too. So, it was safe to say that I used him for certain things but what child doesn't pick some friends off of what they can do for you? We would play games like Mortal Kombat or Street Fighter for hours at a time. When we weren't in their house we would just chill outside and rollerblade or skateboard. But our favorite outside games was "ditch" and "nigga knocking."

Ditch was like hide and go seek for kids who were basically teenagers. There would be two teams and one team would try to find the members of the other team before they got back to the safe zone. Nigga knocking is when you walk up to somebody's house and knock on the door then run and hide. You would keep doing this until the person came outside and started cursing then you earned a point. If you wanted to go for two points you would keep going back to the same house until they came outside and sat on their lawn. These were just some of the childish games we would do to past the time, innocent childhood games that everyone could relate to. When we decided to be on our juvenile delinquency, I would leave Jared with Tonya.

Breaking windows with rocks, stealing from the stores, or beating people up for no reason, is what we called "catching a Mexican." Mexicans would catch you by yourself and jump you. We figured we get them back for all the times we've been jumped. These events were regular routine weekly things. We were just kids being kids was how we saw it. I was usually the designated person to steal from the stores because I was simply good at it. It really didn't matter what it was or how big it was, I would get it if we wanted it.

Robert would usually be the first one to throw a punch at the innocent person we decided to beat up. It wasn't like we really picked anyone out specifically it was just a spur of the moment type thing. No hate crime, it just had a harsh name to what we called it. The odds were, it was going to be a Mexican because the city was full of them. We would normally be walking down the street for whatever reasons and whoever would be like "check this out." Check this out was the hint and we all knew what was about to happen, we would all follow up after the first thrown punch. Sometimes we would take what the person or people had in their pockets. The law calls it a strong-arm robbery, but we called it Tuesday.

If we wanted to crank it up a notch, then sometimes we would just do them dirty. Doing somebody dirty was spitting and peeing on that person. It wasn't a regular thing but it would occur every now and then. I would get a rush doing these types of things. It seemed so normal because that's what was going on with all the kids in my area. We would talk about the dirt we would do at school with other kids. The kids would tell us the same difference that they would do and we would just laugh about it together. Some of the kids would be doing things that made us look like angels. They would be stealing cars, selling drugs, breaking into people's houses, and carrying guns to commit a robbery. We weren't on that level of delinquency yet, but I was sure if we kept doing what we were doing we would be on that level soon. Before we got to that level, we still had fun and did childish things for quite some time.

Chapter 6: The Motherfucking Spot

The Skating Palace, the Boys and Girls Club, or the Police Activities League (P.A.L) dances was where we had our fun and did our childish things at for the most part. The Skating Palace was the teenager's version of the club. This is where I can say I remembered my childhood being as normal as any other American kid's childhood. Just like adults working hard through the week and waiting on the weekend to get wild and loose; we were too. Thursdays, Fridays, and Saturday nights were the days to be at The Skating Palace. If you were anybody and somebody, you would be there at least one of those days. Then you would come to school and talk about what happened over the weekend, who fought who, who hooked up with who, just the plain old gossip. If you weren't there, then you missed all the excitement that went on. Hearing the stories without actually being there just wasn't the same. It wasn't as funny as it could be and it wasn't as breathtaking as being there first hand. Robert, Kris, and I made sure we were there ninety percent of the time.

I remember taking hours to crease down my Dickie pants to get ready. It was like everything had to be perfect from the shoes to the shirt. I would scrub my shoes until they looked brand new, I would have the perfect deep crease in my pants, the fresh black tee on so it can match my black Nike Cortez shoes. This was an event and if you weren't on you're A+ game, then you would be the topic next week at school. I made sure I would lace Robert up with some gear. It wasn't like I had it like that, it was just more than what he had. Robert would keep a pair of fresh one hundred and twenty dollars shoes on, but his clothes were horrible. If I had it, then Robert knew he could get it, and it was vice versa. We were homies, and that's what homies do, get through and go through the struggle together.

Kris would always have the new things, so I never had to help him out. Sometimes I would have to go through his closet just because he had too much stuff that was fresh and I just had to wear it.

The Skating Palace usually started around seven-thirty so we would show up there at about nine. We had to give it time to start jumping and plus, we couldn't be the first ones in there. How un-cool do you look being at any event as the first person in the place? Plus we had to make an entrance because we were the shit. It was three dollars to get into The Skating Palace before ten o'clock and five dollars after. I don't know how we scraped up this money every weekend, but we kept just enough to make sure we were there. I'm pretty sure beating people up and robbing people played a big part in the contribution to my childhood memories at The Skating Palace. The first thing you would see walking into there was arcade games, tables, and the concession stand. Just like the club, an adult would go to the first thing you see, the bar. The concession stand was our bar, and the first thing you do in the club was go to the bar. We would go to the concession stand and grab some drinks and snacks just to let the girls know that we had a little bit of money. Then you would have to make your rounds in the place to see who was all in there.

I would make my rounds to spot out potential floozies to sell dreams to. Robert would be looking for the same, but Kris wouldn't have to because he was a pretty boy. When you're a pretty boy, floozies come to you, so he would just post up by the concession stand trying to look cool. By the time Robert and I made our rounds we had a good idea who we were going to recruit to our team of girls. Now it was time to get some quarters for the arcade games to play later. After the quarters, it was time for getting some quads or roller blades to go skate. Since we rollerblade all the time, those were our choice majority of the time. On the skating floor was where you earned cool points with the ladies. When those girls would see how fast you could go or how smooth you handled yourself while skating, they would go crazy. The average skaters would just skate but not us, we were just above average skaters. We had a certain way to make skating look even cooler than it really was.

Kris was the fastest skater out of all three of us. Robert was the trickster, and I was the smooth one. Kris would skate and circle around us as we skated around the floor the fastest we could. Robert would be skating on the front wheels of the roller blades with nothing but incredible balance. I still don't know how his lanky ass was able to do that. I would be doing some kind of a dance that was smooth while acting like I'm talking on a cell phone which was not activated. When all three of us were doing our thing at the same time, we looked like who you wanted to be out on the skating floor.

People would clap and yell our names out. The DJ would give us a shout out over the music on the microphone. We felt like stars out on the skating floor. After about ten minutes of showing off, we would head back toward the arcade area. It was my favorite part of the night because now it was time to go get the ladies. After seeing what we just did on the skating floor, the ladies were wide open and wanted us to talk to them. I always made sure when I went to talk to a girl that I caught her by herself and out of sight as much as possible. The logic behind this was one, if I got shot down, meaning denied by her, nobody would really see because we were ducked off out of sight out of mind; two, talking to girls in a pack was bad for you. If one girl out the group didn't like you, that meant the one that you wanted to talk to would get influenced not to like you either. You always want to give yourself a fair fight. Trying to game a group of girls is not going to happen so don't even try.

The third reason, last but not least, was you don't want other girls seeing you talking to another girl because then they would know you were a player. The girl I really wanted to talk to would be close to the last recruit. All the girls that I talked to before the number one pick were just practice or runners-up, so if they saw me talking to the number one girl, it really didn't matter. I would have about three or four new numbers so if one got dismissed because she caught me it was no harm. But the number one girl can never see you talking to somebody else because she was always the prettiest. This was how you built a team by gathering the prettiest girls you got and dismissing the others. The other girls are just practice to maintain all the number one picks. I always made sure I grabbed enough practice to keep my game sharp. The Skating Palace was the perfect place to do so, as well as the Boys and Girls Club and P.A.L dances.

After we got our player time in with the ladies, we would converse with kids from school or the neighborhood. Playing the arcade games wasn't really my thing, but Robert would overdose on the situation. Robert was addicted to playing video games, so he would spend a lot of time in that area. Robert would play the game for money with people. From time to time his attitude would get the best of him when he lost and start to fight.

Losing money wasn't the problem, it was losing in general that pissed him off. For some people, loving to win was a passion. It was deeper than that with Robert, he hated to lose with a passion. When he would get in a fight, it was cool because it was close to closing time anyways so when we got thrown out, it was just like if we were done with our mission. Plus, the ladies want to see a bad side of you too. This was a win, win situation.

The Boys and Girls Club dances were another event that we went to often. Every three months they would have a dance. In 1996, dancing was still cool, even the most dangerous gangsters were dancing back then. Being a wallflower just wasn't cool, you had to get up and freak somebody. Freaking somebody was dancing nasty with them. This term came from the "Wreckz N Effects" video Rump Shaker. This video had girls in bikinis shaking their butt and dancing really close to male genitals. This was actually a big movement for hip-hop and an even better one for my childhood. Whenever a dance was coming up we would be prepared for it. These dances thrown by The Boys and Girls Club always had a significant memory to come with them. We would wait and count down the days until the next dance. Every dance was always better than the last one.

There was always a crazy situation on the way to the dance or after. We were always getting suspended from school around the time the school dances were happening, so we never could go to them. The Boys and Girls Club dance were the only time you really had a chance to grind on girls. Unless you've gamed enough girls to mess around with you and, if not, then you were waiting on the dance to do so. It would only be one dollar for the cost of entry at the dance. It was cool that they made the price affordable for everybody to go.

There would be a chaperone present to make sure kids weren't getting out of hand, which we would. Food and drinks were available, so we made sure we got there early to eat up all the free stuff. We would leave and come back about an hour later. The dance would only be three hours, usually around seven to ten o'clock. It wasn't like The Skating Palace that stayed open until twelve or even one sometimes. We would leave and go pick up some of our friends or girls that lived in the area.

There were about four different Boys and Girls Club locations in the city. Depending on which club was having the dance was what determined who we would walk and go get. We had friends and girls all over the city but some areas we just couldn't walk around in and expect nothing to happen to us. Certain areas like Colonial or El Rio was not the area to be black walking around in.

After we would grab whoever from wherever, it was time to get our freak on. We would step up in the dance just as fly as we wanted to be. Fresh haircut, creased pants, cologne, money, and a cell phone or pager. The phone and pager were for fronting. This was all we needed to attract the hoochies. While waiting on this event, you already set up for a bunch of girls to be there so you can grind on them and hopefully more if your game was tight. That's what the whole dance mission was about, freaking girls or getting active in recruiting girls and messing around with them. If you played your hand right, you'll have a girl waiting on you right when you walked in the dance.

Once I spot the girl waiting on me I let my boys know or vice versa. We walk over and introduce everyone to everybody. You wouldn't just have somebody there for you they would have to have friends with them for your friends. It wasn't always a sure thing that the girls you counted on to be there would show up. You know how it is as a kid, you find some way to get in trouble and can't go or find something better to do. There always have to be backup girls also known as runners-up and some for the crew. That's just called good manners where I'm from. Besides, it ain't no fun if the homies can't get none.

When done introducing everybody then it was time to get to the main event. I'll walk my girl to the dance floor and commence to freaking that ass immediately. I'm grinding on her, she's grinding on me, we feel each other up and it's going down. We dance for a couple of songs until we both get hot and sweaty as if we were having sex. Getting all hot and sweaty was the perfect excuse to get away from her and search for the other girls or even new recruits. I would make sure to tell her to stay here; I'll be right back I have to go to the bathroom. That gives me about ten minutes to search around the room to see who's all in here. Eventually, I'll spot another girl that I've been talking to on the phone who's gone through the three-stage process. It's kisses and hugs when we see each other and then immediately grinding on the dance floor. Just like the last girl we get sweaty and hot. That's my signal and it was time to go, I'm on to the next. I tell this girl the same thing I told the last girl. Off to repeat the exact same steps all over again with someone else.

It was just a cycle until I bumped back into the crew. The crew was doing the same thing. Somehow during this cycle, I will find some new players for my team and squeeze their phone number out during the short time I had. I did nothing but freak and grind on girls for two hours. At the end of the dance, I smelled like ten different girls and would have glitter all over my face. Occasionally, I would get caught up talking to another girl. When chasing every skirt moving, you will wind up talking to somebody's sister, cousin, or best friend and you won't even know it. The girl you've been talking too has described you to all of the above or shown a picture and you weren't aware of it.

Yes, you will get caught every now and then but that's the roll of the dice. Getting caught was a good thing because this helps you tighten up your skills on getting out of trouble. You would be amazed at some of the things you can say to girls and they believe you. But for the most part, it was just another good recruiting day and progress was made with the girls you already had.

Chapter 7: Always Into Some Bullshit

Walking home was when those crazy memories were usually made. It can be anything from getting chased by a gang and the magnificent getaway, to breaking into somebody's car, starting a small riot, or going back to a girl's house. When walking home, the first unspoken rule was to walk in the middle of the street. Walking in the middle of the street gives you options in which way to run. You never know who's going to pop out on you and try to jump you or if there was a dog loose. By walking in the middle of the street it gives you the advantage of seeing more of your surroundings and being alert.

The second unspoken rule was if I take off running then you better take off running, no questions asked. Following these rules walking kept us safe for the majority of the time. Occasionally we would get home with just a little bit of drama. After the very first dance that we went to was when we established those rules. Robert, Kris, and I were on our way back to the south side of Hueneme, which is still in Oxnard. We weren't aware of our surrounding and some cholo's popped out on us. Cholo's are Mexican gangsters or want to be's and usually, you know when theirs cholo's around. They have a certain type of whistle for their gang call and if you're in their hood they'll let you know with that whistle.

This particular time we didn't hear that whistle, probably because we were talking too loudly and laughing. We were strolling on the sidewalk having a good old time without a worry in the world. That was our first mistake and out of nowhere, five cholo's pop out and start hitting us up. *Where you from, fool? This is big, bad eastside Colonial Chiques over here, homie.* As soon as somebody asks where you from, you're supposed hit them in the mouth; or let them know what gang you bang. Even if you don't gangbang they wouldn't care, they just want to fight, so it was pointless to explain you don't gangbang. Instead of letting the person get the first hit you always want to get the first punch thrown. When the odds are two people to one person you better try to knock out the first person you punch so you can have an even fight.

Needless to say, we didn't have a good outcome that fight. There would be times where we would rise to the challenge of a handicap match, but not that time. If there was an even number of people fighting, then there was no problem beating those cowards up. Cholo's would rarely hit you up when it's just you and them, they always fought in packs like they were wolves. After that ass whooping, we made sure to be alert at all times. It was a good thing that we got jumped at that time because it made us more street smart. It gave us experience that would grow into a particular skill set of defending yourself against multiple attackers. Every fight and every jump was like gladiator school and we were eventually going to graduate to warriors. It just wasn't going to happen anytime soon for us. I don't know why we thought we could walk around somebody else's hood like everything was peaches. We could have easily got shot because the Mexicans and Blacks were always at war.

We didn't always get into fights on the adventurous walks in somebody else's hood. Sometimes, we would find a car to break into when walking home. We wouldn't break into it to steal a stereo or nothing like that, we were just looking for money or anything valuable that could be easily concealed. You would be surprised how so many people leave money in their car. People would like to leave money in the center console or in the ashtray. You would think, why not take your money in the house where it was safer. Some people just don't have common sense and we were grateful for that. It would be chump change that we would find. Usually, it was about sixty dollars and that meant twenty dollars three ways plus whatever valuables we would take. Portable CD players, pagers, cell phones, watches, bracelets; you name it, we stole it. It would all be in the car with easy access. I never understood how we would luck up all the time and pick the right car. It was so available to us that sometimes I thought maybe we were being set up. Who just leaves those types of valuable lying around in a car?

Occasionally we would get lucky and have a girl say, *why don't you come back to my house, my parents are gone until tomorrow.* We all knew what that meant; a lot of crazy shit was about to happen at that house. Vanessa was one of the girls that I had on my team and after a dance, she invited me and the crew back to her house. Vanessa lived in El Rio but of course, I failed to ask her where she stayed. At that point and time, I was gamed to go back to her house. The excitement and anxiousness got the best of my thoughts. It was during the walk when I realized she lived in El Rio. We knew that was a problem, but being young, dumb, and full of cum, we didn't stand a chance to our hormones. After about a forty-five-minute walk we get to her house. She has her friends, I have my friends, and we're all going to be friends. Vanessa was exactly how I like my girls.

She was five foot two, Hispanic with a beautiful complexion, and she had what we called a "Ghetto Booty". A ghetto booty is hard to find; the requirements for this type of ass were impossible. You had to have the right circumference of ass, with just the right amount of width and it has to sit perfectly on your back. When it sits perfectly, it will leave a nice dip in your back right before it turns into your butt. That dip on the back drove me crazy and that was all I could think about. That moment when we would be in bed or the bathroom floor because it really didn't matter where she got it, it all depended on how much self-respect she had, but she would have to arch her back when sliding her panties off that ghetto booty and that's where the dip is fully exposed to its finest potential.

Vanessa goes to put some music on so we can start to kick it and catch a vibe. Robert breaks out the weed and starts to roll a blunt so we can get our minds right. Vanessa whips out some alcohol from her mom's stash and next thing you know, we got a personal party going on. Everybody was enjoying themselves, my boys are getting to know her girls and it's all good. Thirty minutes into this personal party everybody was kissing, hugging, and getting along just how we planned.

We started to take our girls in different areas of the house to get to know each other better if you know what I mean. I'm in Vanessa's room and we started to mess around. I'm kissing her and feeling on her breast. I attempt to take her bra off, but I'm miserably failing at it. She takes it off and I pounce on her chest like she was prey in my food chain. I'm sucking on her nipples as I work my fingers down into her pants, then I start to finger bang her. At this stage in life, finger banging was really popular and if you weren't doing that, then you were lame. It was equivalent to having sex for me at this age. Remember Vanessa said her parents were out of town until the next day, but she didn't tell me that her brother was still in town.

Her brother was a known gangbanger name Chocolate. He got his name from his lips. Around his lips are darker than his complexion, so it looked like he was eating chocolate. The Blacks and Mexicans were always at war and the saying about Chocolate was he eats black people up and spits them out. This was another reason why he was called Chocolate, but we know that's not possible, but it was a good metaphor for how he felt about black folks. At this point and time when I'm in Vanessa's room, Robert and Kris are downstairs in their own world doing whatever they do. Everything's going fine until we hear a car pull up blasting music. I look at her, she looks at me and she said, *oh shit, Chocolate is back. CHOCOLATE, what the fuck is he doing here? Oh yeah, he's my brother, I didn't tell you huh? He was supposed to be at a party at his homeboy's house.* I should have known better when I saw we were walking to El Rio that this was going to be a bad mission.

She immediately puts her clothes back on and checks the window. *Oh fuck, you guys better get the hell out of here because he's drunk and has two of his homies with him.* Before I had a chance to warn Kris and Robert, Chocolate and his homies were already in the house. Kris and Robert hear them come through the door and try to find somewhere to hide. That didn't work out too well because almost as soon as they came in, I heard, *what the fuck you doing in my pad nigger!* I slowly started to walk downstairs to see what was going on and before I got halfway, Robert and Kris were running upstairs. We ran into Vanessa's room and locked the door. Luckily, she had a window in her room, so we had a way out.

I was the first one out the window, then Robert, and by that time Chocolate and his homeboys broke the door down. We jumped off the roof and waited on Kris. Then it happened, just like a scene out of the movies, we saw Kris dive out the window. He just barely hit the edge of the roof, and he tumbled down to the ground, landing in the bushes on his side. We helped him up and got him on his feet so we could run as if our lives depended on it. Well, it kind of did since we were in the wrong hood and the infamous Chocolate was on our ass. As soon as we get him on his feet, Chocolate hits the bushes right where Kris landed. He lands on his back and we take off running. I guess he hurt himself because he didn't start chasing us. We get about twenty-five yards away and then we hear numerous gunshots. It only took one shot for us to hear and run faster than an Olympic gold medalist. It was like we shifted from first gear to fifth gear all in one motion. We bend a couple corners and hop a few fences before we took a break to breathe.

For some reason, the excitement was funny to us, so we started laughing. I always heard that the fear and laughter senses were very close in the brain so maybe that's the reason for those actions. I sure was scared as shit and they must have been too because we laughed pretty damn hard. That laugh didn't last long because a few seconds later, a dog starts to run up on us. Out of all places to take a breather, we take one in the backyard where there's a pit bull. As quick as we hopped that fence was as quick as we got back over. Unfortunately, we all didn't make it because Robert got stuck on the fence and the dog bit his leg. We pulled him over and he was missing a piece of his pants by his calf. I tell him *at least it wasn't a bullet, way to take one for the team.*

Chocolate and his boys never came looking for us, so we lucked up on that situation. This was just one of the legendary memories that would be created from a P.A.L or Boys and Girls Club dance. I don't think I could count how many times we got ourselves in a situation like that. Chocolate and his homies were the first time that we got shot at, but it sure wouldn't be the last.

Chapter 8: The Foundation of Inner Pain

It sounds funny to say, but it was times like that when I felt like a kid having extreme fun. Not the part of doing wrong but just hanging out with the boys and doing what kids do making memories. I guess doing wrong was normal in my environment, so it didn't seem like wrong was being done. When I was with my boys, we would find a lot of stupid stuff to get into. It was really just a scapegoat from my home lifestyle. Being a teenager but having the responsibilities of a parent at times was complicated. At this age, I was already going through my own problems at school, and I was trying to figure out who I was.

Being a secondary victim to domestic violence on the regular sure didn't help my mental state at school. I would lack sleep from the nights before because of all the arguing and things being thrown at each other. Sometimes I couldn't sleep because I was concerned about my mother's safety. She would always turn out alright, but I wouldn't know it, so I would stay awake until the fighting stopped. It started off approximately three out of seven days of the week they would argue. Half the time I would be sleep, and around twelve midnight they would start to get into it. Can you imagine sleeping and then out of nowhere hearing people beating on the walls and yelling as loud as they physically can with doors slamming? That shit was scary for a kid, especially to be woken up out of sleep because you're already in an unconscious mode, so you're out of it. Then add all the background noise of yelling. It would scare you too. As you finally start to realize what's going on, you have to calm down a child who's screaming bloody murder. Not only was I scared, but my little brother was as well because he was in the early childhood stages.

After calming him down, then I could tune into what's going on with all the commotion in the next room. Majority of the time the arguments would be about Joey's alcohol problem or him not making enough money to help support the family. Joey worked at a place called Keens Hardware, and he only made minimum wages which was five dollars and seventy-five cents an hour. The sad part about it was Joey had child support coming out of his checks. That meant he would only get about half of a forty-hour week paycheck. This would explain why my mom worked two full-time jobs. The little peanut money, as my mom would say, wasn't doing shit for us. When working two jobs and your significant other was barely contributing to the household it could piss anybody off. You would be extremely mad if they always had money for a six-pack of King Cobra beers and cigarettes daily.

My mother had a valid reason to be upset; by taking it to the next level of domestic violence was her inner feeling lashing out. Basically, she was sick and tired of being sick and tired. From time to time police would be called by neighbors because they were completely out of control and too loud. It got to the point that officers knew my parents by their first name whenever they were called out. We weren't the only family with these problems in our apartment complex, but we were the most routinely called on family.

Joey was a whole different person when he was drinking. Usually, he was nice, cool, kind of funny but corny at times when he was sober. He would even give me money when I asked or for no reason at times. But when he was drinking, he was angry, sarcastic, emotionless, just cold blooded.

Joey was born and raised in Oakland, California and he was proud of his city. He would let you know in a heartbeat where he was from and how he used to live. He would always tell my mom that she was born with a silver spoon in her mouth. Joey explained how he grew up with a family of alcoholics and no food in the house. He often expressed how it was rough living where he lived back in the 1970's. When he was drinking it seemed like he would boast about all the wrong he used to do. Being a Pimp or selling drugs and going to jail was something he was proud of, it seemed. He would go as far as boasting about how his children's mother was one of his first hoes, which he called his "Bottom Bitch", and how he used to smack her around for not having his outfit laid out for him to wear for the day.

I think when he was drinking it put him back in a time in life that he wished he was still a part of, but for certain reasons, he changed. I don't know if it was all the drugs he used to use or if it was the trouble he ran from, but he did change for some reason. The expression you can take the man out the hood, but you can't take the hood out the man is true. Even though he had a job and was trying to live a square life, he was still hood.

Joey always had a revolver pistol on him or lying around the house. Hustling was always going on either at the pool hall or him stealing stuff from work and selling it. By him having these flashbacks when he was drunk brought the worst out of him. It was a side that you didn't want to know. Joey would be drunk and ask me if I had any money in my pockets. I would say no, then he would say, *well if you want some come and get it.* He would drop five or ten dollars on the ground, stand over it and say, *take it little nigga.* I would try to grab the money and he would put his hands up to start play fighting. The only problem was I would be playing, and he would be throwing blows at me like he was in a real fight. There were several times he would catch me with a gut or rib check that felt like a Mack truck hitting me. If I would even show a sign that I might start to cry, he would hit me harder and say, *stop being a pussy, you said you want this money now take it.* At the time when it was happening, it seemed like he was trying to make me tougher. As I think about it now, I think he was taking some anger out on me. No grown man should be hitting a kid as hard as he would hit me, even if it was tough love!

One time I complained to my mom that he hit me too hard and my ribs were sore. She said *stop being a sissy, he's just trying to make you tough.* "TOUGH!" I vomited when he hit me in the stomach, that should be proof. But he had my mom fooled that he was making me tough. I believe he would do that because he couldn't whoop me, so he just found another way to put his hands on me that was justified in my mom's eyes.

Besides those times and two other altercations, he never put his hands on me. From time to time Joey's anger would get the best of him. Sometimes he would punch holes in the wall or break my mom's car windows. Shockingly he would never hit my mom. At least that's what I thought. I think he thought twice because he knew that my mom was crazy and would fight back. Joey stood six foot six and one hundred seventy pounds soaked and wet. My mom stood five foot eleven approximately two hundred pounds, so she was a force to be reckoned with.

There was one time I suspected that he finally did something back to her because her left eye was blackish blue for about a week. She said that she was changing the shower rod and it popped out and caught her in the eye, but that story just didn't sit right with me. It wouldn't be until later for it to make sense why Joey would snap like he had bipolar symptoms.

It wasn't always crazy in my household, there was a lot of good times when they weren't arguing. My mom worked hard for her money, but she always tried to make my childhood as much fun as she could. It was an unspoken thing about how I had so much responsibility and expectations to take care of my brother, so every now and then my mom would remind me that I was a child by taking me places like Disney Land or Magic Mountain theme park. It was her way of showing me that she loved me and appreciated me without really talking about the why. I knew we didn't have money for these types of events. As a parent how do you tell a child that I know you're not supposed to be doing this, but I just want to thank you for roughing it out. Silent gestures were always thrown at me, and even if she didn't think I knew what was going on, I sure did.

We didn't always do big things like the theme parks. Sometimes we would just get some good quality time in such as playing dominoes or scrabble, the basic board games everyone grows up with. Whenever Joey would play, he would always get caught cheating and then World War III would start. Joey's motto was, if you're not cheating then you're not trying. Funny because that motto stuck with me, it actually made sense to me. If you want something, then you have to be willing to do anything for it. Well, at least that's what I grasp from it.

Day by day, week by week, and month by month, the same old routine. I felt like something had to change. Robert, Kris, and I were bored of doing the same shit every day; playing basketball, fighting, petty theft, and all of the above. It was time to step our game up some so we can have that excitement like we use to have. This was the point in time that I thought we needed to have a name or something for our clique. I wanted people to know who was doing this stuff around the city. I figured, shit, we all chill together why not just be one name when people see us. Everybody in the clique proved that they were down for theirs, so it was simple to make a name up. (D.F.M) Down for Mine would be the clique.

That's exactly what we all were. People would eventually hear about our clique through word of mouth. Folks were coming to us trying to be down. But we only recruited a few to our crew. It was crazy that by just giving us a name, it changed the way we chilled. It went from childish fun things to bigger fish in the skillet.

Selling weed was incorporated and carrying weapons like knives and a gun. The minor stuff stopped, and the big boy games started. An all-black, nine-millimeter handgun was the first weapon I ever shot. One of the new recruits who became the homie named Jason was the person who introduced me to the weapon. Jason was older, about Kris's age of sixteen. Jason had already been to juvenile hall a few times before, so he wasn't scared to do anything because he had already walked the halls. Jason lived behind me, so it was easy to kick it with him. He told me he can get a gun from his mom's shoe box and she wouldn't miss it. We walked to the alley and he gave it to me and said *shoot that dog*. I can't even lie, I was nervous at first because the alley was right behind my courtyard area and Joey or somebody could see me. I thought for a quick second and said *fuck it, I'm down for mine.* (BANG BANG BANG) That was the loudest sound I had ever heard. The poor dog was shot in the head twice and the side of its body once. When bullets go through flesh, it has a crazy looking outcome. All I could see was the dog's brain fragments hanging out of its head.

We took off running and ducked behind some stairs at another courtyard area. The feeling of shooting a weapon and knowing that I could seriously harm someone was a super adrenaline rush. I mean a rush beyond normal; it wasn't like fighting or running from the cops. The rush was powerful and had a possessive feeling to it. It was more like a crack pipe to a smoker. I was addicted to the rush as if it was a drug; it took over my body like a dope fiend. I instantly fell in love with the feeling, and all I wanted to do was shoot the gun. This new love that I had meant trouble wasn't very far away.

It seemed like almost every day I would ask Jason to bring me the gun and D.F.M would go out and rob people at gunpoint. We got a lot of practice shooting by using animals as targets. It didn't matter what we took when committing a robbery, it was all for the rush and putting our name out on the streets. We figured every clique has to put in work and we weren't an average clique. That meant we had to put in twice as much work. Putting in work was any kind of violence or destruction to public property while representing our clique at all times. These types of acts carried on for weeks. Over that time period, I learned that I had a talent for robbing people, sad to say, it just came naturally to me. I mean it's not like it takes brains to rob someone.

Trouble came quick. Since I was so addicted to the weapon, of course, I had to take it with me to school and show everyone my new love. I'm at school showing it to everybody, and I catch the attention of a girl named Tennille. Tennille was one of the prettiest girls in school and the most popular. I showed her the gun, and she said, *can I hold it?* I tell her not *now there are too many teachers around,* so she said *come to my house after school.* The first thing in my mind was (yes, I got another one on my team). I said, *cool, I'll meet you in the front of the school when we get out.*

After school, we linked up and started walking to her house, and on the way I see my homie Shannon walking down the street. I yell, *what's up fool, its Matt,* he hollered back, *what's up fool,* and starts walking with us. I went to introduce him to Tennille, but they already knew each other. Shannon said, *yeah, I live a block away from her, she pretty cool and down for her shit.*

Shannon and I caught up on times as we walked, and he started talking about how he can't stand living at home. Shannon said he was in juvenile hall for about a year and he had been home for three months. These last three months have been terrible at home he said. Shannon and his mom got into it all the time, and she was always kicking him out of the house. I couldn't blame his mom for that, I mean the nigga was a problem. He also mentioned that he didn't understand things in school, so he got into fights to past the time at school. I believe it was a self-defense mechanism and he displayed violence, so nobody would make fun of his stupid ass.

Shannon said, *I'd rather be back in juvenile hall then living at home, as a matter of fact, I was on my way to rob the gas station, so I can go back, but I'll kick it with you guys before I go. Damn Shannon, it's that bad at home that you want to live in juvenile hall. Hell yeah, nigga, I'm not playing, and I'm going today! Now, what can be so bad that you want to live in jail? Nigga you institutionalized. Look homie I can do what I want, when I want in jail. I don't have to see my brother's dad, and I run shit; I'm a "Shot Caller". Mmmh! If you say so homie.*

We finally got to her house and her aunt was there so we went to her room and chilled. As soon as we got in her room, she said, *well whip it out fool.* Shannon's stupid self said, *hell yeah, I'm going to get some pussy before I go back too. I knew you were down for your shit Tennille.* I started laughing, and she said, *no dummy. No pussy for you, Matt has a gun, and I want to hold it.*

I pulled it out my backpack and let her know it's loaded so be careful. She asked if I've used it yet. I told her that I shot a dog and robbed a couple of folks, but I haven't really got to know it yet. She passes it to Shannon and he checks it out then gives it to me. As I'm getting ready to put it back into my backpack, he said, *hold on let me go outside and shoot it in the air.* As I go to pull it out the backpack, I grabbed it the wrong way, and it fell out my hands onto her dresser. BANG! One shot fired, and we look at each other then we notice Tennille got hit in her leg. She was cool until she seen that blood gushing out then she panicked.

Tears start falling and she was crying extremely loud. Five seconds later her aunt runs in the room and sees what happened. She goes to call the ambulance immediately and, I think, oh shit its game over for me. Shannon looks at me, and it was like he knew what I was thinking. He said I had that same expression on my face when I knew I was going to juvenile hall for the first time. *Don't trip little homie; I was going back today anyways so I'll take this one. Besides I can't stand living at home*. I couldn't even say nothing; I was in shock that I just accidentally shot this fine ass girl, and I'm probably going to jail behind that bullshit.

He told Tennille to tell the cops when they come that he was the one that dropped the gun, it was his, and we were here to mess around with you. Tennille said, *hell no I'm not going to let people think I was going to mess around with your fat ass boy. Look we were here to go swimming in the pool.* We all agreed on that alibi. I asked Shannon if he was sure he wanted to do this for me? *Dog, listen to what I'm telling you, if I don't go now it might be my brother's dad who gets shot and not in his fucking leg you smell me?* All it took was once for me to hear that he got this case and I figured better you than me, so I was down with it. Plus, it wasn't like I bitched out and said take this case for me, so I looked at it as I owed him one. *That's a real nigga move you bout to do, dog. Yeah because I'm a real nigga just don't get uppity on me when I call for my get back. I gotcha you homie*, and then we dapped it up.

The ambulance and police got there and immediately handcuffed Shannon. I didn't even have to say anything because Shannon stayed in trouble so much they didn't even ask who did what. They just said you're under arrest to him, then asked questions. I thought it was crazy how you can arrest somebody then ask questions about what happened. They just assumed he did it. The police walked him to the cruiser and he looked at me and I knew what he was saying even if there weren't words spoken. Shannon was a real ass nigga for that, and I knew that one day I would have to repay him. I'm sure it was going to be huge. But I would cross that bridge when I got there.

Chapter 9: Jumping Off the Porch

I decided that guns might not be what I needed in my life at this time. I guess it takes a specific action to happen before you realize how serious things are. You would think that after that situation and coming so close to jail that I would slow down. However, the reality of that situation wore off quick, and I was back to doing foolish things in a matter of days. It was like I never skipped a beat. The clique was still rolling strong, and within that same week, we started selling more weed. At first, we were selling and getting enough money to have fun, like go to The Skating Palace or buying play station games, shoes, and clothes. The petty amount of drug dealing to have things we wanted and to re-up for another score. We went from nickel and dime bags to half pounds and pounds.

Robert was the primary dealer out the clique; it seemed that he just had a talent for it. We all sold, but he just did better with it. Robert had more clients than all of us. He was like a historian when it came to weed. He smoked it regularly, he talked about it all the time, and it was his field of expertise. It's funny how pretty much everybody had a designated role in the clique. We all knew a little bit about a little bit and a lot about nothing. Some had better talent and skill sets in particular areas. This made us a pretty well-balanced clique. It's never good that just one person knows everything or does everything. When the head gets chopped off, then the body will fall. If Kris, me, or Robert went to jail or got killed, how would this continue?

It was good that people just fell into certain positions. Jason was the live wire out the crew. He was always down to do whatever, whenever, and however. You need someone like that around at all times; we call them type of folks, "Dumb Outs." Then we had the flashy, pretty Ricky guy, Kris. He would be the advertisement for the clique. Kris was well balanced all around as a thug. Kris would be the one to make us look good by how he appeared in people's eyes. He was very approachable with great communication skills, and he knew when to show his gangster. The best aspect was that he could expand us to a different culture of clients. I mean come on, he was light skinned, well dressed with the best clothes, and he had all the new electronics, such as cell phones, pagers, etc. By looking at him, he was that dude you might want to look like. A "Shot Caller" appeal and he had bitches; I mean what guy doesn't want that. This can bring recruitment as well and an opportunity to grow into an organization. When they saw Kris, they thought, damn D.F.M is taking care of each other, they got their shit together, I want to roll with them.

Then we had the dude who can manipulate damn near anybody to do what he wanted. That dude was me, and if you asked me, I could sell a hooker to a preacher. I was that slick! It was amazing how naturally manipulating people came to me. I call it a gift and I used it all the time for good or bad.

We were like an all-star team. Do you remember the TV show "The A-Team?" Everyone had particular roles and was a valuable asset to their clique. You can't make a fist without four fingers and a thumb. If we didn't have all of us, then we couldn't be solid, and solid we were.

Every good clique has structure and organization in it just like a gang. We had the higher ranked people, who I pointed out, then we had the foot soldiers. Foot soldiers took orders and did what was asked of them. There were some loyal soldiers who were down with us before we started this clique, like Deejay and Tyson. They really didn't have a specialty, but they were just loyal soldiers who did whatever we needed them to do. This could consist of beating folks up to the span of robbing people. Regardless what it was, it was a needed task that had to be completed to continue for the clique.

Last but not least, we had the crash test dummies that would do anything just to be down with our clique. We would send them out on exactly what they're called, crash test dummy missions. A crash test dummy mission is stupid and more than likely you're going to get caught. An example is breaking into the school and damaging as much property as you can before the police come. It shows us that you had heart and could be down. But when we knew that you couldn't or wouldn't represent us right, then we had you break into homes or go beat up a girl that Robert got pregnant again and give her all body shots, so she would have a miscarriage. Among us four, we already knew they wouldn't be down with us, but we had them do things anyways for our excitement. Plus, it got our names out in the streets and kept us relevant.

It damn sure didn't take long for our crew to have respect. The type of things that we were doing was crazy compared to other crews. With earning respect from our fellow peers also came hate. Other crews kept hearing, D.F.M this and D.F.M that, and eventually, it sparked a beef with T.S.K.

Town Side Kings were a well-known clique way before we had the idea of becoming one. They were known for having hoes and jumping people. Almost any time you heard about a big brawl or somebody getting put in the hospital over fighting, you knew T.S.K had something to do with it. The thought of having a beef with another respected crew was exactly what we thought we needed, a rival. Our clique name already rung bells through the south side and with this beef, it can be through the whole city.

Robert, Kris, Jason, and I had a meeting about what was the best way to approach this situation. We unknowingly came up with a plan that would turn into a riot. We figured a majority of the T.S.K members went to Sunset Junior High School and Channel Island High School. These schools were ten minutes apart from each other and twenty from Black Stock Junior High and Hueneme High School. If they wanted problems, we weren't going to hide, so we put the word out to meet us halfway. Halfway would be at a school called Bard Elementary. Robert sent word to their clique when and what day to meet us since they had a beef with us. We spread the word to our schools about what was going down and when. Robert had set it up for a week from the current day, so we had time to collect an audience. If we were going to brawl with the most known clique, then we needed witnesses to see how we were going to do them. What's the point of putting our reputation on the line if nobody would be there to tell about what happened? Plus, we wanted mutual parties there, to tell the truth.

Every day up until the brawl all you heard were people talking about it. The hype kept getting bigger and bigger. I was surprised that it didn't get leaked to the principal or teachers. You wouldn't believe how excited people were; it was like the Super Bowl weekend. There were so many homeboys that came up to us letting us know they had our back. That week I don't think I had to spit game to any girls because they were all coming to me. I had a little taste of what it's like to be the top crew, and I knew that I wanted it. It was similar to the gun rush, but it had a strong urge that was somewhat possessive too. It might have created a new persona or self-confidence that made me feel comfortable in my own skin. I mean, all I ever wanted was bitches. Isn't that the reason any man does anything in life?

The week finally came around, and it's Tuesday. School has ended, and the plan was that we were supposed to start walking to Bard Elementary and both cliques would meet up. We didn't want to draw attention to ourselves before we got to the spot. There's nothing like having the police coming and fucking our day up, so we put simple instructions out. No more than nine in a group walking because that was about the average size group of kids walking home from school, so it looks normal. D.F.M was ready to bang, all nine members walking side by side down Bard Road. The crowd behind us was ridiculous, I mean, it didn't even make sense how many people were following us to watch and catch our back. I knew they weren't going to walk in a group of nine, but it didn't matter.

During that time, we felt like Generals in the Army leading and commanding their troops to war. The adrenaline was flowing through my body. As we get closer and closer, it pumps more, and I crave the rush. I look around at my clique and I see nothing but stone-cold killer faces. The lynch mob behind us was getting pretty rowdy themselves as we got closer.

We reach a point where we could see T.S.K and their crowd. We started chanting "I'm down for mine, and I'm going to fuck you up!" We get about a football field apart from our rivals, and then they started breaking out weapons. Little jimmy bats, bricks, sticks, and stone was all we saw, so we did the same and brought out ours. Less than forty yards between us and we take off running, attacking one another. This felt unreal, it felt exciting, and it looked like the start of a slippery slope. It started off my crew versus their crew the first few minutes. It wasn't long until everybody started to fight. I was fighting with a dude named Playboy, who was one of their leaders. Somehow Playboy had me in a bear hug. Playboy was at least seventeen years old. He repeated the eighth grade twice, and he was huge. He had a muscular physique and was Samoan. This bear hug felt like a death grip, the kind that a python would wrap around its prey and squeeze the life out of it. Thankfully he made the wrong move and I got out of it. I swung and hit him in the nose. His nose starts to bleed and I wrap my hands around his head and hit him with a quick, powerful head bunt to the bridge of his nose. He falls to the floor, and I get on top of him and start to choke him. This was the first time that I physically felt possessed, demonic, and unstoppable. It was unreal. I felt like I was watching myself and had no control. I knew what I was doing, but I couldn't stop myself; something or someone else was controlling me. I just kept squeezing his neck with so much anger until he started to turn slightly blue and purple. He's going to die was all I kept thinking. Nigga, you need to stop, he's not going to make it.

Possessed I was, incapable of physically controlling myself. It felt like when you're sleeping, and you wake up, but you're not so alert to what's going on, so you're stuck and can't move because nothing makes sense. All you can do is watch and wait until you come to your senses. Lucky for him, but mostly for me, somebody kicked me on the side of my face, and it snapped me back to reality. I fell over as Playboy frantically starts gasping for air. His homies start stomping me out on the ground. Robert ran up behind them with a brick and cracked one in the back of the head. The noise of his head getting hit with that brick was similar to a damn shotgun being let off. At this point, this was where the fight got completely out of control. Two members of T.S.K whip out knives and come toward us. Jason, the live wire, saw the knives and then he blindsided one of them. He falls, and now it's three on one, we all run up and try to get the knife away from the guy. Keep in mind there was a big crowd of people watching and fighting. While we tussle for the knife, somehow the guy ends up falling toward the crowd watching us. The amount of force he had falling toward the crowd had to be tremendous because he fell into a kid named Peter and stabbed him. Peter got stuck in the bicep, and at that same time the cops pulled up. Somebody had to drive by and see this riot, that we didn't intend to have, and called the rollers.

After ten minutes of brawling, rollers and ambulances show up. Everybody who was able to run did. People scattered like roaches when the lights are turned on. "We out! We out D.F.M!" Everybody takes off every which way. I jumped over somebody's fence to their backyard. Backyard to backyard was how I traveled until I felt I was far enough to run on a street where the cops weren't.

Man, this is crazy, I thought while walking down the street. We just started a big ass riot, and several people were hurt. I wonder if Robert and Kris got away. I bet we got the respect we deserved now. This was the shortest thirty-minute walk ever. I had about a million thoughts going through my head at one time. By the time I got home the rush went away, I acted like nothing just happened. I laid on my bed and replayed the event over and over for the majority of the day. The next morning, I woke up and turned on the television as I got dressed for school. Of course, the first thing I saw was our brawl on the news. Oh shit, this can't be good at all. We made the news. The reporter announced that five people were arrested, and it was only one person from my clique. Jason was the only person to get locked up behind this, and since he was on probation, I knew he would be gone longer than a year. Jason already had a year on the shelf, so it was curtains for him. I didn't have to question if Jason would snitch us out, he was solid, and I wasn't bothered.

I carried on with my day and went to school, so I could hear the gossip. I walked through the hallways and heard, *Peter got stabbed, some other dude got hit in the head with a brick, all kinds of people got beat up. D.F.M was fucking T.S.K up; they're top clique now.* This was all I heard coming out of folk's mouth. It felt good to earn this level of respect from my peers. This was what we thought we wanted, to be top clique. I must have forgotten what I learned in elementary about standing out. When you stand out, you draw attention to yourself, and sometimes it's not all good.

Down For Mine carried out what was expected of the top crew for a solid four months. We maintained stealing, selling drugs, fighting, robbing, tagging, and whatever consist of putting in work. Now that it was Kris, Robert, and I as leaders, we called ourselves (C.O.D) Circle of Darkness, a clique within D. F. M clique. This was who we were since we were so close and couldn't see one without the other. We thought our clique couldn't be touched. We had money, fear, and respect. Nobody would try to test us clique wise after all the work we were putting in. We failed to remember that we tested T.S.K and we wanted their spot because they were the top clique. There was always somebody or some new crew that wants what you got.

Everything was going smooth, and we would routinely fight, drink, smoke, and continue to do dirt. This was our new normal for a while. Then the worst happened. Robert and a soldier named Lil Head went to go slang some weed to a customer. This was supposed to be a routine sell, but it didn't go down like planned. Lil Head was a rider for D.F.M, he loved doing dirt, and he didn't mind putting in work. If anything needed to be done, we would send Lil Head, and it would be done right, no questions asked. He was from Texas and moved down here six months ago. Nobody knew his real name or where he lived. We called him Lil Head because of the obvious. I believe he had a birth defect because his head was noticeably little as fuck. He looked like a cartoon or something. Lil Head wasn't mentally challenged, but he was crazy as hell, and we all liked him off the jump.

The deal that Robert had was bigger than we usually made at one time, so he took our most reliable soldier to catch his back. It wasn't like we had a big connect or was selling a lot, but this deal for three pounds was a lot for us. This was a chance to make about $3600 in one drop off. Usually, we sold a quarter pound, or at the most, a pound of weed. I could understand why he needed to have someone with him and what better soldier to take than Lil Head.

They get to the location at Bubbling Springs Park, which was still close to our area but also not. Robert has the pounds in a backpack, and Lil Head has a butterfly knife in his pocket, in case shit hit the fan. They wait around for a while for the customer to show up and finally when they do, twenty-five minutes late, Robert does what most people would do. He starts flipping out, *what the fuck is this, dog you got all these niggas with you and you late as hell. Chill out,* the customer and his three homies said. *Let's just do this shit, fool. I don't know what the hell you are trying to pull dog, but it's not going down like that. It was supposed to be me and my homeboy and you and your homeboy. Vato, relax holmes, it's cool just give me the shit, and we can do this. You got the money? You got the weed fool? Show me the money first. I got your punk ass $3600 bitch. Matter of fact, you look like one of the niggers who spit on me when I got jumped. He probably is homie, and he's that nigger from D.F.M. You got me fucked up with someone else homie, I've never seen you before so miss me with that shit. Yeah, I'm from D.F.M what the fuck does that have to do with this money,* Robert said. But in the back of his mind, he knew that it was him, and it was about to be all bad from here on out. He knew if they backed out the deal that they would just rob them, so he tried to play it off and continue business.

The customer wouldn't let it go and then his boys started to pump him up. Robert pulls out a pound and shows it to him. *Take this backpack and let me get my punk ass $3600 now so I can get the fuck out of here nigga!* Lil Head knew that it was a bad move to give the weed up without seeing the money, plus they were out numbered two to one. He starts to unravel the knife in his pocket, but one of the customer's homie sees his movements. *Look out vato he's got a gun homie.* The customer pulls out a gun while Robert yells out, *NO! we're not strapped.* The customer started to yell, *you motherfuckers you trying to rob me, and you look like the nigger who spit on me.* BANG, BANG, two shots to Lil Heads chest. Robert said he didn't even see his body drop. Before they had a chance to turn the gun to him, he took off running. They started to shoot BANG, BANG, BANG as they ran after him, but lucky for Robert, the gun jammed. They figured, fuck it, they have the weed and killed somebody, it's time to get the hell out the park.

Robert frantically runs back to his house where the clique was hanging out. He broke through his house door like a Police Swat team during a raid. We all hopped up shocked and confused, *what the hell is wrong with you and where's Lil Head?* We could see that he was startled and in autopilot mode. He wasn't all there he was in a daze, but after he grabbed his breath, he calmed down and told us what went on. *What? Lil Head is dead? Who did it? I don't know dog, but I knew it was all bad when he said I looked like the nigga who spat on him when he got jumped. He knew we were from D.F.M too, so it was definitely going down regardless since everybody wants our spot.*

This was an eye-opener to me. I knew what we were doing was wrong, but I considered it fun and games. I guess I thought we could charge all the wrong to our immaturity and get a pass in life. Instead, immaturity was passed, and all was charged to life, Lil Head's life that is. I mean what else should I have expected? Somebody had to cry for all this laughter we were doing. Sad to say it was Lil Head's mom at his funeral the next week.

Chapter 10: I Still Haven't Forgiven Myself

This was the first homies funeral I attended, and I wish it was the last. Damn, he's really gone, and now it's time to walk up to see him for the last time. As I was walking back to my seat from viewing his body, Ms. Washington looked me in my eyes. This look that she gave me was a cold, cruel, and painful medusa stare. It was a mother's pain. *I hate you; this wasn't your friend, not one of you knew his name before this funeral.* She imitated Kris's voice, *his name was David Earl Washington,* and snickered then she smacked me. *Get out, all of you little bad bastards.*

At that moment, I was feeling like shit on a stick. It was a shameful walk down the aisle and out the church. Seeing all the people who loved him crying and looking at us was an unforgivable moment. Sometimes I still see all those faces, and that feeling comes back. The way we looked walking out was similar to a dog ducking his head and putting his tail between his legs. I never wanted to feel like that again, I told myself. The only way not to feel like that was to stop carrying on the way I was. If I continued on that path, raping or killing somebody was all that was left, and I didn't think those actions were in me.

The only thing that was certain was death or prison. Several thoughts went through my mind over the next few days. I finally gathered my thoughts and called Robert and Kris to tell them to come over. Six thirty at night on a Wednesday we were at my house. We go outside and sit on the stairs to catch up on things. It's been five days since Lil Heads funeral, and we haven't chilled out together. I tell them that over this time I've done some thinking and I don't know if we should continue the things we were doing. *For one, you see where it got Lil Head and Jason. For two, there's nothing left for us to do but murder and rape. Frankly, I'm not with none of that, are you guys?* Robert said *I'm not down with rape, but I will kill if I have to. Yeah, I feel that if a nigga does something to my family or me, then he has to go. Dude, I feel you but the way we are going, it's coming soon. We're moving way to fast in this game, and all that's left is to go to jail, get killed, or kill. I think we need to slow down and just be smooth.*

Me, myself, I'm about to start focusing on these hood rats more and playing basketball or something. I'm not scared, but I don't want to end up like Lil Head, dead before my time. No matter what, you guys are my best friends and I'm always going to have your back and kick it with you guys regardless. Just not the way we always been chilling, so I hope you guys can accept it. You my nigga, Matt, you know this! We're always going to be down for life. So that means no more of that bullshit going on. Whoa, you're going to chill out, we're still going to get to this money. You a fool homeboy; before I got through completing my sentence, screaming and yelling came from my house. Dishes being thrown on the wall and stuff being knocked over followed up the loud yelling. *Man, shit! They always arguing. Let me go get my brother homie. Don't trip, dog, we about to leave anyway, just get at us tomorrow or something. Alright, let me go stop these fools, later dog.*

When I stepped in the house, I can see my mom and Joey going at it like I've never seen before. They were tussling, but no blows were being thrown. I grabbed my little brother and took him to the back room because he was watching, and I didn't want him to see that. I sit him on my mom's bed and put in his favorite Barney the dinosaurs VHS in the VCR player. *Look, you sit here and watch this while I go check on them, okay?* Jared didn't really talk much, and when he did, only the family could really understand him, but this time he said in his funny mumbo jumbo English, *Matthew, I don't like when they fight.* It took me by surprise because I could tell by how he said it that he was starting to understand what was going on between them. It kind of hurt me because I was hoping all this would be over with before he could understand or she would leave Joey. I said, *I know man, me too, but don't worry about it, I got you, just sit here and I'll be right back.*

I walked down the hall and thought; I hope he puts his hands on my mom, so I can stab his ass. I only thought that because I believe that's the only level of a situation where my mom would leave him. At times I felt like she chose her happiness over ours, which wasn't right. I understood that she had to have a life, but when that life was causing us to be a dysfunctional family with domestic violence and alcoholism as our normal, that wasn't right. But as a kid, I guess you don't understand everything you encounter. I got to the end of the hallway and I saw my mom pick Joey up and body slam him on the coffee table. Oh, shit was all I could think. I stood in shock as my mom was talking shit to Joey and taunting him. It was all a muffled noise I heard, but I knew she was mocking and talking shit by her actions. My brain finally let me tune back in two minutes later in the middle of her sentence. *Punk is what you're being right now, get up you're not hurt.*

I was laughing my ass off in the inside but still in shock that she just body slammed this man on the coffee table. Whatever they were arguing about must have been serious because it's never got to this point of physical violence. At this time, it didn't matter what the argument was, I joined in on my mom's side and started taunting him as well. There were times my mom was wrong, just bitching for whatever, but it was balled up frustration more like a lash out. *Yeah, Joey, get up man you not even hurt dude, you acting like a punk.*

Calling Joey a punk was a low blow because he didn't use or like that word. He always said to never call him that and there was an explanation to it. He told us where he's from that word means you're a "Jailhouse Bitch". To us, it was nothing more than saying asshole. This was used by me to be cruel and get some get back. I took advantage of the situation, but my mom used it to disguise that she realized she fucked up, so she had to portray an image of her display and act as if she didn't care. What she really was doing was checking to see if he would react and stand so she would know how much damage she had done out of anger.

I don't believe she meant to take it this far but when you're in a moment of rage, anything can happen. At first, I didn't believe he was hurt because he was lying on his side and was moaning. About an hour went by of this taunting and groaning, then he tried to move, and he was doing something like a low military crawl. I looked into his eyes and seen the pain and somewhat embarrassment. That's when I knew he wasn't lying he was really injured and something was wrong, especially since he never mention anything about us calling him a punk. It took a tear to come out of his eye for my mom to believe him and then she started to show sympathy.

Sherry, it's my hip, I can't move, it hurts too much, call an ambulance. So, she did. I could tell my mom felt bad, only because it was about an hour later before she seeks medical attention. The ambulance gets there and takes him to the hospital and my mom tells me *watch Jared, I'll be back. Mom, wait, what's for dinner? Boy, there's some corndogs and burritos in the freezer, bye.* Damn it corndogs or frozen burritos again. It seemed like that was all we ate besides chicken. If I never saw another one of those again in life, it would be too soon.

My mom comes back the next morning and tells me that Joey has shattered his hip into a thousand different pieces and he's going to need a hip replacement. My reaction was, *man, that's crazy. I thought he was playing at first. Matt, I'm about to grab some clothes and go back up to the hospital so watch your brother, and I'll give you guys a call later.*

Attendance in school at this point was a hit or miss. I was there maybe three out of the five days a week. When I did come, the teachers would all talk shit as well as my peers. Usually, they would say something slick like "I'm glad you can make it today Mr. Sanders" or my favorite, "you still go to this school?"

Chapter 11: Loyalty to the Homies

Ever since I talked to the clique, we got kind of distant from each other. There was a weird vibe between us. We still kicked it, but not as hard as we use to. My niggas felt like I turned my back on them which I didn't, I just was trying to turn my back on the activities that we used to do. I could tell they didn't understand it and felt like I wasn't down anymore, but I was always down for them.

Two months had gone by with this vibe and Robert tried to test me. *Yo, son, my sister is working at Robinsons May, and she got these credit cards that people left at the store. She wants us to come through and charge some shit for her, and we can get whatever we want.* Now I knew that Robert was testing me, but he also was just showing me love as well. This was how I knew it was a test. We had a bad vibe going on between the Circle of Darkness, and if I turned down an easy come up, then he would think I'm not down with him or the crew.

In the hood there's loyalty, not everybody stays loyal or has it, but this was definitely an option to find out if I was. If I have three pairs of shoes and you need a pair, as my brother's keeper, I'm supposed to give you a pair. It's the loyalty and honor that we all go through; the struggle together or whatever it may be because, in the end, we're all we got. When it comes to loyalty, I'm supposed to take the shirt off my back if you need it. This was like an unspoken urban rule that doesn't need to be taught because if you're real or down with your people, it's already within you. You either have it, or you don't.

This was the same difference in situations. Robert had an easy come up where everybody could gain more than what we had. If I turned it down then I'm not my brother's keeper, I'm simply saying in urban communications that I don't want to know you, or I'm not down with you. There were two things you didn't want to be known for in the hood, and that was being a snitch or not being loyal. Usually people who are not loyal turn into snitches, and snitches get put in ditches. Either way you looked at it, you can be ostracized from your neighborhood like an Asian culture who brought shame to their family name.

Robert knows I ain't got any clothes or money like that, so he was putting me on. I say, *fuck it, I'm down dog. When are we doing this shit?* He's like, *I knew you were my nigga and we are doing it next Friday. What's so special about next Friday, why don't we just do it tomorrow? My sister wants to get her paycheck first in case something goes wrong. Ok, I can dig that, but ain't shit going to happen because we fucking G's.*

All week I'm constantly thinking about this come up and playing things out in my head. I'm the type of person that when something is on my mind it's stuck there and the only way to get it out is to accomplish or go through it. I have dreams at night of us getting all the new stuff. Fubu, Tommy Hilfiger, Polo, Nike, Timberland, and whatever else we can get our hands on. By having these popular name brand clothes, this was going to make the chase for hoes so much easier, and since my focus has been rerouted to hood rats, I was all for it.

The days get closer and closer, and I'm beyond excited. It's as if Christmas was coming and I was actually going to have things I wanted and liked no more damn puzzles. Friday shows up slower than an income tax return check that's been waited on since it's been filed. Today's the day we were supposed to meet up at Robert's house, and his mom was going to drop us off at the Ventura Mall. I get to the homies house, and I ask, *where's Kris?* Robert said, *that nigga is being a bitch, he's with Jenifer and said he was good.*

Jenifer was a drop dead, gorgeous Asian and White hoe. She was what everybody in school wanted; sexy, beautiful eyes, nice body, and popular. Jenifer had some of that shit that was to die for. Ironically, I say that because she used to go with a well-known athlete named Jason. Jason was an older guy, maybe four to five years older than us, and he was going places in life. Prime example, he used to model and he was a dancer on the TV show The Soul Train. The story I got was that he and Jenifer broke up for real this time. You know how teenage love goes, the back and forth game. Well, this time it was serious, and once he realized he lost her, he would do stalker shit over a few months. He got the picture one day and decided to take a shotgun to the face over this bitch. He left a note and everything explaining he didn't want life without her. It was a sad story in the hood because even though he was a sucker for love, he was respected in the hood and had a promising future.

So with that, I say she has that shit to die for because that's going to forever be on her resume. Kris already had clothes, shoes, and jewelry, so he wasn't really tripping because that's his norms. I was excited when I found out my homie was on with the hottest thing out. Plus, that was just another element for the city to hate on the clique. It's time to roll, mom dukes dropped us off at the mall, and we proceed to walk to Robinsons May. We had moms drop us off at the other end of the mall, so they couldn't catch her plates on camera if we got caught. I felt that was a smart move, but we were about to go in here and win so losing wasn't really on our minds. We enter the store laughing kind of loud because we don't know how to act and we're cracking jokes, just doing what we normally do. Unfortunately, we had drawn attention to ourselves without even knowing. That was strike number one.

Robinsons May was a little more of an upscale store. Put it this way, these young ghetto black boys didn't belong in there, and we were clowning. Needless to say, all eyes were on us from the start. We stroll into the clothing area and finger through a couple of shirts and pants. I find something I like so I popped my top and tried it on in the middle of the store. Cleary there are dressing rooms right across from me, but I'm not caring because I'm simply not caring, that was strike two. Two young black kids were getting undressed in the middle of the store. I tried on three or four more items like that, and as you should already expect, more employees are paying attention to us.

We're not peeping game at the time because we have tunnel vision. We're like kids in a candy store with more things than we should have, let alone, we shouldn't even be in here. I piled up handfuls of clothes and take it to the register. But on the way to the register, I'm getting so many looks you would have thought I was famous.

What's up girl, you ready? We got some good shit, yo! Nigga, did y'all get my baby something? What do you mean? Robert was supposed to tell you to grab Malik some clothes. Damn, he ain't say all that, but I only got two hands. Azzure was steaming mad, *boy you think this shit was just for y'all to come up, how the fuck am I winning out of this? Go back and get my baby some stuff and I'll ring this up while you do that. Alright then, I'll be right back,* and as I walked away, Robert was coming toward the register with hella shit. Azzure yells out, *get the new Penny Hardaway shoes size 7c, fool.*

By this time, we gained security on us, but we're not even knowing because it's all about the come up. I get back with a gang of stuff for the little homie and she's having problems ringing the shit up. Azzure was still new to the job and just got out of training about a week ago. She was taking so much time that she tells us to sit down while she rings up the other customers that have formed a long ass line. Thirty-five minutes go by and we're looking at her like, nigga you stupid, are you trying to get us caught? Ring that shit up so we can bust a move. Finally, she gets everything processed and then she tells me to write my name as the signature. Now, momma ain't raise no fool, so I scribble x's, o's, triangles, and things of that nature. We got three bags full of things in each hand. The grip from the bag handles was cutting off circulation in my hands from the weight of the shit we had. We walk out the doors and mob through the parking lot. I say, *nigga it's all good,* and as soon as I opened my mouth we hear; *HEY! STOP!*

Robert turned around and said, *oh fuck, its security.* I said, *so its security keep walking fool.* Apparently, we didn't hear buddy creep up behind us. He grabbed Robert by the shoulder and said, *you need to stop and show me a receipt.* Robert punched him in the stomach and said, *Matt, take off!* I grab the bags that I could of Robert's, but it was only two. I head toward the bus that I see across the street, and when I get there, I look back. By that time, there are three security guards on my homie. I quickly think, do I leave the homie on stuck and have all this shit we took? Or do I get to swinging on these busters? As you might remember, I told you before; loyalty is something that has to be within you, it can't be taught. I ran back toward him and got to punching, kicking, and all the above on those poor guys that were just trying do the right thing by working to provide for their families the honest way.

During the altercation, they gained control and placed handcuffs on us. Once we were escorted to the mall holding area, we were cuffed to the benches to wait for the police to take us. Robert was acting a full-blown donkey, all you heard was, *Bitch, let me up out this shit, or I'll beat yo ass cuz! What the fuck we do? We paid for this stuff; this is fucked up man! Y'all harassing us we got receipts, bitches!*

I'm keeping calm, but tripping out like, we really let these soft ass security guards catch us. The police finally showed up, and I told the cop my wrist was numb and asked if he could loosen up the cuffs some. *No problem*, the Officer replies. Robert attempts to get his loosened, but he went about it the wrong way; *Hey man my cuffs tight as fuck, nigga, loosen my shit too. Young man, don't call me a nigger, I'm not black* said the Officer. *You a white nigga*, Robert replies, *and you couldn't wait to call me a nigger huh, fucking pig*. The Officer walks over, appearing to loosen his cuffs, but instead, he tightens them up and then slaps him in the face and said, *I told you I'm not a nigger and don't disrespect me again.* I yell out, *you bitch ass nigga, slapping kids that are handcuffed don't make you tough.* The Officer punches me in the stomach, and I instantly throw up all over the floor. I'm starting to think I must have a weak ass stomach because I can't take any gut punches. Robert begins to get hype and starts trying to kick the Officer from the other side of the bench saying; *I would beat your ass if I weren't handcuffed. Oh yeah, you little skinny shit, let's find out.* He pops the cuffs off, and they get to going at it. I'm still trying to gather myself because that blow to the gut took a lot out of me, but I'm keeping an eye on my homie.

Robert throws a jab, then another jab, now a right hook to the Officer's face. Those punches weren't fazing him, he grabs Robert and body slams him on the floor. BOOM extremely loud was all you heard. During all this, I got myself together and slipped my cuff since it was loosened up for me, which was part of the plan from the beginning. As soon as I get my hand free, here comes Officer Billy Bad Ass with a boot to my face. I had no time to react, so I had to take it to the chin. *You fucking young thugs give this community a bad name. This is my community, and you think you can just take shit you didn't earn? Not on my watch*. Robert hops on his back and screams *run nigga, get the fuck out of here!* After taking that unnecessary ass whooping, you didn't have to tell me again. I run for the door, and as I'm exiting I hear the cop radio for back up and state one suspect fled the scene, and he starts giving my description.

Now, this wasn't my first encounter with rogue police officers, but this was the first time that I've been physically assaulted by one. They call it a reasonable amount of force, but I call it whooping the shit out of young black youth's ass and scarring them for life. How can we trust the law when there's no justice, and they take the law in their own hands? They do what they want, when they want, as far as I'm concerned, law enforcement is just a big gang ran well. Why wouldn't we do what we want, when we want too?

Somehow during the commotion, I made it out of the office without seeing one security guard. I break through the side doors of Robinsons May like a runaway slave. I'm gasping for breath while I'm sweating. I'm a little confused because that kick to the face has me dizzy. I just ran with no direction or no means. I'm running like a madman across the parking lot. Once I get a few streets down the road, I calm down and try not to draw attention to myself. I'm in Ventura, but don't know where the fuck I'm at and I don't have a clue as to how to get back to the south side of Oxnard. I'm walking and thinking, mmmh, who could I call or who do I know that lives out this way?

I decide to stop at a Seven Eleven convenient store and get a bag of hot Cheetos and a Sprite. I'm starving, especially since I had just thrown up everything in my stomach. This was probably going to be dinner like several times before. It was only two bucks, and I needed to watch how much I spent because I only had about eight dollars on me. Now if I decide to call a cab and they ask to see the money first, I can flash a few dollars and then hop out running when I get to where I need to be. So, I got a game plan, and now it's time to put everything in motion.

I walked into the store and as I entered, I saw the pay phone out the side of my eyes to the left of me. I walked to the back of the store in the soda area. The sodas were a few aisles back and just my luck, there are three fools in uniform, kicking it. The uniform of the day was Dickie pants or shorts, flannel shirt, black gloves, Chuck Taylor Converse All-Stars shoes or the Nike Cortez shoes, and if they were wearing shorts, high white socks to the knees were mandatory.

At this time, I already know that I'm about to get hit up. It didn't even take sixty seconds, and I hear *Aye fool, where you from homie?* Here comes the bullshit. I look back and think should I run? Nope because where the hell am I going to run to, I don't know where I am. Then I think, well there's only three fools, I got somewhat of a chance. While I'm thinking, I see the store clerk on the phone, so I'm assuming he's calling the cops anyway because there's too much activity in here for him. I pretend not to hear them and continue with my business by grabbing a Sprite. I start to head toward the chips aisle. *Hey, this pinche negro must be deaf or something holmes. I asked you where the fuck are you from, Homie?* I still didn't say anything hoping they'd give up, which I knew was not going to happen, but shit, it was worth a try I guess.

Then I hear, *This fucking nigger smells like vomit, ese. Hey, you stinky bitch nigger, I'm fucking talking to you dog.* Well, it's time to take this ass whooping like a man, is what I'm thinking, plus I tried to avoid them, and it just didn't work. I transformed and turned into the demon within inside me, *Bitch, what the fuck you say?*

The tall one approaches me and while walking up, he said, *you're in the wrong hood fool, this is Big Bad Ventura Chiques homie.* When he was close enough, I take off to his head and body by throwing haymakers. His two homie's jumped in. One's trying to choke me out from the back and put me in an L.A choke hold. The other one attacks my body with blows to the ribs and blows to the stomach. The tall homie I punched gathered himself and jumped back in, but he's not fucking around this time, he whips out a pocket knife as he walks toward me. Fear can bring out a tremendous amount of cleverness and bravery. You will be surprised at the things you're able to do when under maximum danger. I got one on my back and one in front of me, who was giving powerful body blows like this was Nintendo's Mike Tyson's Punch Out game and I'm King Hippo.

I had recently seen a movie called Rumble in the Bronx with Jackie Chan, so I figured I'd try a move I seen. I jumped up and kicked the ese in front of me with both feet into his chest. I knew that homie behind me wasn't going to let me go because he wants this choke hold too bad, which lets me know he can't really fight because that was his initial move. The choke hold is intended to be used when you are getting beat down, or your opponent is to damn big and you just got to put him sleep because you can't risk the chance of getting hit by any punch they throw. Now knowing he's the scary one, I really only have to fight two people and he will more than likely run off or bitch out.

So, I made the move that I saw in the movie, and it worked; not only did it work, it saved my life. Shout out to Jackie Chan! As I jumped, the tall homie swung the knife, and I got high enough that he missed me then stabbed his friend in the side of his stomach. The momentum of the kick off the chest pushed me and the scary guy back into the aisle which happened to knock us down on all the chips, pickles, Slim Jims, and sunflower seeds. This freed me like I hoped it would, but I didn't really expect it to work. I told you when you're in fear for your life you always figure something clever out.

I popped up and started running. As I ran to the door I saw that I was right, the clerk did call the cops. I'm sure they were already in route due to the shenanigans I had about fifteen minutes ago, but it didn't matter, they were right on time. I ran through the first officer like Bo Jackson on 4th and goal. The second officer grabs me up, *whoa little big fella, why you in such a rush?* The first officer looks around and sees the wounded dude and the disaster of the store. He immediately pulls out his weapon and so does the other officer. *FREEZE, PUT YOUR HANDS UP NOW, SHIT BAG,* as he points to me and gives the command, *YOU SIT DOWN ON THE FLOOR NOW!*

He radios for back up and calls for an ambulance and places zip ties on the tall homie and the fool that was stabbed. I get zipped tied and then the scary homie starts spilling the beans as they detain us. *This fool did some Bruce Lee shit and we fell back, but when he did that he got my homie stabbed by my other homeboy. Damn, are you at least going to let them ask you what happened, fool?*

SHUT YOUR PIE HOLE, said the second officer. One officer performs basic medical treatment for the victim. He gets plastic sheets, or something of that nature, and places it on the wounded skin area, then he tells him to keep pressure there. They talk to the clerk and the clerk goes through the story of what happened. I sat down thinking, boy, what a damn day.

Once the ambulance comes, the officers reviewed the camera footage and saw for themselves what happened. I had the zip ties cut off of me and was told I needed to write a statement at the police station. I told them I was still shaken up and I just wanted to go home. They asked what my phone number was and where I lived. I explained to them that we didn't have a phone then I gave them the address to some random place on J Street. Fortunately, I was able to trick the officers into releasing me and told them that I would come in later or tomorrow with my parents to write the statement. I strongly expressed the fact that I was a minor and didn't want to write anything without my parents' consent. I was polite, respectful, and in the role of an innocent schoolboy, so they fell for it.

I got a few band-aids and minor treatment from the paramedics then bribed the officers to give me a ride home since they couldn't contact my parents. During this ride, I overheard them talking about the mall situation and how the other suspect wasn't found. Boy, these have to be some of the dumbest motherfuckers on the force. They never asked what I was doing in the store, let alone how I got to Ventura from Oxnard. God is good, I tell you. Remember when I said I thought the clerk called the cops? I guess I was wrong because they also brought up how mad they were because they didn't get a chance to get their daily routine donuts from the store. To think a glazed donut played a role in saving my damn life.

Once we arrived at J Street, I was a little paranoid because I didn't think about the perception of the hood. Me stepping out of the police car wasn't a good look at all. There were a few people down the street looking, but thankfully it wasn't any of the homies. The officers tried to walk me to the door, but I told them nobody was home and pointed to the driveway because there was no car parked there. They said they would get in contact with me and to make sure to inform my parents about the events and if they have any questions to call the number on the card. I made sure to take my time acting like I was looking for my keys. I'm hoping these clowns hurry up and leave before the people who really live here decide to look out the window and see me at their door.

Are you locked out? yells one of the officers. *No, I'm fine,* as I pull a set of keys out and mock like I'm opening the door. Lord, please don't let these people hear me jingling the doorknob because I really don't have time for this shit. The police pull off, and I started to walk away. The door opens, *did you want something? I thought I heard my door being messed with? Oh no. I'm sorry, I got the wrong house my friend told me the wrong address.* The Lady looks at me like what the fuck ever and slams the door shut. This was probably the best walk home because it gave me time to reflect and gather my thoughts. Plus, I didn't have any further delays to the crazy day I'd been having.

Chapter 12: Sick and Tired of the Sacrifice

I got home and my mom said, *hey, we got to go get Joey out of jail, this fool got a D.U.I again. Damn! Mom let him stay there; you can't keep bailing him out of jail for the same stuff. Boy, who do you think you're talking to? I'm just saying, mom, I feel like you put him before us and that ain't cool. I'm going to find my dad and stay with him. It's like every day y'all argue and throw things in the middle of the night, waking me up out of my sleep, and Jared is scared to death. I'm the one that has to calm him down, not you. Sometimes ya'll be going for hours and then you be tripping when I don't make it to school. I can't go to school because most of the time you worried about him being alone with his father. I didn't ask for this, and it's not my fault you've got bad choices in love.*

SMACK! SMACK! Mom bitch slaps me in the face while yelling; *you're going to leave me? Huh, you're going to leave me? I'll kill you first! I brought you into this world, and I'll take you out.* The argument started off in the living room, but somehow, we ended up in my room. Mom starts to place a good grip around my neck and commence to choking me out against the wall. For a quick second, I think maybe I should hit her with a right cross, but that thought quickly leaves my mind because I wasn't crazy. She just kept repeating, *you're going to leave me?*

The pain and screech in her voice was so emotional. I heard so much more than are you going to leave me? I heard, how dare you threaten to leave this family for a man that doesn't care if you exist. I know I made a few bad choices, but I'm a good mother. I work hard to provide what food, clothes, shelter, and love you have. I need your help, we're a team, you're my first love, and you want to leave me for someone who doesn't call on your birthday or send you Christmas presents, let alone nurture you when you're sick?

It was evident that I had hurt my mom more than I could explain. I felt like I betrayed her by being honest and asking for a normal childhood. How selfish of me was what ran through my head. I found a way to squeeze out words during her death grip. *No mom, I'm not going to leave you. I promise, I promise.* She lightened her grip and tears rolled down her face and mine. My mom wasn't the type of woman to cry and usually when she did it was from being so angry. But this was both. It was anger within the truth spoken and sadness from the thought that I would even consider leaving her side. We had more of a sibling or friendship type bond. The struggles we overcame together made our relationship strong, but beyond strong, we had a loyalty to each other. *I could never leave you, mom, I'm sorry. I know, Matt, now go get your brother so we can go.*

Due to Joey's alcohol problem and the current situation, it caused us to move. This was my way out of my clique's activities. But it also meant that I wouldn't be able to see my homies, which became more like brothers over time.

We moved all the way up north, which was a fifteen-minute drive and at least an hour and a half walk. There was no way for me to kick it or hang out unless I got a ride. I could walk it, but that was too much walking for Jared, he was only about four at this time.

We moved right before the summer ended and I was going to start high school. I was hoping for a new start, but somehow life had its ways of always putting me behind and playing catch up. It's like I would never get a chance to have an even playing field. Joey was granted work release. This put a strain on the whole family because not only did my mom have to adjust her hours and wake up earlier to pick him up, she also had to take time off work to drop him off at the designated time.

There was no one available to watch Jared during my school hours. That left me to pick up an extra shift. Joey would normally have him in the mornings and go to work at 3:00pm when I got home from school. Daycare wasn't an option because the prices were outrageously expensive and we were barely making rent. I was forced to stay home my first six months of high school. This put me extremely behind if I was to ever think about graduating on time.

There were times my mom was able to find someone to watch my brother, but it wasn't often. Twice a month I would have the opportunity to attend my freshman year. Every day felt like the first day of school at Oxnard High. I would show up and not know where my classes were and get asked a million questions from my teachers about my attendance. I would say things like I had a death in the family, or I was hospitalized for a few weeks. I realized once you say you have sickle cell disease they would normally stop asking. To tell the truth, I didn't even know what it was, but I heard it in a rap song by Mobb Deep that one of the members had it.

This was a condition that people accepted when they weren't able to make concerts and perform. I figured if fans would accept it, the teachers would too. The fans were paying good money to see this group and a teacher was getting paid regardless if I showed up or not, so they had to accept it. I eventually got tired of making excuses up and didn't feel like even going. I can't learn anything twice a month at school, and besides, I accepted that I probably wasn't going to graduate anyway since I was kicked out of elementary school and junior high. The school system doesn't care if I learn and neither did I. All they did was push me forward to the next grade, even when I wasn't going to school at all. Once every other week, the homies would come by and visit me and we would catch up on things. A lot of the times we would go play some basketball or just get high.

Occasionally my house would be the kick it spot when they ditched school. They would bring some girls over and we'd try to get in their pants. At this time in life, I went from finger banging girls to getting oral sex. I wasn't really trying to go all the way and have sex. I think the fact that Robert stayed getting people pregnant and making them have abortions or getting them beat up to have a miscarriage when they wouldn't agree to get an abortion scared me.

There's no way I would be able to take care of a baby, especially knowing how it was having my brother all the time. It was like I basically was raising Jared, I just didn't take care of the finances. The quote "it takes a village to raise a kid" was the right expression because I sure had my hands full with him. The thought of raising him and trying to take care of another one scared me to death, so I was cool on the full sex aspect. But messing around and feeding my teenage hormones was a must, and I was content with what I was doing.

It didn't take long before my mom couldn't make rent and we moved again. This time we moved close to my old area by Lemonwood. This meant I was to attend Channel Island High School. Channel Island was where a majority of T.S.K clique went to school. I knew it would be a lot of problems when I arrived there. I was ready to face the music and see what drama this school was going to bring. When I was able to make classes, it wasn't bad. A lot of the homeboys from Black Stock went there, so it made it easier to adjust. Whenever I would get hit up, I stated my name and my clique, but the few homies I knew wouldn't let shit go down. Most of them were on the football or basketball team and they were always trying to get me to join. But they wouldn't let me get into shit. I wanted to be a part of the football team, so they took me in, and I started working out with them and training on the days I could make it.

My mind started to transition into wanting to be an athlete. I saw that they all had each other's back and hung out together. There was brotherly love and a bond that was similar to my homies and D.F.M. The only difference was they weren't terrorizing the streets but dominating on the field and in the books. I mean come on, everyone wants to belong to something or be a part of something. This could be my new way to get what I was looking for. All I was looking for was to be accepted and shown love. I saw that they had respect, they had love, and the bitches were all over them. This was everything that I wanted, besides some money, but it wasn't a problem because I been broke my whole life, that was just a normal thing.

When I was making money, I wasn't doing anything but buying food and sometimes clothes for me and Jared. I couldn't spend it how I wanted to because that would bring suspicion to my mom and the last thing I needed was for her to find out what I was into. I honestly believe she knew I was into certain things but never said anything because she didn't know how deep it went. I don't know how I balanced two different lifestyles. But I always stayed respectful and appeared to be innocent. If she was to see a black eye or a pair of shoes she didn't buy, it was an easy lie to tell. I would say I got into a fight at school with a bully, or she figured I borrowed shoes and clothes from one of my friends. When I bought Jared things, I would always try to wash the neighbors' cars for five dollars to cover up where the money was from. I would make sure she saw me washing at least one car when she got off work, so it could be believed that I was doing it all day. I made most of my car wash money from a neighbor named Larry. He had money because his daughter Cherry acted on the TV show Family Matters.

Everything was going smoothly. I found something that I wanted to do, and when I was at school, there was no static. Life seems like it could be heading for the better. That was until Joey got out and off work release by completing his time, and then things went back to its norms, which was the domestic violence. It wasn't more than three weeks since he was out, and we got the eviction notice to move again. Having the cops called out all the time and loud fights in the middle of the night caused the neighbors to complain and the landlord kicked us out.

I was happy to move out of the one-bedroom apartment because I had to sleep on the living room floor with a sleeping bag. I could never get rest because my personal space was the general area. Joey would be up drinking all night, playing loud music or playing dominoes with his uncle, Herman. From time to time they would be so drunk and forget I was on the floor and step on me when I was sleeping. There was no respect or designated time for the living room to be off-limits. The television would wake me up when they would try to watch it, or the arguing of the dice games played in the kitchen was a definite no sleep night. I was glad to be moving for those reasons, but I was mad because I just found something I could and wanted to be a part of with some good people. There was no drama for a good two months, and even though it felt unreal, I knew it wasn't going to last forever. I surely appreciated the quick break from my regular life.

Back to the south side of Oxnard in Hueneme, C Street was my new home. This move put me right back to what I thought I was leaving behind. It would be difficult to try and go without taking parts of D.F.M, but I would have to find a way; otherwise, I would be doomed. Now that Joey's back, I'm able to take part in school and be around all the homies. The first day of school at Hueneme I got to meet my new guidance counselor. During our meeting, he informs me I would have to make up half a school year if I wanted to complete schooling. Mr. Saunders worked out a plan where I attended school one hour early and one hour after school for the remainder of high school. I can't fail any classes, or it wouldn't leave much wiggle room for graduation. I told him that I was interested in playing sports and he set me up with the athletic director.

Mr. Miller was the director, and he was the head football coach, so it was perfect. Mr. Miller said, *son, with your frame, you can be the Lawrence Taylor of High School football. Your Six foot three and two hundred and thirty pounds, let's get you in the weight room and start some conditioning. Now you know you won't be able to play this year because of your grades, but we can have you ready for next year. Have you ever played before? No, my mom was afraid I'd get hurt. I had to bribe her to play basketball the times I did. Son, don't worry about it I'll take care of that.*

After that meeting, I felt like this could work, I just have to stay focused. That was easier said than done. I had a consistent lack of sleep because of household activities, and when I did go to school, I didn't understand what was being taught. The last thing I needed was Joey getting a second job. He had to bring in more money because child support was taking more than normal due to him not being able to catch up. That means once, in a blue moon, I would have to take Jared to school with me. Most of the time it was just for the last two classes of school. Joey started a part-time job at Denny's restaurant that required him to be there on his days off from the hardware store at 1:00pm. I lived three minutes from the school, so I would leave for my lunch break at 12:00pm and go get Jared before he left. I don't know how Child Protective Services weren't called on us. A lot of the times I would stay at home because Jared would be acting a fool in class. I had a math class for 7th period, and my 8th period class was weight training, so if I missed the physical education class, it was my coach, and I would pass with an A regardless. Math class was a little difficult to try and not draw attention to us, but how could we not with a four-year-old in the class that's playing and yelling at the top of his lungs. Nobody could study and my teacher, Mr. Cassiano, was cool with the situation. He said he understood and had been in my shoes before. He was kind enough to let me have a packet to complete weekly. As long as I showed up physically two days a week to his class, he could work it out he said.

I got into a pattern, and things seem to be working out. The household situation wasn't any better, but now I had something to look forward to. For the first time I had real goals, and I was striving to reach them. I still attempted to not take part in the type of activities that took place with D.F.M, but it was a struggle. I found the balance and developed the vision to wiggle through major situations and not take part in them over the next three years. There was a fight here or a robbery there but nothing consistent, more of a spur of the moment, unpredictable type things.

During those years, I learned that I was a talented basketball player and had potential with football to do great things if I could only get that juvenile delinquency out my life. I was making grades and playing the sports I wanted while bonding with peers that weren't into the thug life.

Coach Henry was another football coach and probably the main positive male role model in my life, besides Uncle Richard. Coach Henry really believed in me and talked to me like a man. When he spoke, it was inspirational; it was genuine love. He wanted to see me do great things in my life and he wanted to let football put me in a position to get me there as it did for him. He would always tell me I had charisma and I needed to be more aggressive. I understood what he meant by "be aggressive," because I wouldn't play with anger. I was afraid that I would get to the point that I couldn't control it, like when I choked out Playboy. But basketball was where I felt comfortable and really shined. I could be seen on the court; there was no mask to hide my face, it was just the crowd and me. I was a crowd player and when they were into me, I showed out my best.

Basketball was so poetic and smooth to me. When I was on the court, there was nothing to worry about. I was in my own utopia, and I loved it. This was my sanctuary; it has never lied to me, basketball loves me for me. It saw all the hard work I put in. This was more of a rush then any pistol or girl could give me. I literally felt like a GOD on the court. But the thing that meant most to me was that I was looked up to and took pride in leading my team to whatever opponent we faced. All these years I just wanted to belong to something, and now that I did belong to something and it was positive, I didn't want to go back to the old ways.

I loved my homies, but I couldn't love what they wanted to do. This made the loyalty very hard to balance between my own personal growth. I did well enough on the basketball court where I was one of the popular guys at Hueneme High School. I started to slim out to about two hundred pounds and grow to six foot five in height. There were no more fat jokes and bitches were saying I was cute now and they would start approaching me. I went three years in a row as M.V.P of the basketball team and the most improved player to the coaches award for the football team. My confidence was up, and my game was coming together each season.

I developed new bonds and friendships with my teammates. I played football to past the time and to have an excuse to not take part in the activities of the clique that I helped form. So, when we had major plays to make they understood that I couldn't be there because I had obligations already. Robert didn't question me when I couldn't make some things because he knew what I was doing. Plus, he was proud of me for doing something he always wanted to do but couldn't because he could never make the grade point average to be eligible to play. Kris was still going with Jenifer, so he wasn't tripping. Kris was the oldest of all of us, so I think he started to age out of the foolery we were into. Plus, he was on his first year out of high school and working every now and then. From time to time, we'd get high, catch the munchies, and revert back to stealing from stores or beating a few people up, but mostly we all started to transition our focus onto females.

Jan 11th, 2001, it's the middle of my junior year and I'm hanging on the basketball court with my friends during lunch break. Someone ran up and said, *Midget has a gun and he's talking about blowing this bitch's brains out in the cafeteria. Wait what? Midget has a gun?* Everyone started to run in a panic but me. I was curious and had to find out what was going on for myself. I walk towards the cafeteria and hear two gunshots. I don't know what or who he was shooting at, but he definitely fires the gun a couple of times. Sure enough, there he was, Richard, the elementary bully that had the whole school damn near jump me. I guess over time he finally joined a gang and went by Midget. Richard didn't even go to our school, but his girlfriend did. I see him in there cussing and crying. All he kept saying was, *it's all fucked up, I got to do this.* I see him pacing the walkway between the tables. Then he starts talking to himself. I couldn't really make out all that he was saying, but I could hear, *I want to go to heaven, but I can't be here.* Then he would mumble words and cry painfully, as if he was being tortured.

This motherfucker was crazy, and I needed to leave. None of that shit made sense to me. I didn't realize how long I spied on him because when I turned around the SWAT team was about twenty feet from me waving me to the direction they wanted me to go. I slide around the corner to the area they pointed to, and they moved in. I couldn't leave now; it was about to get good.

I stuck around where SWAT or Richard couldn't see me. Richard lured them to the open yard quad style stage we had in the middle of the school. Midget and an Officer exchange a few words, but it didn't take long before I heard, BANG BANG. I see Richard drop and even though he had lost his life, I kind of felt like I got my payback. The only reason I stayed around was to see the cops beat his ass like they have or would have done to me. You never want to see someone lose their life, but it was good enough payback to watch for me, I was satisfied.

I quickly turned around and took off running before they see me and want a statement. Then I would have to explain to my mom why I was there and not on my way to pick Jared up. My mom would've been mad if she knew I went back to see this and had a chance to get away. She wouldn't understand why I did, and neither would any other parent. But it was a must that I saw this with my own eyes. I jumped the fence and ran home, which wasn't far down the street. I got home and thought to myself; man, I sure need a joint. I've been doing pretty good without it for a while. Why not? I deserve it, especially after the type of day this was. Shit, I need it.

This was only Wednesday, who knows what the rest of the week would bring to me. I contemplated and went back and forth with myself for a few minutes. I eventually ended up giving in to my pleasure principle. There's nothing like good old Mary Jane to keep me sane and the occasional drink of Gin and juice.

Chapter 13: Be Careful What You Pray for Because You Might Receive Her

Summer basketball League was over, and I showed out. I was averaging 14pts and 9.5 rebounds for the season. My name was starting to spread in a good way around my city. I would go to the mall and hear people whisper, *Oh, that's Matt Sanders, he's the Center for Hueneme, he's got game.*

I was impressed that people I didn't know knew my name and this was building my confidence and my ego. I didn't let it get to me too much, but it made me that much more comfortable when I would talk to the girls. They would say things like, I heard of you, and I heard you're a player, too. But that told me that they were curious to find out. This was my new normal interaction with the ladies and it just kept improving.

Now that basketball was over, I jumped right into football season. This was my senior year, so it meant if I planned on doing something with this, it was time to go get it. I put my blood, sweat, and tears into every play on the field. This season I was starting as an offensive left tackle and as an outside linebacker on defense. Ironman football was what they called it. I put all of my heart and dedication into the team, but we still came up short with a losing season. It was the last game of the season and after the loss, I was walking off the field with my helmet in hand and tears coming down my eyes because this would be the last time I would ever play football, and I knew it. The thought of not being able to advance my career to the collegiate level hurt. But what really hurt the most was the thought that I couldn't see myself making it out my environment and leaving this life behind. I was going to be trapped like several others from around the way.

Football scholarships are easier to come by because every team is going to have at least a thirty-five-man roster, which means a higher percentage of making it to college sports than basketball.

Basketball teams only hold a twelve-man team. My odds were pretty slim, even if I was as good as I believed and people thought.

As I'm walking off the field toward the gate, I hear *Hey, number ninety-nine it's okay baby, let me take care of you.* I turn my head and there she was, this five foot eight, light brown eyes, box braids, coca cola shape physique, golden brown skin complexion, gorgeous female. She had dimples when she smiled. She was more than gorgeous; she was precious.

She waved me down and said, *come here.* I told her, *you caught me in a moment, beautiful, I'll be alright. My name is Sharlean, and you're Matthew, right? Yeah, that's my name, how did you know that? Oh, I heard of you and your ways. Go get dressed and I'll be right here waiting on you handsome.*

I got excited and tried to play it cool. This was definitely a first, and she was coming on strong, so I knew there was no way I could let this diamond in the rough fall threw my hands. *I'll be right back, precious, you going to be right here when I'm done, right? Trust me, I'm not going anywhere without you.* I walked away and overheard her say to her friend, who I did not meet, *Nikki, girl, you don't even know what I'm going to do to this man.* Then they start giggling.

This had to be my fastest time getting showered and dressed ever. I didn't even stick around to hear my coach speak to us as a team. All I could think about was this fine ass girl who was jocking me outside. I gave a few handshakes and daps to my close friends on the team and told the underclass some quick, inspiring words; then I slid out the side door before the coach could see me.

I got to Sharlean and she said, *let's go get something to eat, I know you're hungry.* Nikki said, *wait, girl, my man ain't come out yet.* I asked her who she went with? Sharlean said that Dean was her boyfriend. *Oh, my wide receiver, that's cool.* I hadn't really kicked it with Dean a lot, but we had hung out sometimes, plus he was always around the people I was with, so this should be cool. Nikki was kind of robust and loud, but a very nice girl. I couldn't see why Dean would be with her because he was skinny and a decent looking dude, so it wasn't adding up to me. But I have realized that a lot of skinny guys like plump girls, plus that's all Robert dated.

Dean comes out and we all walk to the car and Nikki said to meet them at Toppers pizza. I'm shocked because most girls I would talk to didn't have a license let alone their own car. I was trying to squeeze into this four-door Toyota Corolla and Sharlean was laughing. *I'm sorry, baby, I don't think the seat goes back anymore. I'm good; it's not a far drive. Is this your parent's car? Boy, this is my car; I'm a grown ass woman. Okay, I see you got your shit together. How old are you precious? I'm eighteen, how about you? I'm only seventeen but my birthday is in January, so you aren't that much older. My birthday was in October, so I got you by a few months, but it doesn't matter if you're younger. This would be my first time talking to someone younger than me.*

This sparked a nice conversation for the ride to the pizza place. I found out that she was in college, worked, and did hair on the side. She came from a strict background with one younger sister, and Nikki was her best friend. By the time we get to the pizza place, I was ready to eat and get out that damn car. Sharlean liked to talk a lot, but it was cool because all I could do was gaze into those beautiful eyes and stare at her golden-brown skin. She would catch me every now and then staring at her, but she would just smile. Those dimples would drive me crazy every time she smiled.

I believe that she loved the way I looked at her, so she would expose her cleavage more by fixing her shirt and leaning over the table for no reason. I'm picking up on the signs that she's giving me and I'm throwing a few back at her. I would find a way to touch her thigh or whisper something into her ear. Everything seemed to click at the pizza parlor. The chemistry was vibrant and the sexual urge was strong. I just wanted to kiss those luscious lips; I bet they were soft as pillows.

During one of my gazes, I heard a muffled voice. I could not quite make out everything, but I heard all that I needed to hear. Dean said, let's go back to my house. I hurried up and asked the waitress for the check. That was all I needed, just a chance to see what this girl was about. I went to pay for our bill like a gentleman, but she stopped me and said, *I got it.* Oh man, I could get used to this shit, was what I thought.

She paid and we grabbed our things and walked to her car. The ride was right down the street, so it didn't take long to get there. We settled in the living room and snuggled up on the couch. *Y'all want to watch a movie or something? Yeah, throw something in like Poetic Justice or Jason's Lyric.* This movie was not going to get watched at all, it was just for the pre-game.

Do you want to watch a movie really meant are you ready for foreplay? We got five minutes into Poetic Justice, then the kissing and touching started. I was still tripping on how this was going so far. It was no effort at all. That almost never happens; matter of fact it never has.

Okay, enough with the kissing, I started to move my fingers down into her pants. She's gushing wet already and then she does something that I've never experienced. She takes my hand out her pants and puts my fingers in her mouth. I'm in complete shock and find it hard not to ejaculate in my pants. This girl was a freak who apparently has done more things than I've ever tried.

Nikki and Dean don't waste any time and take their night into his room. Before they get to his room, Dean said his dad and sister were gone for the weekend and if we wanted to we could crash at his house. This was the cherry on top of the cake. I knew tonight was going to be the night to go all the way and I was nervous but excited. My emotions were like a rollercoaster, but quickly it was brought back to reality.

Sharlean said, *I wish I could, but my dad would kill me if I'm not home by 12:00am. What time is it anyway? You might want to grab your things because it's 11:41pm. Shit, I've been late the past few times, so I can't be late again. He said he would take my car from me for two weeks.* She buttons her pants up and gives me a kiss. *Sorry, babe, I can't drop you off, I got to go. It's cool, do your thang, but when can I see you again?* She gives me her number as she runs out the door.

Well, I guess I'm here for the night homie, good looking out. No problem man, there is soda and some hot pockets in the fridge if you need something. I'm about to go wear her ass out now if you don't mind. Boy, shut up and get in here and you better not give me three strokes and a grind like last time.

They shut the door and I try to go to sleep on the couch. I keep replaying the night through my head. Damn, I can't wait to tell the homies about this shit. She really put my fingers in her mouth after I just had them inside her. Prayer really works!

Every night and every morning for the past year, I had asked the man upstairs to send me someone for me, someone who I didn't have to game up or front for. This gorgeous girl really liked me for who I am. This was going to be the start of something far past what I could see. I replayed her enough in my head that I was able to calm down and go to sleep. But not before I jacked off into a paper towel. I had to get rid of all that extra testosterone.

It was morning and I slept well. The day after a football game was always rough because you feel all the hits you took the night before. Sore was not a good word to describe the pain I was feeling, but when I started moving around and warming my body up, it usually went away.

Nikki gave me a ride to my house and told me that Sharlean was really into me and she's never seen her like that with anyone. I play it smooth and tell her she might get a chance with me. I was already in love and didn't know it. Walking through my house, I saw my mom. My mom was off work that Saturday morning, which was rare.

You just getting in boy, she asked. *Must have been a long night. How was your game? We lost like usual. I'm glad this season is over because I'm ready for basketball.* I would never talk to my mom about females. All she knew was that they were always calling the phone interrupting her when she would be on the computer trying to get onto America Online.

Mom, I met a girl last night, and she is gorgeous. That's good, boy, you need a nice young lady around you, not these little neighborhood rats. What's her name? Sharlean, and she's in college, works, and has her own car. She is amazing, mom, I met her after my game and we went for pizza. Who are her parents? I didn't get all of that yet, but she seems a little uppity, so I'm sure they're good people. Hmm just make sure you treat her right, Matt. Of course, mom, why wouldn't I!

Throughout the day she was all I could think about. I didn't want to call her and seem desperate, but I also didn't want her to think I wasn't interested. Normally there's a three-day waiting period before I would contact a girl. This situation was different. I didn't have to build up her appetite for me; she was already starving. I can't fight my excitement or hormones, so I called her. *What's up, precious, how was your day? Good, I just got off work. Did you make it home on time? Yes, and my dad was in the kitchen looking at his watch when I walked in. I thought I was late according to my cell phone, but he said I made it on time. Good, I'm glad to hear that because it sounds like he was going to beat that ass. Boy, stop it, I'm a grown ass woman, but my dad is strict.*

What did you do today? A whole lot of nothing I'm still sore from the football game. I can't lie, I've been thinking about you all day. Really! What type of things have you been thinking? I just keep replaying the night over and seeing your fine ass smile with those dimples.

After an hour of playing Mack Daddy on the phone, Sharlean said she was coming to pick me up. I tell her *cool, besides my mom wants me to hang up so she can get on the computer to play some poker online.* I hopped up, threw some music on, and creased my outfit while singing Ginuwine's song "Pony."

I was in playboy mode. I threw on a turtleneck shirt, khaki pants, with some suede wallabee boots. Hell, I even borrowed some of Joey's cologne. Now that I'm fresh, dressed, and smelling like a million bucks, I'm ready to go play with the playas. While waiting on Sharlean, Kris stopped by. *Yo, what's up son. I see you all stupid fresh, what are you about to do?*

Man, I met a fine ass girl last night homie, and she's about to come through to swoop me up. Nigga, you lying, who? Her name is Sharlean, and she got a big ass booty, fool. Word, she ain't got no friends I can get on with? I'll check dog, but I don't think so. She's in college, got a job, and, check this out; she's got her own car. Oh yeah, nigga, you got to put me on. I'm staying right here; I got to see her.

I thought, damn, I was bragging too hard. I didn't want her to see Kris yet because he might take her already. I mean the nigga had green eyes and was light skin, so snatching bitches from niggas was a regular for him. Oh well, if it happens, I can't hate the playa, I got to hate the game.

We walked outside and took a blunt to the face. I needed to calm my nerves anyway, plus I was funnier when I was high. Bitches love a dude that can make them laugh, so I was trying to Eddie Murphy her to death. *Oh shit, here she comes, nigga, she pulling up. Matt, if she steps out this car looking like Freddie Jackson, I'm clowning dude. She's fine as hell, you'll see, I told him.* She rolled her window down and said, *come on.* I hold up the blunt and wave her my way. She stepped out the car with some small white shorts; A.K.A coochie cutters, a black spaghetti strap top with her breast hanging out, she had some big ass hoop earrings on with her Janet Jackson, Poetic Justice, braids wrapped around her head. Her braids looked like an angel's halo around her. Sharlean's golden brown skin was glistening and her make-up was on point.

She was holding her phone and wallet in her hand as she walked up. Her walk was like a model on the catwalk in Milan, the way her hips twisted made her breast jiggle just right. Kris was staring so hard that he barely gets a chance to get out what he wanted to say before she gets to us. *Matt, she looks like a ghetto Beyoncé. I know right, I told you she was fine.*

Hey handsome, what's up? Hey gorgeous, this is my homie Kris, Kris this is Sharlean. Kris extends his hand to shake, but she just made a gesture. *Hmmm, I'll be in the car when you're done. Okay, here I come, just let me finish this really quick.* She walked away as Kris and I stare at her ass. *Matt, I can see all her pussy from the back with them coochie cutters on, my nigga. I know, did you see her ass falling out them shorts? I hit the blunt two more times and told him; I got to go. Hey, what was all that attitude she had towards you for? Oh, nigga, I tried to get with her a few weeks ago at a party. She wasn't going for it, so I called her a bitch and then fucked her friend. Boy, you a fool, I'll get with you when I get back.*

I got in the car and rode to her house. She said her parents were gone until Sunday; they went out of town to visit some family in Los Angeles. *Is your sister gone too? No, she's around somewhere. I see you got a problem with my homie. Yeah, he's an asshole. Long story short, he tried to get with me, and I shut his light skin ass down, so he called me a bitch. How is he going to be mad at me for not wanting to talk to his ugly ass?* This was the first time I heard any girl say that they didn't like Kris, so it threw me for a loop. All this meant to me was I didn't have to worry about the green eye bandit around her now.

We talked and got to know each other more in her room. She told me she was born in Germany because her mom was military and that she once was sent away to a military school for punishment. She seemed so comfortable to tell me her life, and so did I. She learned my background of a dysfunctional family and how I've been trying to leave that menace to society life alone. She was amazed at the activities that I had taken part in. *Matt, I can't see you being like this, I see you have a good heart, and you're so sweet. You need to just focus on your sports because you're really good at them. You have to promise me that you will avoid doing things like that from here on. I will try, but I can't guarantee you that. My life is crazy, and I never know what's going to happen or when, so I just adjust when necessary.*

Matt, I just found you, and I don't want to lose you already. For some reason, she was speaking as if we were a couple and she genuinely cared for me. It felt good to be wanted and cared for. This was the beginning of a forever love. I changed subjects by talking about her huge house. *Where do your people work? This is a nice ass house. Well, my dad owns a construction company, and my mom does life insurance. I thought she was in the military? No that's my real mom that was in the Army. Wait what are you talking about, are you adopted? My dad is really my uncle, and his wife is my mom, they adopted me when I was young, and my real mom was in the military at the time. She gave them guardianship while she deployed, and they never gave me back because she ended up on drugs. I know this is confusing, but this is my life. They treat me different from their real daughter all the time.* Now it made sense to me why she was sent away to military school for punishment. *Damn, that shit sounds crazy, but it's all good.*

We continued to talk for another two hours and found out that we had a lot in common. The only difference between our pain was that hers was covered up with money and materialistic things. Mine was covered up with rage, the rage that comes from being a product of my environment. *Hey handsome, let's go smoke a little. I'm down, where at? I'm going to take you to my spot. It's where I think, cry, and get high.*

We left her house and headed to the beach to go smoke. *So, this is where you like to smoke,* I asked. *Yeah, it's beautiful when the sun sets, and you can see the seagulls fly over the horizon.* We sat on some rocks, far back under the pier. *This is beautiful and very peaceful,* I said, *I like this spot.*

We got higher than Geronimo with a peace pipe. After enjoying the view, we took a walk on the beach in the sand. We held hands looking at each other with a passion and desire that sent frequency waves of lust through our bodies. *I want this feeling forever,* she told me while looking into my eyes. I told her, *I do too.*

We kissed and felt each other up. She stopped and said, *there is somewhere else I want to take you. Cool, where we going, sexy? I have something for you when we get there, you'll see.* Wow, she's already buying me shit, I thought. This was going to be alright, and to think I didn't even have to play any mind games with her.

We pulled up to Bubbling Springs Park, and all I can think about was the homie, Lil Head. *Girl, what do you know about Bubbling Springs Park? This is my go-to spot to smoke if too many people are at the beach. You better be careful out here, this is the south side of Oxnard, motherfuckers will try and snatch your pretty ass up. I'll be okay, and there's never anybody here. Yeah, that's because this is where all the drug deals go down beside Durley Park. Stop being scary, Matthew, you'll be fine. Oh, I ain't scared, I'm just aware of my surroundings. Shit, I lost one of my homeboys over here on some bullshit.*

It's all good, what did you want to give me? Damn, impatient, you're going to get it! Tell me a secret first. Sharlean, I don't have any secrets. Everyone has secrets, tell me something no one else knows about you. Umm, I can't think of anything. Okay, I got it now. I shit before I shower. She looks at me and starts laughing, *boy, you silly.*

Okay, close your eyes. I closed my eyes, but not before talking shit. *What are we, five years old now, you want me to close my eyes and not peek. Just do it, I promise you won't regret it.* Ten seconds later she said open them. I turn my head to look at her, and she has her shirt off. I guess this was the "to be continued" from last night. No words were needed, I go right to her chest like a guided missile that was tracking. I'm sucking on her breast as if I was being breastfed and missed a meal. She tells me to get in the back seat. Oh my god, this was really about to happen. I was finally going to have sex. No more bullshitting, this was the time, and this was who I wanted my first time to be with.

I unbuckled my belt and slid my pants down. She took off her shorts and hopped on top of me. As soon as I felt her insert my Johnson inside her, I let it loose. This was the best feeling in the world. It felt magical, it was surreal. I couldn't believe this was actually happening. The sound of her moan upon the insert was so damn sexy.

I managed to stay hard, and she kept riding me. How she rolled and twisted her hips was poetic. Every noise and breath she took turned me on more and more. My adrenaline was at maximum high, as I'm trying hard to compose myself and make the best of this moment. She screamed out, *Matthew, I'm going to cum.* I felt her vagina clinch up as she slightly trembled.

Yes Baby, Yes Baby, keep me feeling like this. Sharlean speeds up her body motions as I'm grabbing her ass. We start kissing; she bites the bottom of my lip enough to apply a little pain but pleasure. *Oh shit, babe, you better stop you're going to make me cum inside you. Cum inside me baby, cum in this pussy. MATTHEW! MATTHEW!* Damn! We both have an orgasm, but this one was even better than the first one that she didn't know about.

She flicks her hair over her head and with a sexy smile she said, *I told you I had something for you.* I smirked, *yeah, you sure did. But you didn't know I had something for you.* With her finger in her mouth, she said, *this is mine, baby? This is all yours, gorgeous. In that case, I better not hear about you giving away my dick. I don't want anything to do with them hoes. Shit, you better not give my shit up! Trust me this is all yours, handsome.*

We kiss again then fix ourselves. Just as she buttons her shorts there's a "TAP TAP TAP" on the window. We both look up and it's the fucking cops on the driver side. She quickly covered up her nipples. *Ma'am, can you roll down the window?* Sharlean whispers to me, *my parents are going to fucking kill me.* She cracks the window and you can see the steam blow out. *Ma'am put your shirt on.* I hand her the shirt after searching the car for a few minutes. It probably was fifteen seconds, but when dealing with the cops, everything can seem like an eternity.

Do you guys know this is illegal to be doing this in public? I'm sorry, I'm so embarrassed I really am. I know you are ma'am, I can see your cheeks turning red. Sir, you should have more respect for the lady and take her somewhere nice. This is a beautiful colored woman, and if I was with her, I wouldn't treat her like that. This officer of the law said, "colored woman" and tried to shoot his shit at my girlfriend in front of me. The blatant disrespect was normal from police, but I really couldn't say shit because he had the upper hand.

Sir, I think you mean African American woman and yes, you're right, I should take her to a nice place. The thought ran across my mind to say when I take her there I'll make sure your wife is there too, you fucking pig! *Well, today is you guy's lucky day. I'm going to let you go with a warning.* He writes a warning ticket and hands it to Sharlean, he looked me in the eyes and said, *you should thank your girlfriend for having a great set of tits.* He winked at Sharlean and blew a kiss to her then walked away.

This was who I was supposed to respect and seek when in need of help. Yeah right, all police are dick heads and have the false sense of authority because they wear a badge. I don't know why I let this bother me so much, maybe because I was used to this type of treatment, but Sharlean wasn't. Even though I was six foot five, that officer had a way of making me feel small. The fact that I couldn't defend her honor killed me inside, and I was hoping she didn't look at me in a different way.

Yo, drop me off at my house. I should have my dad talk to the chief of police, he knows people. I don't think that would be a good idea. You're going to have to explain why your shirt was off. Maybe your right, I should leave it alone. We parked at my house and gave each other some more kisses before I got out. *I really had a good time with you today. Call me when you get home, so I know you're safe. Ok, handsome, I'll call you when I get there.*

I'm walking up through the courtyard area and I see Joey's uncle, Herman, sitting on the stairs. *Aye, Aye, little nigga what's going down? I see you knocked you a bitch; she looks fine too.* Herman was a trip, I mean he was just a real-life thug. He was always in and out of prison for silly shit. He would go in for five years get out for two and go back for three. Herman was only forty years old, but he had spent over half his life in prison. This was a repeated cycle for him since a juvenile. He was a real loser type with no future and apparently no past.

I'm back baby boy, what's happening? Damn, they finally let you out the cage, huh, that's what up homie. I thought you were going to stay in Oakland this time? I was until them niggas shot me up. He pulls up his shorts and shows me six bullet wounds to his legs. *Mane, I wasn't out for two months before these kats started hating on me. But I'm alright; it ain't nuttin to a playa.* He stands up and we gave each other a hug.

Mane, you look good boy, you done lost some weight and got a few waves in your hair. You still don't have anything on me. He takes his durag off and his hair looked like Redondo Beach. There were waves everywhere, and they were silky too. *Okay, I see you homie, you still got it. You look a little more buff, too. A little? Mane, I was in the five hundred club on that weight bench. I can see it. I also see you got that prison build where you're big up top and skinny on the bottom. You better sit back down before you fall over. Oh, you got jokes huh?* Herman puts me in a headlock while saying; *I can still take your big ass.*

After we play fight, which I never like to do, he apologizes to me. *Nephew listen to me, the last time I was out here that powder had me zooted. I just want to apologize for that shit. I ain't know what I was doing for real. I dig it, shit happens.* But in the back of my mind, I already knew he wasn't to be trusted. Herman decided to jump in when my mom and Joey was arguing a couple of years back. The argument got a little physical, and somehow, I walked into the kitchen to see him grabbing my mom's leg and pulling her. Joey was trying to pull my mom away from him somewhat, but it was more of a fake motion act to show my mom he was defending her. It was written all over Joeys face that he was scared of Herman. I thought I was going to save my mom. But when I ran up, he pushed me and drove me into the refrigerator. The force and impact was so hard that my head put a softball size dent into the freezer door. All I remember after that was Herman yelling, *ya'll better raise up off my love one mane!*

I knew I had a concussion that day because it was hard to sleep that night. I would get dizzy spells for a few weeks after. Two days later, Herman got arrested for stealing his bosses' truck. I forgot to mention that his boss lived across the street from us. Since Herman was at our house all the time, it wasn't hard for his boss to notice his truck. I told you he would get locked up for silly shit.

I'm about to go inside and eat something. Are you coming in? Come walk with me down the street, nephew, I got to grab a brew and some more smokes. The store was just around the corner and I had time to get back before I missed Sharlean's call, so I walked with him. Herman was smoking his hand-rolled cigarette, walking, and talking. He was basically telling me lies that all people fresh out from prison tell. Prison war stories were the best explanation for the conversation at hand.

Nephew, I was in there knocking niggas out, or *nephew, I was a "Shot Caller" on the yard,* blah blah blah. What did catch my attention was when he saw a familiar face walking across the street. *Aye mane! Aye D-Lo, what's going down mane? D-Lo, I know that's you, homeboy why you acting like you don't know a nigga. Herman, you don't know that dude, come on brah.* Right after I said that Herman yells out, *Oh, okay you're walking with that BITCH and acting like you don't know a nigga, huh. I remember when I was fucking you in the ass at San Quentin Nigga! You knew me then!* By the look on D-Lo's face, I believe he did know Herman, and he was trying to leave his prison life in prison. Any person who can yell something that obscene out in public clearly doesn't have the right mindset and shouldn't be trusted.

Herman was a walking time bomb that did what he wanted, when he wanted, and obviously to who he wanted. *Mane, fuck that faggot ass nigga fronting on me.* I didn't have much to say the rest of the walk; I was still in shock over what just occurred. I gathered from that experience that people incarcerated don't perceive themselves to be gay as long as they're doing the fucking. So, this made me think it was more of a power and control for someone asserting dominance instead of a sexual urge. Either way, I philosophically looked at it I understood that they were still homosexual and couldn't accept that fact. I was so grateful to get back from the store and into my bed. Finally, at home and not hearing anybody arguing was a small treat that was oh so needed. I think I might get some rest tonight, but not before I shower and talk to Sharlean.

The school year was going by fast, and I'm on track to graduate on time. Life seemed to be looking halfway decent since Sharlean had come into my life. I didn't have to take care of Jared as much as I did before. My cousin Roshawn, who is now going by the name Rosa, moved in with us at the beginning of the school year, so the responsibility was passed on to her. Rosa was a good girl that had been through some terrible things in life. She was going through adversity and adult situations by the age of ten. I know that wasn't easy to cope with. Sometimes we would talk and she would vent about certain things. To hear her story was motivation for me to keep pushing because it helped me realize that my situation could be worse. Rosa had the balance of legit crazy and somewhat highly smart. I thought she was smart because school was her get away place from all the madness, so she buried herself into book work which made her excel.

Good thing for me, I gave her a lot of my assignments and she didn't mind doing them for me. Rosa was a big part of keeping me on track with school my last year. I was starting to focus on the wrong things more than I should. But isn't that what all teenagers do when they find their first love?

Basketball season was going great and I was looking forward to the all-star game in March. But then it happened. I managed to fuck up and make a poor decision that actually affected me. It was a few days after my birthday in January, and I'm feeling grown. The motto was, "Bitch I'm eighteen." Anything that was said to me or asked of me I would reply back with "Bitch I'm eighteen." This phrase was intended to be for fun and to show my sense of humor. Unfortunately, I had to use it with the seriousness of almost whooping someone's ass. It had been a rough start of the day for me at school. My first-period teacher was upset because I showed up to class with four minutes left. I felt like I at least attempted to make class, so she should have been happy with that. I walked in and took a seat at my desk while her back was facing the class. She turned around and caught me in the middle of squatting. *I'm glad you can bless us with your presence, Matt, now if only you can get here on time and stop disrupting my class. I'm sorry, something popped up this morning, my bad, it's all good. No, Mr. Sanders, it's not all good, you have a letter grade of a D minus in my class. So, unless you want to be a super senior sit down, shut up, and stop disrupting my class, ALL STAR!*

I was fine with the usual teacher ranting, but I felt that her saying shut up was unnecessary and the all-star was uncalled for. I believed she was trying to provoke me. Her tactics worked indeed. *I promise I was on time until my girl kept me hostage in the car. She wanted to give this All-Star some morning coochie! I told you, Mrs. Phillips, something POPPED UP.*

The classroom goes to a roar of laughter. *Quiet, quiet class! Don't entertain him; this is not funny.* Someone shouts out, *yeah it is, I seen them parked on C street, the car was rocking too.* The class laughs even louder than before. This really made her mad. *Go to the principal's office now.* I grabbed my backpack and headed out the door, but before the door shuts, I hear her say, *he probably didn't wash up before he came here.* I yelled out, *nope, I'm a dirty dick boy.* The class goes back into another uproar.

I got to the principal's office, but he was out, so his secretary writes me up and sends me to my next period. It's science class with Mr. Lewis. He was a cool teacher and he used to coach football for the school, so we had a good rapport. The whole class period people were joking on each other, and he was getting upset. Yeah, I started most of it, but when I saw he had enough, I stopped. I can honestly say the match that lit the fire didn't start with me. Everyone was calm for a few minutes then Mike yells out, *hey Matt, I found your Chapstick.* Everyone looks up and he's holding a big thick ass glue stick. It was the kind that would be used in third grade for arts and craft. It was dead silent then everyone stares at me confused on what type of reaction I was going to have. I started laughing, *Mike, my lips ain't that damn big, are they?* Once they saw it was okay, then they joined in laughing.

By this time, it was too late, Mr. Lewis had enough it was the final straw. *Matt, go to the principal's office.* I take my things and leave. I respected that teacher, so I didn't give him any shit. Damn this was the start of a terrible day. I contemplated ditching school, but I already woke up, and that was half the battle, so I stayed.

The secretary wrote me up again and said the principal was still out but that she would leave the write-ups on his desk. She told me to stay in the office area until this period is over. I was waiting on my class to start, but while doing that I heard somebody's mom acting ghetto on the other side of the office. *How the fuck my son miss this many days of school and I'm just Muthafuckin getting notified? Where's his ass at? Go get him before I do.* That went on for another fifteen minutes or so. I was glad when my next period started. I survived third and fourth period with no issues and made it to lunch time. There was five minutes before lunch ends and across the campus quad I hear a familiar yelling voice. *Muthafucka, you want to play and have me up here missing work because your monkey ass done lost your rabbit ass mind and not go to school? Did you think I wasn't going to find out with your silly ass?* I look up and see someone's mom with a belt in the air as she's whooping some guy. I get a better view of the situation and it was the homie, Lemar. This was the funniest thing I had ever seen. I'm literally in tears from laughing so hard. The homie got an ass whooping in front of the whole school as a senior. He would never be able to live this down. This was how he would forever be remembered.

The lunch bell rings and it's time for class. I arrive in fifth-period still laughing like everyone else. I put my things at my desk; then I asked the teacher if I could go to the vending machine really quick to get a soda. The tardy bell rang as I finished my sentence, but she still said, yes, just hurry up so she could go over her lessons. I ran to the vending machine and got the soda. When I started to run back, I heard, *you're late, come here.* I looked, and it was the newly promoted Principal, Mr. Saunders.

Well, well, well, Mr. Sanders, you sure have been busy today, haven't you? Sir, I have permission from my teacher to get this soda. No, you don't, as he snatched the drink out my hand and took my three dollars out of the other hand. *Matt, I have two write-ups on my desk from you terrorizing your teachers this morning. How do you expect to graduate with behavior like this young man? Sir, I had a bad start to first period, and second period wasn't me, he just heard my name and saw everyone looking at me, then he kicked me out the class. Now I understand you're allowed to take my soda, but you can't take my money, Mr. Saunders. Can I have my money back?*

With a nasty demeanor, Mr. Saunders said, *no, I can do whatever I want, I'm the principal, and you're the kid. BITCH, I'm eighteen, I ain't no kid, plus you can't take my money. Well, I just did kid. I told you I'm not a kid; I'm a grown ass man like you. Now if I go in your pockets and take your money, I would be wrong right?* He turns around and starts to walk away, but I run in front of him and demand my money. He tries to avoid me. *Look, kid, I'm not about to play your childish games, get out of my way.*

That was my boiling point and where I decided to make a terrible decision. I felt I was a man now since I was legally an adult, I was getting pussy, and I had a little bit of money. I couldn't just let this man punk me. I yelled out; *I told you I ain't no kid* and then I pushed him with enough aggression that his soul possibly left his body and didn't find itself until he hit the ground. Then I stood over him and took my money back like a man. *Since you want the damn soda so bad, here you go.* I snatched the orange soda and poured it over his scared shaking body and called him a bitch. He yells out, *you're expelled, get off this campus before I call the cops!* When I walked away, I knew all the hard work and discipline was thrown down the drain. All those hours I came early and stayed after school to make up credits over the past three years didn't mean shit now. I told myself I would never invest so much time and effort into something again without completing it.

The walk home felt incredibly long. Thoughts kept racing through my mind of going back and vandalizing his car. But that would be a coward move, everything would point to me, so I just accepted the choice I made. By the time I got home, I saw my mom and she was packing our things in a box. *What are you doing, mom? We're moving across the street from Durley Park.* This was how it was sometimes; we would just get up and move with short notice or no notice at all. I was cool with it because I never really unpacked all my things because I knew that it was bound to happen again at a moment's notice.

Okay, what's for dinner? It's go for what you know. There are corndogs and some burritos in the freezer. Of course there were, why wouldn't there be.

Chapter 14: Old Habits Die Hard

My great-grandmother let my mom rent out her house across from Durley Park. It wasn't a bad house, but it smelled like a geriatric home. The good thing was that I not only had my own room, but I had my own space. There was an attachment to the house that was about thirty feet by fifteen, so my mom let me and two of my homies rent that area out. I had a new circle of homies but still ran with the old ones.

They were complete opposites of each other. Camilo was super athletic and into football. He was also very popular. I would joke and call him the mayor because he knew everyone and everyone knew him. Then there was RJ, a bad attitude not afraid to punch you in the mouth type of guy. RJ was someone who came from nothing but had a good heart and only meant good intentions. Things never seemed to work out his way so when it didn't; he would lash out and start a fight.

We would use the side entrance to the house, so it felt like we had a studio apartment. Sharlean would be over all the time, which was a problem with her parents. Shortly, she would move in. We all got along, so that was good.

I got my first job at a shoe store in the Ventura mall. My mom made it clear that I wasn't going to be living in her home while not going to school or working. My first day on the job and I was already scheming on how to steal shoes. I noticed the cameras and the angles they faced. There were only two cameras and the way they were set up; it would be easy to get shoes.

I waited for a week to find out who was cool and who was a snitch. I made jokes and mentioned to the ones that I believed would be with the scheme to see if they were down. *Man, all these shoes back here, who would know that the inventory was low if we're the ones that do the inventory?* Johnny said, *I know right, nobody from corporate ever calls, and they only check inventory once at the beginning of the year.* I thought, perfect, we're covered in that area, plus I didn't plan on being there that long.

I make another joking, but true statement. *Look homie; I could scale these walls at an angle where the camera couldn't see and walk out with hella shoes. I mean, I would need someone to look at the camera and tell me if I was exposing myself.*

Oscar, the store manager, said, *dude, I've always thought of that.* That was all I needed to hear to know that I could start boosting things out the store. I told Oscar, *look and tell me if you see me.* I grabbed a box of shoes and scaled the walls until I made it to the door. Oscar said, *I'm next,* so he followed my same path and had his pair of shoes.

Johnny got him a pair as well, and then we made a deal only to take one pair a week. We didn't tell Miriam because we thought that she would tell. Besides, she was too pretty to steal she could just have any guy buy what she wanted. This went on every week for about four months. I started selling my product and kept a few for myself. I was able to take Sharlean out to eat and to the movies whenever we wanted to. I wish I can say I stuck to one pair of shoes a week, but it went up to about three pairs a week. I'm selling a majority of them for seventy-five dollars a pair. Over time, I accumulated fourteen pairs of shoes for myself and I was making a good profit.

Some people started to hear about what was going on and started showing up to the store and just walking out with shoes. I guess they thought there were no cameras, so at least once a day someone would walk out with a pair.

As you can guess, inventory was extremely low, and there were too many reports to corporate of theft from the store. I was smart and quit before the shit hit the fan. I got used to having the consistent flow of money, and I couldn't stop the new lifestyle that I now created. I had rented a sixty-five-inch TV from Rent -A- Center and I wasn't going to let that go because I couldn't make payments. Plus, I liked buying and doing nice things with Sharlean, and I didn't want that to change.

I remembered that I was smart enough to use the address three houses down from us on the corner when I got the TV. When the people moved out, I jumped the fence and went through the window to unlock the front door. I made sure if something was to happen that they couldn't repossess the TV because they didn't know the location. When they dropped the TV off, I told them I was just moving in. I gave my employment number as my contact, so they wouldn't harass me. Then I got a few of the homies and we moved it to my house. I was good with the TV, but now the concern of cash flow was the issue.

I stated before; it doesn't take brains to rob people. I hung out with the old crew more than usual now. I was at a once a week pace of seeing them, but this spiked up to three times a week. The same shit was going on when I tried to leave this lifestyle alone, but now the difference was there were new niggas.

The new niggas couldn't understand why or how I had so much say so in the activities. Some didn't even know I was the one to start D.F.M, but that was cool with me because I wasn't trying to be recognized for that anymore. All they knew was that I played basketball and had a fine ass girlfriend, so it didn't make sense to them.

I jumped back in the game like I never left. We started breaking into people's houses and taking their valuable possessions. Anything that we could sell without a trace was the name of the game. Jewelry, Play Stations, TV's, camcorders, and sometimes money was stolen. People would leave two or three hundred dollars in their dresser drawers; I couldn't believe it.

Every now and then we would find a gun or a rifle. Those weren't hard to sell at all; usually the gangbangers would buy them for any price. To think, they had the nerve to be mad when I sold them guns without bullets. They must have thought I was a "Mark" if they thought I would show up with a gun and bullets so they could rob me after I sell it to them. I'm sure there are plenty of idiots out here doing it so I couldn't get mad, I would just laugh at them.

Sharlean was starting to ask a lot of question about where I was getting my money from and saying that my attitude was changing. I told her that I was out hustling, playing basketball for twenty dollars a person. This was very believable because I still would find time to play ball a lot during the day, especially since we lived across the street from the basketball courts. That was the only thing that I liked about moving on G Street. Camilo, RJ, and I could catch a basketball game at 2:00am any day of the week, and there would be a crowd out there. I'm glad she went for it because she didn't particularly care for Robert or Kris. I think it was more of the shit we were into that bothered her.

Everything was going well, and then I got a call from Oscar out the blue one day while I'm sitting in the bed. *Hey, Matt, Johnny got busted for all that inventory being gone with no explanation. Damn, sorry for him but what does this have to do with me? Johnny is a bitch, and I didn't think that he would be down for something like that, which is why I never brought up my plan to him because I thought he would snitch. He better not and, plus, I don't even work there anymore. Yeah, that's true, I told him it was going to go down soon, I quit a week after you did. Then, that fool started taking those three hundred dollar leather jackets and shit. I knew he was going to get caught, so I bounced. Hmm, well keep me updated, man, my clique might have to pay him a visit. Cool, I'm with that homie I'll let you know, peace.*

Stinky butt, who was that on the phone? Precious, stop calling me that shit. No, you're my stinky butt, handsome. Whatever, but if you must know, it was Oscar telling me Johnny got jammed up with that shit at my old job. The look in Sharlean's eyes was as if she had seen a ghost.

What's wrong with you? Matt, I need to tell you something. What's up, babe, what do you want to tell me? Matt, I'm pregnant! Whoa, what! She said, *I knew you would hate me,* and then she burst out in tears. *No, baby, don't cry and I don't hate you. Why would you say that? Well, you didn't quite have the response I was looking to hear. I'm sorry, it just fucked me up when you said it. So, what are you going to do? I don't know, what do you want to do? There's nothing more I would love to do than to have a baby with you. But right now is not the right time, precious. I don't have a high school diploma or a job, and I would like to be married before I have a kid.* She looked at me, and all I think she heard was marriage. She paused and gazed at me with a smile. *Okay, handsome I'll take care of it.* We didn't have this conversation again. I didn't even ask where she was going to get the money from or who was going to take her to get an abortion.

Sharlean walked in the backyard and said to come outside, that she had something else to tell me. Once outside, she said, *I smoke cigarettes.* I didn't believe her until she sparked one up. *Damn, it's been about six months since we've been together, how did I not notice this.* I guess I had tunnel vision regarding her and everything else. I told her, *it's cool, don't trip.* She asked me if I wanted one and I took it. So, we smoked a cigarette and then a blunt right after. Little did I know, this would be the start to a nicotine addiction.

Chapter 15: Something Has Got To Change

Today is like yesterday and tomorrow will be like today. The same hustle chasing a dollar will never stop. I started playing basketball less and started getting active with the homies more. RJ moved out of the house, but he did it like a sucka. He stole all my basketball and football jerseys and a few pairs of shoes when he left. I wasn't too mad because I knew that he needed it but it was the fact that I open my house to this nigga and he does that. Plus, he still owed my momma rent of $150. All he had to do was ask and it was his. He's a real-life clown for that.

Sharlean was beyond mad because she bought a lot of those things and she told me that he was trying to get with her when I wasn't around. She wasn't trying to start anything because she knew how I could get and didn't like seeing me like that.

Camilo stuck around for another two months, then he moved out in August. We had the spot to ourselves, so you know what comes with teenage privacy; sex, sex, and more sex. It wasn't just every day; it was two or three times a day. We were learning each other's body more than we did before and it was making our bond stronger. We were madly in love and enjoying life as we knew it.

Almost everyone in my family had met Sharlean, and they loved her. From time to time when we were out in the city, an Original Gangster (O.G) would walk up to me and say *Damn, L.O.C,* (Love Of Crip) or (Loss Of Control) depending on how you use it, *you doing alright for yourself.* When a nigga you don't know says that to you, that means your bitch is fine. For some reason in the hood, you can be dead broke and fucked up, but if your bitch was fine, you were doing alright in life.

Sharlean was a trophy, so I would catch compliments all day for her. I would also catch a significant amount of player haters and have to beat their ass because they were disrespectful and didn't know how to act. The good outweighed the bad, but at least once a week I would get into it with someone because they would try and grab her ass or say something sideways out their mouth. When they would do that, it was nothing more than a challenge to me so they could try and win her with their masculinity. It was safe to say that I had been fighting my whole life, so I was trained as a warrior on these streets to survive and I kept prevailing. Every time was more of a turn on to her to see me in action. It got to the point that she would call me if someone was at the store and got out of line. She knew I would be on my way and from there I wasn't playing any games.

Sharlean was naïve, gullible, and not street smart. She would go to the store at three in the morning with shorts that had her ass hanging out and a shirt with no bra. She basically was an easy target for anyone. They could have an easy rob, easy rape, easy anything. It was best to try and make sure she was always with me when possible if she was going to be living in the hood. We were attached at the hip. We did everything together. It got to the point that we were finishing each other's sentences and starting to sound alike.

Then it happened, Sharlean got down on one knee and proposed to me one day. I was flattered and in complete shock. I told her to get up and gave her a kiss with a long hug. *Precious, I'm sorry I can't marry you right now. I don't have my shit together, and I still want to try and play basketball somewhere.* She was embarrassed and hurt, but understood that I wasn't ready to be her husband just yet. I think she respected the fact that I was honest and wanted to be the best that I could for her, as she deserved.

After she finished crying, she told me that we needed to talk. I could only imagine what she had to say because her tone and emotion behind it was familiar. *Babe, I'm pregnant again and want to keep it.* This pull and pray method that I had going on was not working for me. *Oh man again, already? Boy, don't act like I'm just doing this by myself; I think you had a part in this too. You're right, and I need to do better. You got that gold between your legs and it's not easy to pull out all the time. I think we should start wearing condoms.*

Who? We're not about to start wearing them now. Besides, I want to feel all of you every time we're together, so condoms are out the question and it's a little too late for that. Sharlean we're not ready for a kid right now, just like marriage. Look, I know you want a child, and I would like to have one too, but this just ain't the time, Precious. She started crying again and threw a temper tantrum that was so adorable; I couldn't help but to agree to her conditions.

Matt, I will take care of this again because I love you and if you say this is best then I believe you. You have to pinky promise that if and when I get pregnant again that we keep the baby! I felt it was only fair to agree since I had asked her to sacrifice to the highest notion of sacrifices. *Yes, baby when and if you get pregnant again, we will bring a child into this world, and we will figure it out if we're not ready.* She smiled and had a glow to her even after being denied marriage and a baby, all within thirty minutes. Any woman who can still be madly in love and glow after events like today must be in love. I thought I knew she loved me before and I loved her, but this really showed her character. I knew that she really was a ride or die type of chick and would have my back for life. It hurt me to know that I hurt her, even when it wasn't intentionally.

The pain that we shared made our love stronger. I thought to myself; I bet this was what Bonnie and Clyde felt. They felt a love that you would be willing to do anything for; the happiness of your lover, friend, and confidant. Their love was dangerous and crazy, but I can see how love will and can take you down that course. I did some self-reflecting throughout the rest of that day and came to the conclusion again that if I wanted to make her happy, then I needed to tighten up and get back focused.

The next day I looked into getting my general education diploma (G.E.D). I got signed up and started the process. The adult school gave me a few packets to take home and complete. I never realized how much basic education I didn't know. This all looked foreign to me and very difficult to understand. All those years of class clowning and not showing up to school half the time sure showed when it came time to study. I didn't know shit, and it was discouraging. But this was my own fault; I couldn't be mad at the school system for pushing me forward to the next grade because they didn't want to deal with me. Sharlean would help me the majority of the time, as a matter of fact; she would do all my work because I was embarrassed and ashamed about what I didn't know.

I tried my hardest to stick with the plan, but I would slowly find a way to be lured back to my norms. At this time in life, Sharlean and I were potheads, and during a smoking session one-night, Robert and Kris were at the house, and we got to talking about money and how we needed more. Sharlean chimes in and overhears Kris say that his girlfriend's dad has a lot of guns and jewelry at his house. He went into detail about how we could get in without any problems. It was simple, he would leave the side door unlocked when he left at night, and we would go in the morning when everybody was gone.

Sharlean stopped and looked surprised. *I know you're not thinking about doing this Matthew?* Robert cuts her off before she had a chance to play investigator on me. *Chill out; this shit is easy. We've been doing this type shit for a while. This time it'll be much easier because we can just walk in.*

She stared at me with a look of disgust and anger. *How do you think he has been getting money to take your fancy ass out to eat or buy you things?* I wanted to stop Robert, but sooner or later she was going to find out, so I just let it play out and prayed for the best. *Well, he's not going to be doing this anymore if he has been.* In the middle of the discussion, I got a phone call. Whew, saved by the bell, this call came right on time, I thought.

Hello, Yo, Matt, it's Oscar. Hey, the police came by questioning my mom about shit. She told them I wasn't here and they said that they needed me to come in for questioning about a grand theft situation. I just wanted to give you the heads up because they'll probably be coming to see you soon. Good looking out Oscar. Before I hung up, I told him, *you better find Johnny before I do!*

Great, just what I needed, the police looking for me now. I thought I said that in my head but I didn't and Sharlean heard me. *What are you talking about?* I go ahead and let her know what was going on because she already knew about the other shit. Besides, this way she can't say I didn't give her a choice to be part of this crazy life I live.

Kris said, *this is why we need to make this move on the house soon, so you can get your bail money up, nigga.* Sharlean was so upset that she left right in the middle of rotation with the blunt. She whispered, *I'll take care of this* under her breath as she walked out the door. *Well, nigga, since that's your girl and she took the blunt, it's on you to roll up.* They started throwing hella Backwoods cigars and weed bags at me.

Sharlean stayed gone till about 2:00am. I knew she was mad, so I left it alone, plus, I didn't have the energy to fight, I was too high. A few weeks went by and everything was cool. I thought she would be bitching about stuff, but she was calm like nothing ever happened.

One day, riding down the street coming back from the burrito shop, Sharlean said, *hey, you know I always wanted to go into the Army right? Yeah, what's up? Well, I thought we should check it out.* I said, *okay let's do it.* I wasn't thinking that she wanted to check it out right then and there. While Sharlean was driving, we started to go away from the direction of the house. *Where you going, sexy? I'm going to the military recruiter's office. Right now, are you sure? Yeah, you said we could check it out.* I sure put my foot in my mouth. *It's cool we can do that, I just didn't think you meant right now.*

We pulled up to the office, and there were four doors, one for each branch. We look for a few seconds and then we were greeted by an Army Sergeant named Fisher. She was short, plump, ugly, and had bad posture. This was a terrible representation of the United States Army. But we still listened to her spill. She offered us a seat in her office and handed us a brochure. I sat down to eat this beautifully rolled Carne Asada burrito with extra cheese and sour cream. Needless to say, I wasn't paying attention to anything she had to put out. Sharlean's body language was showing signs that she was interested. She kept leaning forward and repeating things that the recruiter was telling her to me. I was halfway through with my small pleasure in life, and I heard Sharlean say, *see babe, she can help you get your high school diploma, not a G.E.D.* My ears tune in somewhat now. *How can you do that? I can only get a G.E.D is what the counselor at the adult school told me? No, that's not true* said Sgt. Fisher. *They usually don't tell people about the high school diploma because it means you have to come back to their school and complete all the courses you're missing. A lot of people want to study for a week, take a test and be done. It's really about numbers for them to provide and show that they're an adult school and keep their grant money for the next year. It's all politics, don't worry, a lot of people have been misled, but that's why the United States Army is here for you.*

Well, that doesn't sound like the California school system to mislead and not help people further their knowledge in education. She informs me that there is a school in Santa Maria that they use for this program and that she can have a diploma for me in one month. I told her, *I'm with it!* Sgt. Fisher then explained to me that there's a buddy program and that we can go into the military together and be stationed within a fifty miles radius max of each other.

Sharlean and I looked at each other, and she said, *do you want to do it?* I said, *yeah, why not if they can get me my diploma.* The recruiter explained that I would have to get the school part done first before I could sign up, but she said she was going to mark yes on my high school diploma for me and get us scheduled for the ASVAB test. Once we passed this, then she would help me with the school thing. This was perfect! I could use the military to get my diploma and then not go into the military because I couldn't sign up until it was completed.

The ASVAB was just a test to see if I qualify to be in the Army. She signed us up on a delayed entry program. This was no more than a pinky promise saying I planned on being a soldier. After all the paperwork and getting scheduled for a test, we were able to go and had to report back a month later to test out. We left the office motivated and excited about our future. Sharlean said not to tell anybody what we did and just surprise people once we're official. I agreed, and we headed back to the house to smoke a blunt. Getting my high school diploma was all I could think about and using the Army was beautiful. I felt the Army had been using people for years so to be able to get over on them was a win for everyone that signed up and was just a number.

I thought about joining the military when I was younger because my dad was in it. I figured if he was able to do it, so could I. I knew he was in the Navy so I would have to go one step higher than him.

The only thing that was better than the Army was the Marines. Everyone I ever knew that went to the Marines were crazy and always had flashbacks of the war. At least that's what was perceived from television because the only Marine I knew was my Aunt Tasha's boyfriend, who had a short temper and was a drunk. Then there was Herman; he was flat out insane. He told me that the judge gave him a choice to go to war for four years or go to prison for six, so that was a no-brainer of a decision. The sad part was that Herman said the core gave him discipline and straightened him out. I couldn't imagine what he was like before, knowing how much of a wild card he was now.

The Army was just right for me because it was one step higher than that coward of a father I knew of and I always said I was going to be better than him at anything in life, especially fatherhood. I never thought much of the military in my later teenage years because I was into so much that I didn't think I would be alive to sign up at the legal age. To tell the truth, I always wanted better for myself, Jared, and my mom. By joining the Army, this could be the chance to get us out the environment that we were used to and have a fair chance at life.

Multiple events with Joey and my mom's choices to stay with him proved to me that she would never leave him and I would be stuck. The obligation to take care of my brother and to make sure my mom was safe was a burden to me at times. This was what families did, I guess. They stick together, even if they're hazardous to each other. A million different scenarios ran through my mind about the military. The more I smoked, the more I thought and daydreamed about a better life. My main focus was to get that diploma, then separate the rest of my thoughts as I go through the motions in life.

Chapter 16: Sometimes You Lie to the Ones You love for Their Best Interest

We passed the ASVAB test, and a week later I got my high school diploma. The best present I could have ever given myself, and my mom was earning my diploma on her birthday in mid-December. I was upset that my mom couldn't attend my graduation ceremony because she had to work. But I understood that you have to pay bills because the bill collectors don't give a damn about what's going on in your life. I couldn't be to mad at my mom because I didn't really earn this diploma. Sgt. Fisher did all my homework packets and turned them in for me. She must have really needed me recruited. I would have never thought that the Army would cheat me into a diploma that I didn't earn just to enlist me into the military.

Sharlean and Sgt. Fisher attended my seven-class member graduation ceremony. Big Sgt. took us out to eat, and after the dinner meal, something very unexpected happened. We were riding back into town and Sgt. Fisher asked, *do you know where I can get some weed?* The music was playing, but it was as if all noises were drowned out and I could hear everyone breathing in the car.

I looked back at Sharlean and we're both confused at the circumstances. Sgt. said, *come on, I know you guys smoke because you walk into my office smelling like Chronic all the time.* I told her, *yeah, I got some on me, are you serious?* Fisher said, *yes, I'm human too. What, you think a white girl from Wyoming doesn't smoke a little bit of weed?* I handed Sharlean the bag and she started to roll up a blunt.

We weren't far from town, so when she was done rolling, we went to the beach and parked. I couldn't believe we were about to smoke with Sgt. in her Army uniform. Sgt. inhaled the smoke and then she started to get in her feelings. *Matt, don't become a shit bag when you get out of basic training. The Army has enough of them, and you're a good kid. Use the military to your advantage and go see the world. It's a big place out there, and you're not going to miss anything going on in Oxnard. Everyone you know will still be doing the same shit when you come back, you'll see.*

I couldn't understand why she was just telling me this because as far as the Sgt. knew, Sharlean and I were signing up on the buddy system. I didn't say anything because I didn't plan on enlisting anyway. I got what I needed and as far as I was concerned, I was going to hit that blunt with Fisher and not pick up any more phone calls from her after that night.

Sharlean would be easy to talk out of going to the military. We were in love, and I was going to express to her that we would be separated if we went in together, and she wouldn't go for that. We were like two peas in a pod and nothing could separate us.

After indulging in the finest Chronic weed that Oxnard had to offer, we got dropped off at the house. I was pumped to show my mom my accomplishment and to give it to her on her birthday. We walked into the house, and just like any other day, I heard them arguing. My whole mood changed. The adrenaline of a proud moment was stripped away from me. Couldn't I have one day just for myself? I couldn't acknowledge that I received a diploma, which was a milestone in my life? More than half the people I knew didn't graduate or have a G.E.D; this was the harsh reality of my neighborhood. Statistically, I wasn't supposed to have this, and in reality, I didn't earn it. But I damn sure deserved it, all the hard work and effort I put in to make up for someone else's fault.

I was crushed, but it hurt more when I went to hand it to her. *Here, mom, I got my high school diploma today, Happy Birthday!* She said, *good job, Matt Man, I'm proud of you.* Then she doesn't skip a beat and starts back yelling at Joey all within the same sentence. *See, that's your damn problem, you're fucking with that shit again because you're tripping man.*

This angered me more because I realized that this was just another piece of paper. We knew Joey would toot his nose with a little bit of cocaine once in a blue moon, but we thought he left that alone. I don't see how we could have thought that with Herman being around again. I decided at that moment that I would go in the Army and leave this shit behind.

I always felt like I had to protect my mother and play a father figure in Jared's life. But, I couldn't keep living my life for someone else and sacrificing my future for things that wouldn't change. This may have sounded selfish to some, but it was more selfish in my book to take away my moment with all the adult responsibilities that had been put upon me at an early age. I felt I should have been praised for this. More than that, I needed to know that I was doing well and that I could make it in this cold world. I needed the attention, love, and support from my mother to tell me everything is going to be okay. I finally did something right, but it still felt like I can't get right. I told myself, it's okay, I can love my family from a distance. My emotions helped me make my decision. I felt like I needed to take my love away because I wasn't appreciated and I was sick of having my feelings hurt.

I walked back to my area of the house, and when passing through the kitchen, I saw Herman. I didn't know how he got out of jail so quick, but his story was that he got sentenced to nine months only. That didn't add up to me, but whatever.

Herman was pouring a glass of Canadian Mist liquor, and at this point, I needed a drink too. *Aye, homie, pour me up one, too. Mane, don't have the "General" on my ass. You see she's on a roll right now. Yeah, I noticed, but she ain't tripping, she'd rather me be at home getting faded than in the streets where she can't keep an eye on me. Yeah, you right, here you go take mine. Hey, I bet you can't out drink me. Probably not, but tonight I sure feel like I can, you're on. Loser owes one hundred push-ups on demand. That sounds like square business to me.*

Herman and I started going drink for drink for about an hour. I drowned out all the arguing and my feelings and just lived in the moment. It didn't take long for that moment to slap me in the face. My head started spinning, and I got nauseous. *Yo, I'll be right back I got to take a shit. Whatever, little nigga, go ahead and throw up. I'll collect my push-ups tomorrow. Man, ain't nobody about to throw up, I said I got to take a shit.* I went to the bathroom and started vomiting in the sink. I wouldn't dare let him see me like that, but eventually, he would because I stayed in the restroom for a half an hour before Sharlean came in to check on me.

She walked in and I was on the toilet throwing up on myself. It looked like I wasn't even trying to get it in the trash can. She started wiping up the vomit, and I felt embarrassed, so I attempted to help her clean up. I forgot that I was still taking a deuce, and when I went to bend over, shit flew on the toilet stool. *MATTHEW, stop baby, let me take care of you. Why would you try to drink with a stone-cold alcoholic, boy?* I mumbled, *yeah, that was stupid, huh.* Yes, Matthew, she said, *very stupid, very stupid.*

In the midst of this gorgeous woman cleaning up my vomit and shit; there was no way I couldn't marry her. Any human that can love someone enough to nurture them while in the condition I presented was definitely the one for me. She wasn't upset or even disappointed in me. She looked at me with so much passion. Her eyes were speaking to me, and they were saying, I will love you and take care of you no matter what.

I had seen my soul mate, the person I prayed for all those nights, and I wasn't going to wait another day to ask her. *Sharlean, will you marry me, beautiful? Matthew, your drunk let's get you cleaned up, babe.* That was the last thing I remembered before I blacked out.

I woke up the next day feeling appreciative that my life didn't end on a bathroom toilet covered in vomit. Surprisingly, I didn't have a hangover or feel sick. I rolled over and kissed Sharlean to wake her snoring ass up. She said, *Good morning, baby! Good morning, sexy, thank you for taking care of me. I know you probably thought I was drunk, but I meant what I said last night.*

Sharlean sprouted up and said, *are you serious? Yes, will you marry me?* She started crying and told me that I had just made her the happiest woman in the world. We kissed, but not for long because we were interrupted by a phone call from Sgt. Fisher.

Hello. Hey, Matt, good morning, when can you and Sharlean come to the station so we can get you all signed up? I told her that we would be there in an hour, *just give us time to get dressed and showered.*

We got ourselves together and went to the station to make another big decision in life. All the paperwork got signed, and we were official, the only thing left was to go see the doctor to clear us medically, and we were on our way.

Due to the high demand the Army had, we couldn't be seen by their doctor until the middle of January. During that time, we were informed to exercise and stop smoking weed. That was easier for Sharlean than it was for me. It was like she quit instantly one day, but me, I couldn't. I smoked all the way up to the day to see the doctor, and sometimes with Sgt. Fisher. She gave me some funny color liquid to drink one hour before we were to see the doctor so it could clear my system. I didn't think it would work, but it did.

Finally, everything was good to go, and we were on our way, I thought. Yeah right, nothing in my life works out just that smooth or according to plans. Sgt. Fisher gives us a call three days after seeing the doctor and tells us to report to the station; she wants to talk to us about a dramatic change.

We arrived thinking, what could it be now? I was nervous at the possibility that I could have a warrant out for my arrest because of the stealing of the shoes situation. This was another reason that helped encourage my choice. For some reason, people get off of their crimes when they enlist in the military. I believe the judge sees the records and thinks, well why not let another hoodlum fight for his freedom while he sits back and takes someone else's freedom.

I thought I was in the clear because it had been so long but, I guess it's only a matter of time before things catch up. We got to the office and Fisher said, *we have a problem with your buddy system. Sharlean can't go into the Army at this time. What do you mean at this time?* She looked at her and said, *do you want to tell him?* I looked at her and said, *tell me what?* Sharlean drops her head, and with the cutest, sexiest face tells me that she was pregnant. I was happy, and asked her, *how far along?* She said, *six weeks. Are you really happy? Yeah, this is great, why didn't you tell me? Babe, I had to find a way to get you out of here, and this is what I came up with, I'm just glad it all worked.*

111

So, you knew you were pregnant when we started this? Well, not initially, I was going to go with you, but then I found out I was pregnant the day you graduated. I talked to Sgt. about it the day we signed papers because I knew that she would understand. Matthew, you're headed down a road of destruction, and I want you to be the best man that I know you can be. Sgt Fisher knows everything that you're into, and she sees the good in you as well. She can't believe that you're into to that type of life.

When I heard this, I was caught in the mixture of feelings. I was confused, sad, happy, angry, and feeling betrayed, but loved at the same time. *I thought I was going to see the world with you and we were going to be soldiers.* I came to the realization that this woman loved me enough to mislead me to a better path. This wasn't betrayal; this was unconditional love. I owed this to her, especially with all the sacrifices she made to this point.

Oh shit! I just signed up for the Army. I really didn't have any choice. I couldn't stay where I was because it was dysfunctional, and I needed a job to raise the baby that I promised we could have. *Hmm, Sgt, isn't there a basketball team in the Army or something? Yeah, sure, we have the All-Army team that has a lot of talent, and many of the players were D1 collegiate athletes, and some played professional ball overseas. Ok, I'm all in, Sgt. I want to do this. Good,* she said, *because I would hate to tell you that you already signed on the dotted line and, besides, I need to meet my four recruits for this quota.*

We shook hands, and she let me know that my leave date was pushed back because she wanted to give me time to take this all in and prepare mentally. March 13th, 2003 was my day to report to basic training in Fort Knox, Kentucky.

For the next month and a half, I was in the delayed entry program. All I did was exercise and stayed focused. Exercising was easy because I had a workout partner. Camilo decided to go into the Army as well because he had his own personal issues to work out, so the military was the choice for him.

The only time we heard about someone going into the military was because they had utterly failed at everything else in life or that they were in trouble with the law. It was usually the last resort. You never heard of anyone that signed up because they just loved their country so much and wanted to fight for another person's freedom. It was pretty much a trump card that you could use if you needed shelter, food, and some money. They were always taking dummies.

The only issue I had for the next month was to try and figure out how to tell my mom everything that was going on. I finally worked up my speech a week or so later and came to the conclusion that there was no way to tell her but straight out. I knew my mom would be sad that I wasn't around to help out and there was a strong possibility that I could die. The way I looked at it was, shit; I could die in these fucked-up ass streets a lot quicker than at war.

Sharlean and I walked into my mom's room. She was watching the television with Joey. I turned the TV off and said; *we need to talk because a lot is about to change for me.* My mom sat up, and I could tell that she knew that I was about to drop a bomb on her. Plus, I never talked like that, and what could be so important that would make me turn of my momma's TV while she was watching her show M.A.S.H? *Well, Y'all get ready because you're going to be grandparents.*

Joey hopped up with what appeared to be excitement, and that was a shocker. He walked over and gave us both a hug and said congrats. My mom was calm and said, *well, I guess it was going to happen sooner or later,* and then congratulated us. *Well, shit you took that well, mom. I have more to say, so you should probably have a seat, the shows just beginning.* She looks with fear and anxiousness; what the hell else could I have to say. *On March 7th Sharlean and I are getting married.*

Joey and my mom looked at each other speechless, and after a ten-second pause of silence, she said, *you're telling me I'm gaining a daughter in law and I'm going to be a grandmother? Yup, you're getting old mom. Shit, boy, you're trying to give me more grey hair. Well if that doesn't do it, then this will. I leave for the Army on March 13th! Yeah right, boy, stop playing. No, he's serious, Miss Sherry, I think it will be good for him.* With a frantic voice my mom said, *Joey, I need a drink.* Joey and I look at each other because my mom doesn't engage in drinking too often. If I had to guess, I would say three or four times a year, and that's usually because it's a BBQ type holiday that calls for alcoholic beverages. Joey saw this as an opportunity to drink without getting bitched at, so he piggybacked off her.

You're right; I need a drink too, this is too much going on, I'll make you one, my sweets. I said, *Mom, we're going to let you digest all this, I'll be in the back on my side of the house.* Before I turned around, I glanced at my mom one last time, and I saw her eyes were tearing up. Sherry wasn't the type of woman to cry unless she was furious and then it would be tears of anger, but these tears had fear and sorrow written all over them.

Over the next few weeks, Sharlean and I continued to plan our future and thinking of names for our baby. All I remember was the deal led to me picking the name for a boy and her picking a name for a girl. We didn't want to know the sex until she gave birth. I think this made the pregnancy more exciting as if we didn't have enough already.

We both hounded my mom and Joey about coming to watch us get married because, yes, there was going to be a wedding, but more of a blessing by her grandfather, who was a preacher. Every time I would walk by my mom or Joey, I'd ask, *are you guys still coming to see us get married at her grandparent's house?* They would say, yes, or, of course, every time.

Finally, the big day was here, and it was no more than the equivalency of going down to the local courthouse and getting married. But I was excited and couldn't wait to see my mom see me do something right in life, a real milestone. It wasn't a traditional marriage ceremony, but it was ours, and all we had was each other, so that's all that really mattered. Our love for one another overlooked the fact that I was wearing a black South Pole shirt and grey Dickies pants with some black Nike Cortez tennis shoes. Sharlean's make-up and hairstyle was so immaculate, and she was so beautiful that it didn't matter if she had on a shirt and jeans.

We didn't care that we had to borrow a ring from her aunt so I can place it on her finger when it was time to do so. The black rubber band that cut my circulation off my ring finger was just as symbolic to us as if it was gold and had diamonds. On that day it was our day, and the love we shared was the only thing that mattered. I must say, it did hurt not to see my mom or Joey in her grandparent's backyard to support us. For Joey not to be there wasn't as hurtful, but for my mother, the person who I adored, loved, protected, and sacrificed things with, my loyalty to not be there was very painful. Yet, once again, I can't have a day for myself. Not even thirty minutes to take out of her day to just be a part of something that's only meant to happen once in life.

Seeing all my new wife's family members, there was reassurance because even though I knew they felt a certain way about me and where I came from, they couldn't deny and say I wouldn't give her my life if it came down to it. The love and happiness that I had for her was expressed in my actions and speech. I would swim to France and back for this woman.

Her father, Jimmy, gave me a big hug and said, *welcome to the family son.* He then asked me where my parents were. I didn't know, so I made up a lie to cover for the absence of my side of the family. *My little brother got rushed to the hospital; he had an allergic reaction to something. They were in route, but they noticed it as they were riding in the car.*

He looked like he knew what was going on but chose not to comment any further. I'm glad he didn't because I think I would have broken down crying. This was embarrassing, hurtful, and once again selfish. This wasn't anything new for my mom to not be a part of something that I really wanted and needed her to be a part of. I didn't know why I wasn't numb to the pain yet. I guess the bill collectors still needed their money and didn't give a damn if you were sick, late, or getting married.

I figured my mom was at work and Joey was probably drunk talking shit with Herman. The song Butterflies, by Michael Jackson, came on and this was what my wife and I danced to. It was similar to a first dance at a wedding, but since we had a ghetto fabulous ceremony, it was just a song that we would forever make ours.

Dancing, dinner, and conversation with my in-laws, was how the rest of our day went. When we got home, I didn't even ask what happened to them showing up. I just laid down with my wife and thought, six more days and I'm out this bitch.

Chapter 17: The Beginning of a New Bad Start

The six days went by fast, and it was time to go and be courageous. It was eight o'clock at night, and we heard a knock at the door. *Hi, I'm Sgt. Howard, and I'm here for Private Sanders.* Herman said, *let me get him Sgt.* I give my wife a hug and kiss then I kiss her belly. I go say goodbye to Joey and my mom. Jared and my mom walk me outside. We give each other one final hug and something new happened, something I was not familiar with. My mom said, *I love you, Matt,* as she was crying.

I couldn't think of any other time I heard my mother say I love you growing up. I knew she loved me and I knew my family was not emotional people, and the only feeling they expressed was anger. So, to hear my mom say that was weird and uncomfortable. I told her that I loved her too, not knowing that feeling that I was having while saying it. That feeling was the only thing that kept me from crying like a baby. It was especially hard to not cry after seeing my mom in tears.

This made it easier for me to go and that's exactly what I did. Sharlean couldn't watch me go, even though this was her idea. It was best for her to stay in the house. I got in the car and another female that wasn't Sgt. Fisher was there to drive me to the hotel in Los Angeles. *Who are you?* I asked. *I'm Sgt. Howard, and I take it no one contacted you about Sgt. Fisher, huh? Nope, what happened to her? Where do I start? She's been discharged due to inappropriate relationships with recruits and doing drugs with them. Someone turned her in a few months ago, and she finally got kicked out. She told me you were fine as hell, but she says that about everyone. She wasn't lying this time, mmh, mmh, mmh. She's funny she thought she had a chance with you and your girlfriend until she became pregnant.*

This Sgt. had a country accent and was pretty, but kind of flirtatious, if you ask me. Shit, I wasn't tripping, it was something to take my mind off of the pain I was holding inside. The destination was only an hour away, but it took us damn near two hours to get there.

Sgt. Howard took the scenic route down the 101 Pacific Coast Highway. We finally got to the hotel after two hours of flirting with each other. I grabbed my green duffle bag, and she grabbed my backpack. *I'm okay, Sgt., I can carry it. I got it Private; besides, I want to make sure you get to where you're supposed to be.*

We talked to the clerk and checked into the room. She walked me to my door. As soon as I opened the door, she barged in the room and threw my backpack on the floor. The door closed behind us with a loud and furious slam. I turned around and looked because it startled me. After I saw that it was nothing I was cool.

When I turned back around, Sgt. Howard was starting to unbutton her Battle Dress Uniform (B.D.U) top. *What are you doing? Come here, Private!* By this time she had her top off and was in the process of taking her brown tee shirt off. *Hey, I just got married, and I have a baby on the way, Sgt., you're going to have to leave.*

I'm married too, Private, and nobody is going to find out. She walked toward me and started kissing on my neck. This was not an easy task to tell a woman that I'll pass, and I don't want what she has to offer me. I tried to express to her that I loved my wife and that this was not a good start to any marriage, especially one less than a week into it.

Howard was not trying to hear anything I was saying, and she continued to kiss on my neck while grabbing my dick. She then unbuttoned my pants, and I can't fight the urge anymore. The flesh is weak, and I was vulnerable. This was no excuse for my actions, but for the record, I tried my hardest, and I became victim to my first sin of adultery.

The Sgt. starts to wrap her plump, luscious lips around the shaft of my Johnson. She started licking the tip with her tongue ring, and it drove me crazy. I attempted to stop her one last time because I really didn't want to be this type of husband and I just took an oath before GOD. The devil brought his finest distraction for my pleasure, and it worked liked a charm.

Hey, get up here, that's it, we can't be doing this. Oh, you don't want me to do this? She starts sucking my scrotum while giving me a hand job. This was a very talented woman, and after that last attempt, there was no more fighting it.

I took my shirt off while still leaving my tank top on. She saw that I had no more fight in me, so she magically takes all her clothes off in one motion. It was similar to Superman walking into the phone booth and one second later walking out fully dressed in another uniform.

I started to get assertive and demanded her to get on the bed. Sgt. Howard said, *yes private, that's what I'm talking about. Toot your ass up and put your face in that pillow bitch.* I spat on her pussy and shoved my dick in her. I gave her a few good strokes then I smacked her on her ass, POP! Sgt had the type of complexion where it left a handprint on her right butt cheek. That shit turned me on even more. *Yes, Private, harder, harder, Private, yes!*

I smacked her on the ass again, just enough where the pain was pleasure. The pop echoed in the room like surround sound effects in a stereo system. I start thrusting hard enough that she said, *Fuck me, baby, keep them balls slapping on my pussy.* After five minutes or so, I flipped her over to her back. I raised the left leg up, because I knew that was the leg that Sharlean liked to be raised up because the curve in my dick hits her spot better.

Sgt. was screaming, *Motherfucker, hit that shit, yes!* This was when it got strange. She yelled out, *choke me, private, choke me!* I was confused and nervous like what the hell type of shit was her nasty self into. I delayed for as long as I could, but she demands me to choke her. I wrapped my right hand around her neck while holding her left leg up with my left hand. At least I thought I was choking her. *Private, stop being a little bitch and choke me, motherfucker!*

I gripped tighter, and she was able to moan out, *I'm going to cum, private!* With her last moan, she said, *tighter baby.* By this time, she had a purplish blue color to her face. All I could think was this bitch is crazy, and if all of the women in the Army were like this, then I didn't know what I was going to do. She climaxed and then said, *I want to taste myself.* I stood up by the edge of the bed, and she started to lick all the cream off my Johnson.

I looked at her, and she loved every minute of tasting herself. She gripped both hands on my ass then smashed her face into my groin. I moved her hair out of her face because there's nothing like looking at your dick in a fine ass bitch's mouth. The way she looked up at me while making slurping and gagging noises made me ready to cum. I tried to have some sexual ethics, and I told her, *hey, I'm getting ready to bust a nut.* She threw me for a loop again. *You better cum in my mouth, Private, and that's a direct order.* I exploded before she could finish her sentence. Sgt. opens her mouth and shows me all the sperm she had collected then flips her tongue like a snake. She acted as if it was her own personal trophy and was proud to show it off. She swallowed all of it and then showed me that her mouth was empty. I wasn't impressed because I didn't need her to prove it; I already knew she was nasty when she gave me a direct order to complete my first military task.

Mission complete! I pulled my pants up and sat on the bed while she got dressed. She gathered her items and told me, *good luck out there.* Before leaving she said, *this man's Army is small, and I'm sure we'll run into each other again. Here's my contact, hit me up from time to time so we can see how far we are from each other.*

She handed me a paper with her email address on it. *I wish you weren't leaving just yet, private; I would love some more of that dick.* She walked out of the room and reality immediately kicked in like a roundhouse from Chuck Norris to the face. I thought, what the hell have I done, as I smacked my face with the palm of my hand. I jumped in the shower feeling like a real loser. My emotions were all over the place. I couldn't control them. I stopped fighting it and started crying in the shower.

That was the most emotional I've been in a long time. The fact that I got married, had a kid on the way, and joined the Army was a lot to deal with. The thing that hurt the most was that I betrayed my best friend, my lover, and my wife.

Chapter 18: Being All That I Can Be Is Challenging

Day Zero is what they call the first day in basic training. My first step off the bus and I was greeted by four different Drill Sergeants (DS) yelling and screaming, with spit flying out their mouths. I was quickly aware that I was going to be in a world of hurt. *Get your big lanky ass off my damn bus, Private. You've got the nerve to walk off my bus private?* I tried to speak, but that was the wrong answer. *I KNOW YOU'RE NOT SPEAKING WITHOUT PERMISSION PRIVATE? Drop and give me fifty. Beat your face private. Every word out your mouth will start with Drill Sergeant and end with Drill Sergeant; you got that, Private. Drill Sergeant, yes, Drill Sergeant.* I started doing push-ups in front of the steps on the bus.

My peers were falling out of the bus trying not to step on me. One dropped his duffle bag that wasn't secured properly, and his blue underwear fell out. I thought the Drill Sergeant was going to have a heart attack. *Private, I know you don't have some blue boxers packed in your duffle bag? We gave specific instruction to only have seven brown underwear, seven black pairs of socks, and seven brown tee shirts with your personal hygiene. Everyone, dump all your shit out of your duffle bags now.*

I got up to dump my bag and I got what they called "Sharked." That is when all the DS's get in your face with their brown round hat brims on your forehead screaming at you with a bunch of polite words. One said, *motherfucker, are you stupid or are you dumb?* Another was yelling, *who the fuck told you to get off the floor?* The next one was saying; *I wish I could get in a three-point stance and Jim Brown your ass.* The last DS was barking like a rabid infected dog with drool coming out his mouth.

I was confused about what to do next. *Beat your face, Private, beat your face, Private.* I dropped down to the push-up position then another DS said, *get your ass up and dump out your bag, Private.* I got back up, and a different DS yells out, *get on the floor, Private, what are you doing? Oh, I see he does what the fuck he wants to. Don't worry about it; I know how to fix that.*

As I'm doing push-ups, I hear, sound off, private. I yell out, *seven, eight... No, Private, that's not how we count in the military.* DS yells, *everyone get in the front leaning rest position,* which was the push-up position. *On my count ladies,* DS yells out in harmony, *one, two, three, ONE. One, two, three, TWO.* For every push-up in the Army was really two in the real world. We did this for about twenty minutes, and everyone was tired, and some were already vomiting.

They finally let us up after sweating about ten pounds off. We grabbed our things and fell into a formation. By this time, all the DS's had already thrown everyone's things into a pile, so there was no way of knowing whose stuff was whose. This was a great introduction to the United States Army.

After gathering someone else's dirty underwear and packing it into my duffle bag, we headed to the barracks where I would spend the next nine weeks of my life. The barracks was similar to a jailhouse pod. There were only metal frame double bunk beds and footlockers in the bay. I was lucky enough to get a bottom bunk.

We got assigned a battle buddy, which was a partner that we always had to be with. My battle buddy was a guy name Shafer. Shafer was a white dude from Iowa with a Confederate flag tattooed on his forearm. He wasn't tall, but he had an athletic built, so my first thought was that he was a wildcard type person that probably played football. I had seen his type before, so I wasn't too impressed. I felt like I already knew what he was about. To my surprise, he actually was a good dude and wasn't who I thought he was.

Shafer and I got to know each other over the first week. He told me that he had never seen a black person before in real life, only on television. I thought that was insane. On our second day in training, he asked me if he could touch my hair. I looked at him with disbelief, but I knew that he didn't mean anything by it. He was genuinely curious and wanted to see what it felt like. I told him, *look homie, I'm not a dog, fool. Oh, I'm sorry Sanders I didn't mean to come off disrespectful. I'm fucking with you, man, go ahead and feel it.* He touched it and said, *man, this feels fluffy like cotton or something. Alright, fool, you're doing a little bit too much now homie. Hey, you better not tell anybody I let you feel my hair, dude.* We laughed and then hurried up to formation.

Shafer had a good heart, and he was a solid battle buddy. I couldn't complain because I could've gotten stuck with a bum. The first week was tough on everyone. Our schedule consisted of waking up at 4:30am to be in the platoon formation at 5:00am. From 5:00am, we conducted physical training (PT), which was a two-mile run and a million push-ups and sit-ups on Mondays, Wednesdays, and Fridays, until 6:30am. On Tuesday, Thursday, and Saturdays, we only did two million push-ups and sit-ups with a few different exercises. I was the sorest I've ever been in my life. Thank the Lord that I was an athlete, and I had some wind when it came to running, but I had zero upper body strength. Needless to say, the push-ups killed me.

After PT, we showered up in the "Circle of Life," which was what they called it. There were numerous showerheads in the restroom in a circle. We all showered together and conducted personal hygiene at each showerhead until you ran out of showerheads. When one would walk out then, another would walk in.

There were approximately twelve dudes walking in a circle to shower, and your shower was no longer than ninety seconds until the next soldier walked in the circle of life. I had showered in front of people while in junior high, so it wasn't a complete shock to me. Uncomfortable maybe, but you would be so exhausted that you didn't have time to be shy.

After showers, it was chow time at 7:00am. If you weren't in the platoon formation on time, you would get what they liked to call "Smoked." Being smoked was your single punishment in the form of extra PT, and the exercises were whatever they could think of. Getting smoked would take anywhere from ten minutes to an hour. It was very rare if someone got smoked longer than that. Once we marched to the chow hall singing cadence, we would stand in line at attention until it was your turn to get your meal tray. When you had your tray, you would have to stand at the table with it in hand and wait on the last person to get theirs before you were allowed to eat. After everyone had a tray, the DS would yell out, *eat privates!* That meant you had about six minutes to eat your meal before they said to move out. Finished or not, your meal was done, so you learned to quickly scarf your food down like an animal that had been starved for several days.

By this time it was 7:30am, and the DS would find some way every time after chow to smoke you and watch you throw up all the calories you just took in. It could be the pettiest thing, such as having a string on your uniform to one button not being buttoned on your uniform. I think they liked doing this to see how many soldiers they could make vomit. Can you imagine doing exercises in other people's vomit and trying not to vomit yourself? This was no fun, and they showed no mercy. It was as if they wanted to be cruel and got excitement out of it. It was all mind games, and they sure were good at playing with your mind. By that time, everyone was dog shit tired and hungry again because everything you ate was on the pavement.

Once the smoking session was complete, then it would be classroom style training from 8:00am to 11:00am. The videos were the longest and the most boring things you had ever seen. A lot of the videos were demonstrations of tactical training and safety expectations with weapons. We were usually exhausted and sleep deprived from the night before because somehow they worked out a schedule where you had fire watch duty. This was nothing more than a two-hour window of staying awake while everyone else was asleep. You were supposed to make rounds through the barracks and make sure there was no fire happening. I'm sure the building had a fire alarm system, but of course, they wanted to make things harder on you in basic training.

You would pray that within the rotation of shifts you didn't get the 12:00am to 2:00am shift because your sleep would be messed up. Some days I was lucky and got the 2:00am to 4:00am shift, which was a blessing. It didn't take long for someone to get caught in class sleeping. No more than five minutes of classroom training and people were caught snoozing. This would bring another smoking session on that woke everyone up.

The overhead clapper was usually the choice of exercise for punishment, or should I say discipline. It was exactly what it was called, clapping over your head with your arms not lowered past your shoulders fully extended. That sounds easy, but when doing it for fifteen to twenty minutes; it would cause you to go into muscle failure.

After the boring class work, then it was cadence calling, my favorite part of the day. From 11:00am to 12:00pm we would learn how to march and sing cadence. When done correctly, it sounds and looks outstanding. This was when I felt like a soldier in the Army. We would all move as one unit and sound off at the same time. This part of the training came easy for me, but a significant amount of troops found it hard to do.

Lunch chow started at twelve, and then we would repeat the breakfast chow process all over again. After lunch, the DS would put us at attention in the formation and then walk away. They would hide in a window somewhere and spy to see if anyone moved. The slightest movement was not permitted when standing at attention. The best way to achieve this was to find a mark and stare at it for as long as you could. If you had an itch, it better not get scratched. The DS didn't give a damn if a bug landed on your nose, you better not move because they would see it and put everyone in the front-leaning rest position. They would keep you like that for as long as they felt like it and you weren't allowed to do a push-up, you just had to hold that position until you fell on the floor and they cursed you out. Some people fell on their face and broke their nose, at times, due to muscle failure. You could arch your back in the air or sag in the middle, this was the same amount of strength used, but it just mentally felt like you got relief.

From 1:30pm to 5:00pm, they would find other training for us to do. This might consist of a road march with a seventy-pound backpack and a dummy rifle to carry while walking five to ten miles. When done with a road march your body would feel like Jell-O. Some days they would have us go through an obstacle course or repel down from a two hundred foot wall. If you were afraid of heights, then this was terrorizing to you. I was afraid of heights, but I wouldn't think about it. I think because I was so tired and weak that my brain just blocked it out and performed all the actions required of us.

Dinner chow was next on the schedule, followed by another platoon smoking session. We weren't allowed back in the barracks until 8:00pm, so they kept us busy with any and everything. Once we were in the barracks, you had two hours before lights out. This was the time for you to shower, shine your boots, and do laundry if needed. We weren't allowed to be on our beds until 9:00pm.

The last hour went by quick, so if you were able to get those tasks done before then, you could go to sleep before lights out. That was rare, but it would happen every now and then. As soon as your head touched that hard ass pillow and you put the scratchiest blanket on earth on you, you were out for the count. It always felt like you had just laid down and five minutes later the DS would come in waking everyone up, banging on that metal trash can lid.

This was the repeated cycle for the next nine weeks. This was pure hell, and it wasn't often that you were able to make a phone call to your family or friends. My first phone call came the second week of being there after a serious incident occurred. During the middle of the second week, a soldier name Thomas jumped out the window and committed suicide from the third-floor building. It was a tough environment, and he couldn't take the stress or physical discipline anymore. The DS gave us all a phone call to make because of how drastic the situation was. When I first heard my mother's voice, I couldn't help but cry. This highly stressful place and new life was extremely hard to adapt to. I talked to her, and she told me that she had to tell me about my aunt, Lisa, and Sharlean. I heard Sharlean in the background yelling, *is that Matt, let me talk to him, Miss Sherry, let me talk to him now!*

Precious never talked like that, so I knew it was something serious. My first thought was something was wrong with the baby, so I was nervous to hear what she was going say. Sharlean gets on the phone, and she's crying while trying to explain something to me, but I couldn't really make out all of the words. I pieced together that Lisa pushed me, and I almost fell, and your mom didn't do anything. My mom snatched the phone back and told me that Sharlean and Lisa got into an altercation and Sharlean was pushed. Sharlean gathers herself enough so I can understand what she was saying after she took the phone from my mom again.

While sniffling, she said, *Baby, me and your aunt got into an argument, and it escalated quickly, then she pushed me, I almost fell, and she threw a punch at me. I told her that I was pregnant, and she said, I don't give a fuck, bitch! Your mom just watched, she didn't try and help me until Joey came down the hallway and stepped in to stop Lisa from attacking me.*

I had so many questions and so little time to figure out what was going on because we were only allowed ten minutes a call and five of them were wasted trying to understand her. *Baby, your mom let her beat me up while I'm pregnant with your child; please come home baby, please. Sharlean, I can't, I'm stuck out here in Kentucky. The military will bring me up on charges if I leave.* I was so emotional while talking that my voice started to crack when I spoke. The DS yells out, *that's time, maggots, get off the phone so your battle buddy can use it.* I told her I had to go and that the DS was going to hang up. *I love you, Matthew, please come...* CLICK. The DS had hung the phone up, and I'm mad as hell, but I kept my composure.

I never did get to ask my mom what the hell happened or how it started. When my mom said altercation, it seemed a little funny to me because that word wasn't in her vocabulary. My thoughts were that she might have downplayed the situation to me, and Sharlean probably exaggerated it. Either way, it was foul play, and I needed answers. I didn't think my mom would watch her get attacked, but if Lisa was involved, there's no doubt in my mind that something physical happened.

This was too much shit to deal with, and the fact that I couldn't do anything about it was the hardest thing to swallow. I told my battle, Shafer, about it when he was done with his phone call. I wasn't into letting people know about me, but I needed to vent to someone. Shafer consoled me and assured me that everything would be alright.

I was sure that he was right, but this unnecessary stress was not needed.

I got back to being focused and continued the rest of the day, which was pure hell, I might add. It was the same old routine day in and day out for the next few weeks. During those weeks, there were rumors of soldiers in the platoon getting raped. I didn't think much of it; I figured it was all talk. Apparently, it was true because one night, for some strange reason, it was hard to sleep so I went to the restroom, hoping this would help me. I had the bladder pains that you get from holding your urine too long, and it was time to relieve the pressure.

I got to a urinal stall, and I heard whimpering coming from the shower bay. I peeked around the corner and saw Gutierrez behind someone pulling his pants up while saying *if you tell anyone I'll fucking kill you, faggot!* I crept back out on my tippy toes and slid into my bunk like I stole home base in the bottom of the ninth inning. I didn't get a chance to see who the punk was, but I sure was going to find out. I wondered who I would see walk out of the restroom after Gutierrez.

Five minutes went by, and I was starting to get sleepy, but no one had walked out behind him. I couldn't hold my piss any longer, so I walked back to the latrine. I heard the shower running, but then it stopped. I used the latrine, and by the time I washed my hands, I saw Wilson walk out with his shower shoes and underwear on while wiping his hair with a towel. His eyes were bloodshot red and puffy. I tried to play it off as if I didn't know what had just taken place. *Hey, you know DS would flip out if he saw you in the shower troop. Yeah, I know Sanders, but it was hard to sleep.*

I thought in my head, yeah, I bet it was hard. When he walked past me, he had a blood stain on his underwear by his asshole region. I wasn't looking at the man's ass, but this was plain as day, you couldn't miss it. Wilson was an average size man; it wasn't like he was small and could be easily taking advantage of. Well, I guess looks could be deceiving because that's exactly what just happened to him. For a brief second, I started to feel bad for him, but I quickly snapped back to reality. I didn't have any room in my heart to pick up someone else's pain. I had my own shit to deal with.

Chapter 19: The Flesh Is Weak

The last three weeks of basic training was fun. All the DS's eased up and showed that they were human like us and they didn't smoke us as much. The last few weeks we had a lot of weapons training. Shooting weapons like the M16A2 rifle, M249 SAW weapon, the 203 grenade launcher, and the AT4 weapon, which was kind of like a missile launcher, was a one of a kind experience.

Tactics training made the last part of basic training go by extremely fast. Before we knew it, we were graduating from the nine-week program. Sharlean rented a car and drove all the way out to Kentucky on her own to watch me graduate. The crazy part was my dad and his brother showed up as well. I had only seen or visited my dad four times out of the nineteen years I was alive. I collectively had spent four weeks with him and his family my whole life. The majority of the time it was with his family, so I never had time to get to know him. Our relationship was more of I knew of this person, and the knowledge was based on whatever my mother had told me about him.

I was very surprised to see him there, and I thought it was weird that he would just pop up on a major event in my life like everything was copasetic. I wished my mother would have been there to see this but, of course, it was the same story. She had to work again. It was like she wasn't able to request a day off with nine weeks prior notice. I tried not to let it bother me or ruin my day, so I pretended to be happy to see them. I hugged and kissed my wife, and she looked just as amazing as when I left, even though she was thirty pounds heavier. It was clear that the pregnancy was kicking her ass.

I greeted my dad and he introduces me to my uncle William, someone I had never heard of before. We had a short talk before the ceremony started. This was another proud moment, and my sense of achievement was truly earned, not just deserved. While joining the Army, I was able to find out more about myself during this training. My body could get pushed to extreme limits, and I could still perform by being mentally strong and disciplined. Mentally strong was something I was familiar with; it was as if I had been in basic training my whole life. I would get broken down to be built back up. The only difference was that I would get broken down by family affairs and have to find a way to build myself up. Turning my emotions to wood so I could be numb to the bullshit was the rebuilding stage. I know this doesn't sound too healthy and it could have backfired, but I was disciplined enough to not let things out of my control affect me.

I still couldn't believe that I overcame repelling down a two hundred foot wall by facing my fear of heights and believing that I could do it. I survived being sleep deprived for nine weeks. I had seen grown men cry during those hard times in unusual environments. I stood tall and had my chest out through it all. Shit, I'm from Oxnard, California the land of Playas, Pimps, Gangstas, and Hustlers. I Lived On Struggled Times and the Streets Obligated an Unusual Life. I'm the real definition of a LOST SOUL. That military training gave me more confidence than I already had and, Lord knows I didn't need any more. This was my day that I shared with a band of brothers and lifetime friendships.

After the ceremony, we were given twenty-four hours off post with our families. Dinner with my pops was uncomfortable and seemed forced. I had so many questions now that I was older and I needed explanations. But this wasn't the right time, so I just enjoyed the evening being able to act normal and not militant. Twenty four hours went by faster than a night sleep in the barracks. With the snap of your fingers, it was time to report back to duty and go on to advanced individual training (A.I.T) at Fort Lee, Virginia. This training was for learning your specific job trait in the Army. I signed up to be a 92A, an Automated Logistical Specialist. This was a bunch of big words to say I was the supply guy. That was actually the only job I qualified for since I scored the bare minimum on my ASVAB test. The Army had to spot me a few points because I only scored a thirty-four.

It didn't matter because I was here now and I was ready to train and become more than what I had seen from my home environment. The motivation to keep going and become better came from the scary thought that I was going to be a father. Someone was going to depend on me, and I had to set the right example, better yet, lead by example.

I focused hard and took every aspect of training seriously. I took a competitive approach to all assignments. Now, this might sound corny, but I wanted to be the best soldier this Army had ever seen. When it came to calling cadence and marching troops, I took pride that I was elected as platoon guy (PG). PG was the leader of all the soldiers in their platoon. I called the platoon to attention or parade rest. I made sure everyone was where they're supposed to be and on time. I was damn good at it, but every strong leader has a weakness, and mine was women.

A.I.T. wasn't like basic training in Fort Knox, Kentucky with all men. I now had women around me, and if I didn't know anything at all, I knew how to charm a woman. Being away from my wife and not having sex damn near every night was difficult, but I made it through basic training simply because there were no women. This would be my most challenging obstacle during this training, and it didn't take long before a gorgeous Puerto Rican named Rodriguez caught my eye and I caught hers.

Two weeks into a sixteen-week individual job training and we started communicating. It started off with talking at the chow hall and flirting in class to calling each other on the cell phone. This was one of the great benefits of graduating to A.I.T from basic training. Now we were allowed to have weekend passes and stay overnight in hotels off post. Rodriguez and I exchanged numbers and started pillow talking at night, almost every night for a month. I really didn't know much about her; it was all entertainment and something to do. Friendly flirting escalated quickly. We both had our first-weekend pass, and after eight weeks of putting quarters in the slot machine, I knew I was bound to hit the jackpot.

It was Friday night, and everyone would get a hotel room off post at the Howard Johnson, better known as "The Motherfucking Howard Johnson." The Motherfucking Howard Johnson was where it all went down. We would buy cigarettes, alcohol, and condoms. I had a homie named Williams, he was from Baltimore and was a cool guy, we immediately clicked from go. Williams had put in some work with Rodriguez's homegirl, so we had a thing going on. We invited them to our room to get drunk, smoke some cigarettes, and hopefully get into those panties. If one of the girls happened to be on it and the other one wasn't, then the one with guaranteed pussy would go back to their hotel room, as their friend was occupied for at least an hour. The code phrase was, "hey, I got to walk to the store, you want me to pick you up something?" That meant someone was about to get fucked and I'll be back in an hour. If someone said, "hey, I got to walk to the store and grab a durag," that meant, I'm going to lay up at her room when we're done fucking, see you in the morning.

Everything was going to plan. We were all drunk, talking shit, smoking like a train, and getting mad sexual. Williams said, "hey, I got to walk to the store and grab a durag." He told his lady friend to walk with him. I thought, cool, it's about to be game time. I'm going to put it on her ass tonight. That was wishful thinking because little did I know, I wasn't going to have sex with her. When it came time to perform I was too drunk and couldn't get it up. But I'm a playa, so of course, I didn't let her know that. She was dying to be fucked, and I was dying inside that I couldn't fuck her, but somehow I played it off as if I wasn't trying to have sex with her.

I did the caress thing to her body while holding and kissing her. She was making little sexy moaning noises and tried to feel my junk. I redirected her hands and turned her around in a spooning position so I could grab her breast while she held my hand as we both cuffed her chest. I whispered a bunch of bullshit in her ear, and she loved every word out my mouth. After I accepted the fact that I will not be getting my dick to work right, I fell asleep, but when I drifted off, I heard her say, *Sandy, you make me feel safe, and you respected my mind and body.* She rolled over and gave me a kiss, and then we knocked out.

We had to report back to post on Saturday because there was a program that allowed us to go to Kings Island amusement park that morning. After my failed attempt to feed my sexual urge, it was morning, and we were all on time. It was 9:00am and we were on post loading up on the bus to go have some unwind time and fun at the park. Kings Island was a nice park; it reminded me of a Magic

Mountain amusement park. We rode the rides and ate cotton candy with all the other fun foods that came with the event. All day Rodriguez and I were holding hands and kissing.

It was about 2:00pm, and I got a phone call. Sharlean's name came across the phone screen, and I quickly turned the volume down, so baby girl doesn't hear it go off. I looked at Williams and whispered to him that I needed an interference ran for about twenty minutes, my wife was calling me. He said, *say no more, bro, I got you.* I slid away and called her back. *Hey, precious, what are you doing? Just gave birth to your child, that's all. Is it a boy? Yes, you have a Matthew Lamar Sanders junior, my love. Yes, I knew it was going to be a boy; I told you. Whatever, boy, I'm so tired, baby, I can't even hold the phone, my aunt is holding it for me. Well, I'm proud of you, baby, you did it. I love you.* Sharlean started blabbing about a whole lot of nothing, but I was no longer listening anyways. I was too focused on trying to fuck Rodriguez still.

August 2nd, 2003, I became a father, and the only thing I could think of was fucking a pretty ass Puerto Rican chick. Shame on me, but everyone has a weakness and mine was no different from the next man's, at least my weakness came with a nice set of titties and a fat ass. I figured I had already committed adultery so, hey, a sin is a sin is a sin. I couldn't undo what I had done already, so if I was labeled as an adulterer, then I was going to be an infamous adulterer. Why go to hell for one sin, it may as well be for all of them.

I saw Williams and the girls walking my way, so I rushed my wife off the phone. *Hey love, the phone is getting static, and I can't hear you. What? Say that again, Babe, I can't hear you...* click. I hung up the phone before they were close enough to hear me and I acted like nothing was going on. Sharlean called back a few minutes later, and during this time me and baby girl were holding hands. Rodriguez liked to call me Sandy. *Sandy, your phone is ringing, babe, you don't hear that? What? Your phone, Sandy. Oh, let me get it.* I pressed the end button and acted like the person hung up. *Oh, it's just my mom, I can call her later.* I then turned my phone on vibrate to avoid baby girl from knowing that I had a wife.

We wrapped up the day at the park a few hours later. We were still technically on a weekend pass and didn't have to report to post until Sunday 2:00pm for roll call. We decided to continue where we left off last night. More drinks, more smokes, and more drinks. At "The Motherfucking Howard Johnson," it's going down again. We stopped by a few soldier's rooms and played a game of spades and dominoes. There was music blasting, and a few people got drunk and started fighting.

I knew the outcome to this scene, so I told baby girl, lets bust a move to the room before the Military Police (MP) show up. We get to the room, and it's me, her, Williams and her friend. After playing and teasing each other all day, we were both ready for show time. I told Williams I had to walk to the store and get a durag. He gave me the nod that was unspoken words, but he really said beat that pussy up boy, show her how niggas get down. I gave him the nod back.

We got to her room and didn't waste any time. I was kissing her; she was kissing me, I was sucking on her neck, she was sucking on mine. We started getting hot and heavy with the foreplay. I took her shirt off and laid her down on the bed. I slowly kissed her body from her neck down to her pierced belly button. She leaned forward, and I started to undo her bra, and I took forever and a day until she said, *stop, let me do it.* She slung that over the shoulder boulder holder across the room like a scene from a porno. Then she coddled her beautiful perky breast while moving her finger to come to her. The color of her areolas was a beautiful light brown and red color. Her nipples were small but plump. I dove on that woman and I let my tongue lead the way around her breasts. As I licked and sucked her nipples, I started to slide her pants off. Her pants got thrown across the room like her bra. I couldn't wait to take her panties off; I pull them to the side and begin licking on her clitoris. She tasted like strawberries, and I wanted to taste all that she had to offer.

I played downstairs for about ten minutes. I wanted to get good and hard, plus, I wanted her body to yearn for me. She creamed once, then creamed twice, and then she couldn't stand it anymore and told me to put it in, *I want it, Papi.* I couldn't hold off any longer than her, so I ripped her panties off, I didn't have time to wait for the arch, lift, and slide off move. I inserted myself, and she made a loud, sexy moan. She looked at me with seductive eyes. I could feel what she was saying without words. Slow grinds to fast grinds I gave her. She loved when I grinded hard and fast. Rodriguez turned into a moaning machine, and she was the loudest I've ever heard any woman moan. Even though this was only my third sex partner, I knew enough to know that she was getting that vagina worked out like she never had before.

I slowed down, and it drove her crazy, she started a whine and beg type moan. *Papi, give it to me, stop playing with me.* I climbed out the pussy and laid down, so she could do her thang. She hopped on top and started to ride me nice and slow. Then she did a hip twist rotation that was so perfect and so beautiful that I couldn't help it. I didn't even tell her I was going to cum. I let myself climax, and she saw my facial expression change. *Sandy, did I just make you cum, Papi? Hell yeah, sexy, I couldn't hold that shit in. It's okay, Papi, I'm on the pill anyways.* Once I heard her say that I stayed hard and continued to give her my Howard Johnson. She had an orgasm and screamed bloody murder while having it. *Fuck Papi, this shit is good, turn me around, Sandy.*

She got off of me and assumed the doggy style position. This was where I felt I dominated in the sex game. I slide in from the back, and she said, *not right there, Sandy, the other one, Papi.* That was a real eyebrow-raiser, I've never been there before, but during the heat of the moment and the nasty shit, I was willing to do anything to this woman off of backed up testosterone, it was a minor jump. I spat on her ass hole and slowly tried to maneuver myself in the back door. It wasn't too much of a struggle before the door opened up. Once I entered, it was a completely different feeling than the vagina. It still felt amazing, but it had more of a firm grip to it, and I had to keep spitting on her to be able to give her strokes. She was enjoying every minute of this because her moans got louder and louder. She started to request that I pull her hair and smack her ass. For a second or two I felt like I had to be acrobatic to continue pleasing her sexual needs. She had a few more orgasms, and then I started to join her. I began to pull out when it was my turn to climax again, but she yelled out, *nut in my ass, Papi!* That's precisely what I did, and she was able to feel every last drop because she said it was a lot.

That was my first time doing that, and it wasn't bad. We both showered up together and called it a night. Early Sunday morning we grabbed some breakfast and linked up with Williams and his lady friend. I was ready to get back on post, so I could call my wife and check on my newborn son since I had been dodging her calls all night. The girls decided to go to the mall before going back. Me and the homie headed to post to shine our boots and be ready for formation. It didn't take long for me to be in the barracks before all my battles were telling me that the DS was looking for me and trying to inform me that I was a father. Oh shit, everyone knew about me being a father and that Rodriguez and I were seeing each other. I knew it was going to be some shit when she got back on post. I couldn't control the talk, it was already out, and it was going to go down.

I continued to prepare for formation, and I tried to think of something to tell her, but I couldn't come up with anything no matter how hard I tried. Williams' advice was, *fuck it, bro, you don't owe her anything, and she never asked.* That's what I had to go with because it was already time for formation. Two hours flew by, and it was time to take that walk and see what she had to say. I got downstairs and fell in for roll call. The opening words of formation were, *where is Private Sanders? DS here DS. Private Sanders, your wife has been calling all weekend to tell you that you're a father. Why haven't you been answering her calls? She called twenty-three times in the past nineteen hours. DS, my phone got wet and stopped working DS. Fall out of formation and call that woman before I smoke you. Drill Sergeant, yes, Drill Sergeant.*

I ran to the barracks to make the call but on the way I passed by Rodriguez, and I saw she had a tear rolling down her left eye. That wasn't what I wanted to do. But hey, Williams was right, I didn't owe her shit. Later on at dinner chow, we ended up close to each other in the chow line. Rodriguez was two people behind me, and by this time I worked up enough courage to face the music. I sidestepped out of line and attempted to say I'm sorry, but all I could get out was I apologize for... SMACK, SMACK to my face and then extreme yelling in Spanish. She knocked my food tray out of my hand with a vicious force. This brought attention to the DS. *Hey, what the hell is going on, Privates?* I scurried to clean up the mess, and Williams thought fast and told the DS that we accidentally ran into each other and my food tray spilled. Rodriguez and her battle buddy walked off saying things in Spanish, but I was sure it was something to the fact that I never want to see you again, you sorry excuse for a man.

That was the polite version of what was probably said. I cleaned up the mess with Williams' help, and we headed back to the barracks. I just wanted that day to be over. I made it an early night and went to sleep. I got the silent treatment from baby girl for the remainder of the training. After the second week of trying to communicate with her, I gave up and moved onto the next three females. It was the day before graduation, and I previously had orders to report to Savannah, Georgia.

Sharlean and I were excited and ready to get there. I wish I could have been stationed there because, at the last eighteen hours notice, my orders got changed to report to Camp Humphreys, Korea. This would have been a good thing to be excited about if my wife was able to come. The DS told me that it's a hardship tour for one year and no spouses were allowed. I didn't know how I was going to tell Sharlean, but I figured it would be best to do it in person.

After graduation, we were allotted a one week time off pass to be with family before we reported to our first post assignment. Home, sweet home, I thought. There's nothing like the smell of the beach and gunpowder in the air. I spent six months and some change away from Oxnard and my family. Everything looked the same, and everyone was still doing the same shit. I walked through my home doors, and I was greeted with hugs and kisses from my mom and wife. Sharlean told me to sit down because she wanted to introduce me to my son.

It was an amazing feeling to hold him in my hands and know that I'm his father. It was enough to almost bring tears to my eyes, but I didn't let it happen because I was a soldier now and soldiers have no emotions, they just take orders and move out. Yeah, right, I wiped the tears from my face and cherished that one of a kind moment.

My mom and Sharlean had a weird vibe going on, and it was very obvious that they were putting on a front for me. I didn't think either one of them let the fighting incident go. I didn't waste any time, and I let Sharlean know that we needed to talk. She was nervous to hear what I had to say because it was showing. I told my mom to watch little Matt, and I took my wife to our area of the house.

Baby, listen, you're not going to like it, but I don't have any say in it. What is it, stinky butt? I came right out and said it. *We're not going to be stationed in Georgia, babe. That's fine, where are we going? That's the problem; we're not going anywhere. I'm getting stationed in South Korea, and I'm not allowed to take family.* What was supposed to be an exciting and happy day turned into a sad, heartbreaking one. Sharlean burst into tears sobbing loudly, and she kept saying, *I don't understand why I can't come.* I had no answer for her and only knew what the Drill Sergeant had told me.

After fifteen minutes of torture and watching my wife get her heart ripped out her chest, we had make-up sex. Twenty minutes later, she was back to feeling fine, as if I didn't tell her any terrible news. Before we went back to get junior from my mom, Sharlean said, *you sure whipped out a few new moves, babe.* I told her, *yeah, I had nothing to do but watch pornography in A.I.T.* I knew it was more like making pornography, but I wasn't going to volunteer that information. She looked at me and said, *mmmhh,* and carried on with her business.

The day went by quick, and before it was time to sleep, Sharlean told me that she and my mom had planned a surprise cookout for me tomorrow and everyone would be there from both our families. Sharlean was terrible with holding in surprises. Finally, a good night's sleep in my own bed with my wife. I dreamed of this for half a year, and it was finally happening.

The next day came fast, and it was already time for the cookout. My grandparents, uncle, and all my aunts were there, except for Lisa, which was probably a good thing. Sharlean's parents and sister showed up, which I thought was odd because at times they acted as if they were too good to be associated with people like us. Everything was going well, just a casual day with family. I broke the news to my family after we ate that I would be reporting to Korea for my first duty station of a one year tour. Sharlean's parents were concerned about her being left back with a child, but I explained to them that it was out of my control. I said my mom would be able to help her and we would find a way to get through this small obstacle together.

Her dad spoke with a snooty and disgusted tone, *well she definitely can't stay here.* Everyone looked up and I turned to him, with a look that displayed a concern, *finish your sentence, and why can't Sharlean stay here, tell us how you really feel.* He must have caught himself after a nudge from his wife. He cleared his throat and said, *she can't be a burden on you guys, that's not what this family does. They need their own home for their own family. I will give them my old house as a present.* I looked at my side of the family with the look of, "I'll take care of this please, nobody set it off up in here." Thank God it didn't get serious in there because I just knew Herman was going to act a fool.

Everyone respected the wishes of my body-language and stayed calm. I told him, *thank you for that gesture and we would be happy to have a home of our own.* Her dad was a controlling man and he had to have the final say so in anything concerning his family. It didn't matter if it was controlling his immediate family or his sibling's life. His word was gold in his family's eyes.

I knew what he was doing, but I played dumb to the fact. All he wanted was to be able to dictate what goes on in his daughter's life. By having ownership of the home we stayed in, he would be able to still pull her strings, especially while I was away overseas.

It didn't take long after his disruptive outburst for them to gather their things and leave. Soon my family would follow. It was a successful cookout, I would say. There was no fighting between Joey and my mother or among family, and no one got belligerent. I would take this small appreciative memory and add it to the few collections that I had stored.

The rest of the week, my wife and I enjoyed each other's company and the fact that we were parents. The night of my flight, Sharlean drove me to L.A.X airport, and we both cried our eyes out. This was harder than the first time. We been away from each other for six months and then only had a week to spend with each other. Plus, we had an addition to our family.

The thought that I wasn't there for my son's birth, and that I wouldn't be there for his first birthday, first steps, and first words cut deep, like a machete to my heart.

I straightened my face up and calmed her down. We smoked a cigarette and then I gave her a kiss goodbye. I had an eighteen-hour flight ahead of me that I wasn't looking forward to. I managed to get drunk and sleep on three different occasions on the plane. I still had four hours left on the flight once I gave up on trying to fall asleep through the pain. I was miserable, uncomfortable, and it stunk. I had someone sitting next to me getting toe jam out of their feet and another sleeping on my shoulder. I couldn't wait for wheels down.

I arrived in Korea a day and a half ahead of time from the United States. After getting my luggage and finding the United Service Organization (USO), which is where you report for transportation to your duty station by fellow military peers, I was ready to take on this one-year hardship tour. Being from California, I wasn't thinking about the four seasons of weather changes. I stepped out of the airport to load up on my bus, and there was a blizzard occurring. The idiot in me decided to wear a Kobe Bryant Lakers jersey and shorts. I saw people looking at me as if I was stupid, but I wasn't, I just didn't know about their weather. I'm from where it's seventy-five degrees year-round, so why the fuck would I own a coat or even think about buying one.

The ride to Camp Humphreys was nothing short of amazing. I saw people with no driving awareness run red lights and damn near cause accidents on their mopeds. The streets were so crowded, and they were full of activities. Vendors were on the streets selling merchandise of every sort, and there were food stands on all the corners.

It was an eye-opener, seeing how other countries lived. Their houses were similar to metal shacks that were poorly put together. Senior citizens had big baskets of food on their back that were so heavy; they walked bent all the way over. Some people just walked bent over as if it was an extreme medical condition with little or no treatment.

The bus I was riding did a full U-turn in the middle of the intersection while running a red light. It was the worst driving I had ever witnessed. I was somewhat scared that I wasn't going to make it to my assigned duty station, but I did. When I arrived, I was greeted by Specialist Carmichael. She was sweet and showed me around. In the back of my mind I thought, yeah, I'm going to fuck her.

She took me to my barracks room, and I was lucky enough not to have a roommate at that time. I settled in, and then I went on an adventure. I found myself walking the post. It was big, and you had to take the bus around to get where you were going. So I got on the bus for the rest of the adventure. My stomach started to growl right on time when the bus stopped at the PX. I don't know what PX stands for, but it was a place where soldiers went to get clothes, food, furniture, and alcohol. It was basically an on post Walmart with a few extra departments to make life as normal as they could for the troops.

I got off and walked to the food court area. I wasn't willing to try anything that wasn't in my normal settings, so I got some pizza. I went to pay for it on my debit card, but it was declined. I didn't know how it was declined because I had just got paid the night of my flight. I didn't have any money on me because I used it all attempting to get drunk on the plane. It was seven o'clock and already past chow time to go eat at the chow hall. That didn't matter anyway because I didn't know where it was located.

I handed my pizza back to the clerk, but she said, *just take it, I got you this time, but you owe me.* She was cute, short, thick, and was mixed with white and some type of Asian, which was probably Korean. I smiled and said, *thanks,* and she said, *no problem handsome.* I knew that I would catch her on the rebound sooner or later.

I had done enough adventuring for the day, so I headed back to the barracks. I wasn't in my room five minutes before I heard a knock at the door. It was two females, and Carmichael was one of them. They were about to go hang out in the 800 bldg. with some people and wanted to know if I wanted to come. *Yeah, let's do it, why not.*

Carmichael told me that she was from North Carolina and that she was the chaplain's assistant. Her friend, whose name I didn't get, didn't say too much, but her and Carmichael kept whispering and making comments while giggling. Their whispers weren't successful because I overheard them saying, *girl, he is cute,* and how they were going to be all over me. I acted like I never heard them, but I knew that they were plotting and I was alright with getting chose.

We arrived at a different barracks and it's a room full of niggas. Music was blasting and spades were being played. I saw people walking by with plates of food and alcohol being spilled on the floor. *Man, Y'all getting it in out here, huh. Sanders, this is Lil Yo and N.O. This is their room. What's cracking homie? Homie? Where you from, dog? I'm from Cali, why what's happening? Oh, don't trip, Big Cali, I just ain't heard nobody say homie unless it was in a movie. That's how y'all Cali niggas really talk, huh Bo!*

Lil Yo was a short dude. He stood five-seven in height, but I would soon witness that he had the heart of a six-four giant. N.O was shorter than him and pudgy. They both had gold teeth in their mouths and had a southern style language. Lil Yo said, *I'm from Bama,* and N.O said, *I'm from New Orleans,* but it sure didn't sound like how it's spelled. It was a slow, slurred speech; I figured it was because he was sipping on some Hennessy and that's what the cognac will do to you.

They introduced me to the rest of their crew and apparently I was the only person that wasn't from the south. Everyone was so proud of what state they were from and represented it to the fullest whenever the opportunity was available. It was twenty minutes into the kickback that they were having, and I got to see what Lil Yo was about. Some clown named Vet gets drunk and starts talking shit at the dice game. Talking shit is a must during any gambling game, but he was out of pocket, and I knew as soon as he called this man a bitch that it was going to get real. Calling a man a bitch is never going sit right in the hood and doing it in front of women was defiantly a no-go. That word challenges a man's masculinity and is one of the highest forms of disrespect regardless of how it's said.

Lil Yo stood up and asked him, *what did you say, little nigga?* I thought it was funny because short people always refer to other people as small to make themselves feel better. I think it's a complex and a short man's complex was exactly what Lil Yo displayed.

Before Vet had a chance to repeat the full word, Lil Yo smashes a beer bottle over his head. It didn't take long to escalate from there. N.O jumps in, and they tag team Vet. Vet got whooped like a stepchild that you can't stand but have to deal with because you want to be with their parent. The girls and some other people broke it up after too much blood was seen leaking from his head. There was a soldier that happened to be a medic in the room, so she tended to his wounds, and then Lil Yo kicked his ass out, but not after giving him a slap to the face. Slapping a man was another form of the highest level of disrespect besides calling someone a bitch. Slapping a man is the physical action of verbally calling a man a bitch, so I guess they were even now.

Liquor with women usually leads to sex after a good fight. That's exactly what started to happen and in that order. The women in the room changed the vibe by dancing and being flirtatious. Juvenile's song, "Back That Azz Up" started playing, and that was all it took for the freaks to come out. A lot of touchy-feely began to happen in the room, then they kicked it up a notch when N.O started to throw dollar bills at the ladies. Shirts began to come off, and niggas started to get rowdy.

I was tired from the jet lag and really deep down inside I didn't want to be the cheating husband that I already was, so when the time was right, I found my exit. I got to my bldg.755, which took a while to find, but I made it to my room and finally called Sharlean to let her know that I made it. The first night was rough to sleep, so I had a hard time waking up for the platoon formation, but I made it on time.

It was cold as shit and we were out in the snow with some tiny physical training (PT) shorts and a long sleeve shirt. It was Monday, and the regiment of exercise didn't change much from basic training to now. We stretched before a two-mile Indian relay run. This was easy work compared to what I had just come from doing. I quickly learned about black ice as I stepped on a patch and fell.

For some strange reason, the Major of our company was running with us, and he helped me up. *Easy there Private Sanders, let me help you up, troop. Thank you, sir, I didn't see the ice there. Be careful; it's everywhere, we don't need you getting hurt before I beat you in the run on the PT test next month. What makes you think you're going to beat me, sir? I've seen your PT runtime, and you're pretty fast, but I'm faster. I believe you ran a twelve minute and thirty-four seconds two-mile run right, Private? Yes, sir. Well, I will run it in twelve minutes flat. I look forward to giving you some competition, sir. Hurry up and catch up with the platoon, Private. Yes, sir.*

Great, now I had the Major on my damn head, that wasn't what I wanted or needed. After PT, it was time to eat at the chow hall and then report to work. I got to the motor pool, which was my designated area to work as a supply guy. It was either there or the warehouse, and I didn't want the warehouse because they really worked. The inventory would be a significant amount, and all eyes were on you if your numbers didn't add up. Plus you know how I can get with inventory.

The motor pool was easy; I just had to issue vehicles to soldiers and order, pick up, or turn in parts. When I walked in the doors, I saw a Korean soldier, and it baffled my mind because he wasn't in the United States military uniform, it was a Korean military uniform. He asked me if I was Sands? His native tongue wouldn't allow him to say Sanders correctly, so Sands was all I understood. *Yes, that's me. Yes, Sergeant Park, you mean I'm Kutusa Soldier. Oh, sorry Sergeant, I didn't know who you were. Now you know, give me push-ups, push-ups now you give me.*

I start knocking out push-ups until he said get up. It was about fifty before he released me. *I'm Sergeant Park, you, my soldier, you listen and pay attention. I teach you how to work, and you then show me how you do.* I was so thrown off by his native tongue and his assertive attitude, that most of the day, I kept asking him to repeat himself. He thought I was being funny and kept dropping me to do push-ups. I liked him from the beginning because he was a passionate person when he spoke and he knew his shit. Sergeant Park wasn't an asshole, he was just very structured, and he went about things the right way. So, I respected him and his position.

After a long day, I got off work at 5:00pm, but I couldn't complain because we had a lunch break from 11:30am until 1:00pm. I decided not to go to the chow hall. Instead of free food for troops, I wanted to spend my money on Taco Bell or Burger King. I remembered before I got to the PX that my debit card wasn't working, so I called the bank. After a tense and heated discussion with the customer service department, I found out some bullshit. I was told that the bank was taking all of my wages to repay my overdraft fee of four thousand dollars. They told me that on the same day that I arrived in Korea, that I was seen on camera in their branch cashing a twenty-six hundred dollar check and that I came back two hours later and cashed a fourteen-hundred-dollar check.

The level of anger was extreme because I knew that I didn't do it. I was in another country when it was claimed that I was seen on camera. I was informed to expect no pay for the next month and a half until the debt was paid in full. The only thing I could think of was that Sharlean had asked me if she could lend her real sister nine hundred dollars. When she did, she wrote her a check, but on the flip side her sister previously just got out of jail for writing or cashing bad checks. I thought maybe she had some foul play with this, but there was no way to prove it. Also, they claimed that I had cashed the checks, which meant a man was on the footage. Either way it went down, playing murder she wrote wasn't going to get me fed or paid for the next month and a half.

I called Sharlean hoping that she would pick up so I could tell her to send me some money, but she never answered. I went ahead and called my mom, but I already knew what she was going to say. *Hey mom, I'm in a bad situation right now, my bank account has been garnished for some bullshit.* I give her the run down, and of course, she's not able to send me anything, not even twenty dollars. I wasn't mad because I had already known the answer.

She said to me, *Don't they have a place for you to eat and sleep for free, right?* I said, *yeah, but I still need to get laundry done, grab some personal hygiene things, and get phone cards to call home.* That conversation ended quickly because, like always, she and Joey found time to argue even when she's was on the phone. I told her, *I'll find my own way and I'll call you later when I can.*

Chapter 20: It's a Slippery Slope

I went to my room and put on some basketball clothes so I could find the nearest gym and go hustle. I found the gym and caught a game or two before I started talking shit and getting in people's heads. When I felt that they had enough, I tried to embarrass them with my words and then offer the challenge to play for money. This was the set up to get them to play for money. Now they wanted to shut me up bad, and the only way to win overall was to beat me by taking my money.

That wasn't going to happen; for one I was good, and two, I was dead broke in a foreign country. I was hungry and needed that money more than they did. After the sixth game played and four for money, I earned eighty dollars playing twenty- dollar one on one games. I played one person twice and two other people. I made sure not to exceed playing twice with one person and not to take too much money from them because if you take their confidence and dominate them, they'll realize they can't win, and then you can't earn any money. By leaving them with the hope that they could possibly beat me one day, it left the doors open for me to make more money when needed.

Before I left, one of them yells out, *hey, what's your name?* I said, *Cali, why what's cracking? I was just wondering because I've never seen you here before. You just got here? Yeah, last night, homie. Oh yeah, you definitely from Cali. My name is Cue. Big Cali, you got game, Folk! Thanks, man, I'm about to run and get something to eat, I'll catch you next time. Shit, you headed to the PX? I'm going that way too. Yeah, come on, I'm hungry as a motherfucker.*

We walked to the food court area, and Cue tells me that he's in my company 3rd Military Intelligent (M.I) and he lives in the same building as me. He actually was two doors down the hall from me. After a decent meal, I told him what was going on with me, and he told me that he had my back if I needed anything. I thought it was a nice gesture, but ain't shit free in life, so I wasn't trying to get in debt with a nigga I didn't even know. The last thing I was going to do was ask another man for help when I knew how to make money.

We ended up kicking it through the week and then the weekend came. That's when I got introduced to all his homeboys before we went out to the nightclub. I met a dude named Kountry, and he was rock solid in tip-top shape and didn't give two fucks about anything. Kountry was from the south too, and he had gold teeth in his mouth as well.

The other homeboys I met were D.C and Lil Will. Obviously, D.C was from Washington D.C, and Lil Will was from Virginia. Lil Will was a funny dude that cracked jokes a lot and could make a hell of a drink with Grey Goose Vodka. D.C was a basketball player and had a good head on his shoulders. Lil Yo and N.O came to his room, and we were all drinking that one of a kind drink called the "Good Will Punch" that Lil Will made. When talking they all sounded the same because the majority of them were from the south and had that country grammar going on. I couldn't understand much, but the little I did understand was clear.

Aye, Bo, when we go out, we together my nigga, ya dig that? Like a shovel, homie. Listen, we the muthafuckin show when we get in the club. We got a lot of haters that want what we got but don't know how to get it. But I tell you this, if a nigga subscribes, he's going to get his issue, you feel me, Folk? Enough said, homie. Oh, last thing partna, don't be fucking any of those hoes in the clubs with the big pile of salt outside the door. Brah, what the fuck are you talking about, salt piles outside the door? Big Cali, you're going to see, Bo. Them muthafuckin Juicy Girls are going to run your pockets tonight, nigga.

I didn't know what the hell they were talking about, but Lil Will seemed like the only one that hadn't gotten drunk yet and could break it down to me. I whispered to Lil Will, *what's a Juicy Girl, brah? It's a bunch of Korean hoes that be in the club serving drinks in their thongs and shit. Sometimes them hoes will fuck, but most of the time they are pushing orange juice and vodka drinks on you for five dollars. You will be so drunk that you end up a hundred dollars in the hole. Stay away from them bitches unless you plan on fucking. Oh yeah, and if the salt pile is outside the door, that means one of those hoes got a sexually transmitted disease.*

We finished our drinks and headed off post for a few hours to get live. I was excited to see what Korea had to offer, plus I was with some cool ass niggas so this was going to be a night to remember. We were loud and talking shit as we got off the bus that took us to the front gates. We walked through the processing system to show our I.D's and I noticed a Kutusa soldier who had a sword on his back. I thought I was drunk, so I whispered to Lil Will again. *Hey, homie, does this fool have a motherfucking sword on his back, dog? Yup, and he'll swing that bitch too, I have seen him do it. This nigga ain't swinging no sword at nobody, brah, stop playing with me. You got a lot to learn, you Big Dummy!* Once Will said that, I knew he was serious and all I could think about was when my granddaddy would say, you Big Dummy! He was always serious when it was being said so I figured Will was telling the truth.

The crew was loud, laughing and talking big shit when we walked through the city of Pyeongtaek. I was observant of my surroundings because everything was so amazing. Pink lights were flashing everywhere. People were riding unicycles with a person on their shoulders, and food vendors were spread out through the streets. It was like a circus on every block.

We walked by a clothing store that was well familiar with the homies. N.O said, *Big Cali, this is where we get our jerseys and shoes from; throwback Joe has everything you need. At this time in life, throwback jerseys of all sports teams were the fashion to wear, and we were in the middle of where they were made. See Cali, we ain't got to pay the United States prices of two hundred fifty plus dollars for a jersey because they're only thirty dollars here in Korea. Me and Lil Yo buy them a hundred at a time and ship them back to the states and charge niggas one fifty a jersey. We will put you on game so you can get your money up. The only thing is, don't send more than one hundred at a time because, I think, at one twenty-five they call it redlining and they will lock yo ass up and hit you with a big ass fine. We knew a fool name Raymond that got caught up on that shit and that nigga sitting in the joint right now. But fuck all that, let's get at these hoes, nigga, the club is right around the corner.*

We walked into a small bar-style spot. I wouldn't call it a club, but it had a dance floor and hoes. I guess this was the closest to a club we were going to get to while stationed out here. I looked to my left, and I spotted a Juicy Girl immediately. Will was right, she had a thong on with her ass out and a bikini style top. She walked up to me because, I believe, I was staring too hard at her and she knew that I was new to this environment. *G.I., you want juice? I give juice for you, baby.* Before I could say no, she handed me two drinks off her server's tray. I took it anyway; besides, it looked like a long line at the bar, so I didn't mind having two.

The boys had started to get even rowdier as soon as we entered. A song called "Throw It Up" by Lil Jon and The East Side Boyz came on, and that was all it took for them to start throwing up gang signs and mean mugging other cliques in the club. I learned fast that a lot of them were affiliated with the Folk Nation. Pitchforks signs were put in the air onsite, and the testosterone level reached an all-time high. I sat back and looked at the scene to get a better understanding of what the mission was for the night. It was clear as day that with the group of characters I was rolling with, it was all about fighting and fucking. I was with whatever they were on because I was already treated like family.

It didn't take long before Kountry got into it with a nigga. Midway through the song, I see out of the corner of my eye, Kountry talking to some dude with more hostility than was needed. I knew what it was already, so I played the outskirts to be able to see if any of the other dude's clique was going to jump in. I eased my way in closer, so if it were to go down, I would be at a good angle to punch the shit out of somebody.

There it goes; Kountry slapped this man with thunder. I say thunder because even with the loud music and niggas yelling out the song lyrics, you still heard the palm of Kountry's hand slapping the life out of this dude's face. This grown ass man got smacked in the club, and he took it like a G. I didn't expect that at all, but buddy must have had some common sense and realized that we had a gang of rowdy fighting ass niggas and he didn't want any part of that.

Cue grabs Kountry and the clique gathered up in a circle on the dance floor. They started chanting, *seven-five-five, we go live, seven-five-five, we go live!* All I saw was gold teeth, throwback jerseys, and cups of Long Island Ice Tea. This was the moment I knew that I was going to have an extreme amount of fun in Korea.

Bitches started to flock over to the clique, and a whole lot of ass shaking started. A little bitch pulled up on me and started shaking her ass like an exotic dancer. I got a few good feels in and started dancing with her through a song or two. Lil Yo came over and said, *damn, Cali, I ain't never seen her before, you got you one, Bo.* Then he said, *let me show you how a dirty south nigga gets down.* He placed his hand on her pussy, while she stood up from being bent over from backing that ass up on me. She then raised her right leg on his left shoulder and made a move that I had never seen before while she was still shaking her ass. Lil Yo was a small dude so it probably was like she was just stretching because if she had tried that with me, she might have hurt herself.

While she had her leg up on him dancing, he was still holding on to her pussy. I was looking in shock because I didn't know we could do that. My niggas came over to see what was going on, and then the dollars started being thrown on her. It felt like a rap video shoot in the bar. Her friends started to compete with her dancing and tried to top her. One fine, thick chick started doing leg splits and plopping her ass on the floor. This made the fellas throw even more money at them. Before I knew it, we were the center of attention at the club all within fifteen minutes of being there.

D.C gave me fifty dollars and said, *go get more drinks, Big Cali, we about to show out tonight.* I went to the bar to get more drinks, and it felt like the majority of the women were eyeballing me because I was a part of the clique that they wanted to go be around, but it was too crowded on the dance floor for hoes to get close to us. I saw the lust in their eyes, and it didn't matter if they were there with someone. That person they were with didn't exist at that time. I now knew what Lil Yo meant when he said niggas want what we got and can't have it. They were the muthafuckin show and bitches loved them. Now that I'm cliqued up, I'm the muthafuckin show!

We were slapping niggas and grabbing bitches pussy while throwing money. At any given time, we would yell out the clique motto that made people know who was in there presence. I saw a chick staring hard at me, so I decided to stunt and test it out. I yell

SEVEN-FIVE-FIVE, and the homies finished it, *WE GO LIVE!* Lil Yo yelled, *okay, Big Cali, I see you, Bo!* That was the acceptance letter of confirmation I needed. Somehow I hopped right back into a clique without seeking initiation. These types of activities went on all night throughout different nightclubs and bars.

After a good night of partying, we got back to post at 1:00am. We hit the on post club, which was similar to the after-hours club spots in the states. We were there long enough to pick up a crew of five females. They came back to the barracks with us, and people chose who they wanted. I tried to be a good nigga again and went to my room to go to sleep. But that didn't happen at all. I figured that there were about eight of us and three people would come up short. Taking myself out the game was fine, plus, I'm married to my gorgeous wife and I have a newborn baby at home waiting on me. The devil sure has a way to find your weakness, and it was safe to say he knew mine.

Twenty minutes into my attempt to sleep, I heard a knock at the door. I answered the door with my shirt off and boxers on. I figured it was one of the less fortunate niggas that didn't get a bitch and needed to crash in my room because his roommate was fucking. I opened the door and it was a tall, slim, dark skinned lady that was with the crew of females that were brought back to the barracks. *Hey, what's up?* She said, *I was told to come to this room now.* With a confused face and hesitant words, I said, *you were told to come to this room?* She didn't answer me and kind of barged her way in my room while saying I was cute. I didn't understand what the hell was going on, but she asked if she could use the restroom. I thought it was funny that she asked because she sure didn't ask to come in my room, but I told her to go ahead and pointed to the restroom.

She was in there for about eight minutes, which was seven minutes too long. When I got concerned, she came out and sat on the bed. At that time I had the television on so there was some type of light in the room. I went to ask her what she wanted, but before I had the chance, she started kissing on my neck. I attempted to say I have a wife but for some reason, I was highly distracted, and the words wouldn't come out. Women always say it's the thought that counts. So this should count for something. Because I sure tried, but before I knew it, she was taking my boxers off. She was kind of mannish with the way she took the lead, but I wasn't tripping, just shocked.

She pushed me back and hiked up her mini skirt. She either took her panties off in the restroom, or she just wasn't wearing any at all. It probably was best to think she wasn't wearing any at all due to her behavior. It was like she was on business. She had a straight face from what I could see from the light coming off the TV. She got on top of me and started grinding on my Johnson like it was the last one on earth. I felt on her breast and tried to take her shirt off, but she smacked my hand then placed her hand on the middle off my chest and grinded harder.

Business was exactly what it felt like. I was butt ass naked while she was fully dressed and I couldn't even remember if this bitch took her shoes off before she hopped on top. At this point, I was not intrigued by this hoe, and I felt like the bitch because I didn't fuck this woman, she was fucking me. I focused up enough to get my nut off and before I was ready to cum I told her. She got off of me and slid down to lick on my testicles while she stroked my penis. I was almost there, and I told her to keep going, then this bitch shows me how filthy she really is. She took me by surprise by throwing my legs up one at a time; then she started licking my ass while stroking me off. That was by far the best nut I ever had and the freakiest. I cum all over her hand and a little in her mouth. After she felt the semen drizzle down her knuckles, she took that as a sign to suck the head of my dick. I was very surprised that she didn't swallow the semen after the nasty shit she just did.

She went back to the restroom and took a hooker's bath. I knew this because when she left, my towel was wet on the corner and the rest of the towel was dry. I didn't have to let her out because she took off on her own when she was done. I didn't know her name, and she didn't know mine, it was strictly business. I felt like shit again when I was done because I couldn't fight the lust and had betrayed my wife for no reason again.

The next day, I talked to Lil Will and told him he would never believe what that bitch did to me last night. He said try me, very calm and unimpressed with what I was going to say. *Nigga this bitch threw my legs up while stroking my meat and licked my ass.* He laughed and said, *what you've never been in the "Huckle Buck," fool? Hell no. I didn't know that shit even existed. You've got a lot to learn, you Big Dummy. So, you had Nakita in your room last night, huh? Shit, I didn't get her name, she said she was sent to me. Yeah, it was Nakita. She is tall, slim, and fine? Yeah, that sounds about right. I think Cue sent her to you because I sent her homegirl to him quick. I gave that bitch three strokes and a grind, boy, that pussy was so good. Who you send Nakita too? I didn't, she walked out on her own. Listen, man we be hitting the same hoes half the time, and you're supposed to send her to another room when you're done. But she probably fucked everyone already out the clique, and that's why she left.*

Wait a minute; I was the last nigga to fuck out of all of us? Not last night, she probably fucked with Cue only because everyone picked who they wanted already and Cue was all that was left. But technically, yeah, you were the last nigga to fuck out the crew. This how we get down, Big Cali, seven five five, we go live! So we just some dirty dick boys, huh. Will laughed and said, *I like that I'll let the niggas know we dirty dick boys (D.D.B).*

Chapter 21: These Hoes Are for Everybody

The first month went by fast, but it was hard. I still wasn't getting paid, and I was in need of a lot of shit to survive. I would go to the PX and steal bologna, bread, and top ramen noodles to have food in my refrigerator for after hours when my stomach began to rumble and the chow hall was closed. I didn't go off post a lot because I didn't have money and I didn't want to be who we called Don, "Dat One Nigga" who was always begging. That has never been my style.

I didn't get any support from my family, and half the time they didn't pick up the phone. Sharlean wasn't answering her phone as much either. I tried to take into consideration that I was eighteen hours ahead of them, but it didn't matter if I called at 6:00pm their time, I still didn't have any luck. After hustling all I could on the basketball courts, no one wanted to play me after the first three weeks.

Shit was bad. I was able to smell myself sometimes at work when I wasn't able to steal soap and the rest of the personal hygiene because muthfuckas wanted to stare and keep an eye on me in the PX store aisles when I was trying to survive. I ended up changing bank accounts for my direct deposit when I found out there was a very small bank on post. This still took me up to a month and a half to get paid. At least that lying ass bank didn't get another dime of my hard earned money.

I still found time to fuck around with bitches during that month and a half. I came to terms with myself that I wasn't strong enough to fight my temptations and I accepted it. It made it easier to have multiple sex partners since I wasn't able to get in contact with my wife like I should have been. I probably talked to her three or four times since I arrived. She was out of sight and out of mind, but when I was able to get a hold of her, I was still in love. My perspective was that I was fucking these women and I made love to my wife. They got DICK and a nickname; Sharlean knew me, and she had my heart.

I was deeply in love with my wife and looked at my extracurricular activities as nothing more than a sport. However, this sport was easy to get addicted to, especially when I felt like I was on the basketball court and dominated every opponent. By this time, I had fucked about twenty women from the day I left to join the military eight months ago.

A couple of months went by with the same activities on the weekends that had taken place my first week. The only change was that I started to get into fights and my name gained rank. I was already an equal leader of the clique and most of the time all the pre-drinking events took place at my room. Every now and then I would meet a woman, and she would say, *I've seen you before with the seven five five clique. You're the one with all the bitches around you in the club, just like a player. You're probably married and be lying to them girls to get them in bed.*

But they would be wrong because the discussion of my personal life was never brought up. I would have one night stands, or I would keep a few around to throw in a rotation. I tried to be careful, well, not really. I thought if I kept a few hoes around that it would lower the odds of catching an STD. That only works if you're wearing condoms. I didn't like condoms because I didn't get to feel the real them, and it was just different, and I wasn't able to climax when I put on a condom. Raw was how ninety-nine percent of my women were getting it.

Chapter 22: Words Can Hurt

It was November, and I was still having fewer conversations with my wife. I managed to get Robert's number from her the last time we talked. I thought it would be good to check on my homies since they didn't check on me. I called him up and we had a good ass conversation. Robert told me that he needed to talk to me about something, but didn't know how to tell me. *What's up, brah, tell me, man. Matt, I think Sharlean is using the drug crystal meth.* I paused and laughed at him. *What the hell are you talking about, homie? Yeah, Matt, I didn't want to believe it, but my homie said that he had served her about a month ago. Robert, Sharlean is not even that type of person, fool; I think he got her mixed up with someone else.* He said, *I don't think so dog, but I love you, and I got to go, my mom's tripping all out because my little brother had the scale in his backpack for show and tell today at school. Alright homie, I'll talk to you soon. I love you too, brah.*

Not one ounce in my body believed that Sharlean was on drugs, let alone crystal meth. I continued with my daily routine, which consisted of PT, work, alcohol, random bitches, and an occasional fight. Another month went by with the same old routine. I received a phone call from my nigga, Cory, from back home. Cory was hands down the best dresser I had ever known. That boy stayed fresh. Cory and I were cool, but we weren't that cool to where he should be calling me in Korea.

Hello, my nigga Matt Sanders, what's up homie, it's Cory. Cory, is this you homie? Yuppers. What's upper, dude? Just kicking it homie, you know how I do. How's the Army treating you, brah? Everything good, man, I can't complain. It's hella different though, but you know I needed a change. True that homeboy, you did. Have you seen Camilo yet? I did when I was leaving Virginia; he was coming in on a new class. I'm shocked, brah, that you called me. Yeah, I wish it was good news big homie, but it's not. What do you mean it's not good news? Listen, playboy, I asked Nikki for your number because I had to tell you because nobody else wanted to.

When Cory was speaking, I thought he was going to say something happened with one of the homies, not the devastating life bomb that he so willingly and voluntarily told me. *Matt, last week I was riding on the freeway and, um, damn, I don't know how to say this. Just say it, brah. Listen when I was driving, I saw Sharlean sleeping on the side of the freeway.* I was confused, and I was instantly heartbroken because I didn't understand why my wife was on the side of the freeway sleeping. Cory said, *brah, I don't know if you know, but she's been using crystal meth for a few months now.* I knew it was true when he told me because, for one, he wasn't the type of homie that would call me in Oxnard, yet he was calling me in Korea. And, two, what would he gain from making up a horrible lie like this.

Every word Cory spoke was true because he was passionate, sincere, and thought about my feelings when he explained it to me. Cory was a real nigga for that, and I knew that I would always rock with him for life. The thought that people knew my wife was fucked up on drugs and sleeping on the side of the freeway was stomach turning. I didn't understand why people wouldn't say anything to me. Why didn't my mom tell me? That explained why she wasn't picking up and why I could barely get in contact with Sharlean.

I was so hurt; I hung up the phone on Cory. I was glad that I was in my room when I received this information because I broke down and cried. The thought of my precious woman that I was madly in love with, being out in the cold, tired, broke, and drugged out was an unbearable pain. It felt like my heart had been ripped out of my chest and smashed in my face.

I had so many questions, and the most important question was; where was our son? After an hour of trying to gain control of myself, I was able to calm down and rethink the situation. I still needed to be able to ask her without accusing my wife of what I had just learned to be true about her newly founded activity. I worked up the courage to call and question her.

Sharlean picked up on the first attempt. *Hey, what's going on babe? What are you doing? I'm fine just lying around getting ready to start my day,* she said. *Listen, I want to ask you something and it might sound crazy, but it needs to be asked. Okay, what is it? Sharlean, are you smoking any drugs besides weed?* There was a long extended pause. I asked her, *are you smoking crystal meth?* She went into defense mode and replied back with a snappy attitude. *It's not like I'm strung out or nothing, I only tried it a few times.*

By the way, she admitted she was using the drug; I already knew she was spun out of control. My pain started to turn into anger, and I started to yell at her with rapid questions. *Why the fuck are you smoking that shit? Who the fuck put you on with this shit? I can't fucking believe you? Why would you want to smoke this shit? Are you stupid or something?* Sharlean yells, *fine I won't do it anymore, I promise. I only tried it occasionally.* I yelled back at her, *you better fucking not, and where's my son? He's sleeping right next to me. Sharlean you better not smoke that shit again. I promise I won't babe. I'm not strung out either.* I hung up on her and went further into a rage. I started throwing my belongings on the floor and against the wall. I was so mad and hurt that I could have turned into the Incredible Hulk.

The pain came back because I realized that she continued to plead that she wasn't strung out and she went from trying it, to occasionally doing it. That was her really saying, I'm strung out, and I do it all the time. I was no dummy. I understand people well and could read between the lines. Sharlean was dusted, disgusted, and now, couldn't be trusted. I knew that I was going to have a long and curvy road ahead of me, like my life hadn't been hard enough already.

I thought since I had left my environment that I would get a chance to start fresh and do something with myself. But little did I know, I was already falling back into my old ways by finding fun through my weekend shenanigans.

Chapter 23: Someone Has to Pay for My Pain

Those weekend shenanigans turned into every other day shenanigans. I was drinking more, fighting more, and fucking more women out of anger. Before, it was boredom and a weakness of lust. Now, it was just pure self-hatred and not wanting to face my problems.

I thought by releasing my anger on random people and starting fights that it would release some pain. I would let people get the first punch or two, so I could feel the pain because I wasn't able to self-inflict any injuries onto myself. Those punches were what I needed to turn into the inner beast that was inside of me. Fucking different women now went from lust to a semi-sadistic sexual mindset. I wasn't just having sex, I was choking bitches with anger, and when I would fuck them in the ass, I would shove it in and watch them scream or say that is too hard. The part that I didn't understand was that they never told me to stop. They would sometimes cry and take the pain. I felt that I had to inflict pain on them because, in my mind, I associated Sharlean with all the women that I encountered from that point on. She hurt me, so I wanted to hurt her back, but since I couldn't, I took it out on my sex partners.

I began to go further and further with testing the limits to what those women would let me do. I started off with aggressive sex by pulling, slapping, and choking. I left welt marks on their face, breast, ass, or whatever part of the body I chose to slap. I once choked this female so hard and long that after she gained her breath and natural color back, she put her clothes on and stormed out of the room. She told me that I was sick and had problems while tears rolled down her eyes. I spat on her and called her a bitch as she walked out of my room. I didn't give a damn what she had to say, she didn't mean anything to me.

There was another hoe that I butt fucked so hard that her ass hole ripped, and shit started to fly everywhere. It was all over my bed and stomach. Blood and shit is a terrible mixture and smell. She was already screaming in pain, but when it ripped, I didn't feel bad for her. I felt powerful, and it gave me some pleasure to know that I could hurt her like that. I laughed at it in the shower while she took a taxi to the hospital. From time to time women would stay the night, so when she came back, I was shocked because she wasn't one of the hoes that would normally do that. She told me that it was painful, but the best sex she ever had.

Most of the women loved it and never complained. I took that as a challenge and as disrespect. So, I thought I would crank it up a notch since they're enjoying all this pain and pleasure. I had a Korean bitch that I met off post that was a bartender and spoke broken English. A few days later, after manipulating her on the phone, she invited me to her home. I knew I was going to fuck her and I was going to go far past the line because she was a foreigner and I wanted to disrespect her. Ironically, I was really the foreigner because I'm in her country, but I didn't give two shits about what she had to say. During our sex session, she was already showing signs that she was into some freaky shit, but couldn't take any dick. While on top of her, I was easing her into a choke, and when I had a good grip, she started to moan with her mouth open. That was my chance; I started to let my saliva drool down into her mouth. She shocked me and began to lick her lips and swallowed it. I, again, took this as a challenge, so I upped the boundaries. I was drunk and full of urine, so I said fuck it, I pulled out of her and began to pee on her stomach. She takes her hands and rubs it all over her body with a passionate caress while I'm still urinating.

At this point, I'm mentally not in my right mind because I slapped her out of anger. I couldn't disrespect her, and she was being turned on by all of this weird shit. I couldn't believe that she wanted and accepted this freaky, nasty, sick, mentally ill stuff that I was doing. I wasn't fucked up in the head enough to try and take a shit on her, so I let her have that victory. She vigorously rubbed her clit and started to squirt. At this time, I didn't even know women could squirt, so I thought that this bitch was trying to pee back on me. I stood up and continued to watch, and during her rubbing on her clit with her liquid shooting out like a broke super soaker water gun, it got me to climax. I stroked my shaft until I ejaculated on her face.

I owned the fact that I was fucked up in the head and probably needed to talk to someone about my mental state. The behavior that I had been engaged in was not normal, but it slowly became normal for me. I never urinated on another sex partner again, but there would be plenty of other shameful nights with a mass amount of different sex partners.

I started to fall into a deep depression and a suicidal state of mind. I was living life recklessly, even more than before. My drinking habit turned into an everyday drinking ritual. Big Cali was knocking dudes out and getting more hoes. I would get drunk to the point that I would be able to drink myself sober. I would have so much in me that in a moment's notice, I would snap back into a normal functioning reality. I thought that I was crazy. I could be having a good time with slurred speech, blurry vision, and the room spinning. But at the snap of the finger, everything cleared up, and I got annoyed. It was frustrating because I wasn't able to drown my problems in my misery. This was when I would get angry and have to start a fight. Sometimes it would be with a new guy who just got to the post. I didn't care who it was. In the midst of everything, I would think, maybe my life would be better if I didn't exist.

My life had been shit from the beginning, and now, the person who I prayed for, was on that shit. She came to me at a very valuable time in my life, and she was all for me. She loved and only wanted me, but now, I was going to have to share her with this new addiction. Some days I gave myself false hope and told myself; she's not strung out, she really just tried it a few times. I made myself start believing that again.

Chapter 24: From Lust to Love

It was January 20th, 2004, and I was walking on post as I saw this pretty brown skin lady with a gorgeous smile. I walked up to her and introduced myself. She said that her name was Shametta, but her friends called her Meme. Meme had a very southern accent that turned me on, and it was ghetto too. I asked her where she was from and she told me Alabama. I told her that I was from California. She was excited when I told her that, and she said that she had never met anyone from there. *Is it really as bad as seen on T.V.?* I told her it could be, but that we also had some good parts and that you could definitely get what you were looking for there.

We exchanged numbers, and over the next few days, we got to know each other. Usually, I'm selling dreams to people and manipulating them, but I didn't do that with her. I just enjoyed her conversation and got to know her, as she did the same. We went on a real date to dinner about an hour away by the Osan Air Force base. The restaurant that we went to was one that served good American food. We enjoyed our evening with dinner and a movie; I even bought her a stuffed animal from one of the street vendors.

She was different from all the other women that I was dealing with. I had no desire to bring her into my little sick world of sex. I wanted normal, compassionate sex. Within the first five days, we had sex. She was a little shy, but after I test drove that thang a few times, she opened up and let herself go. She was a good girl; she wouldn't give me oral sex because she said that her mom told her that's what hoes did and she was a woman. I respected her for staying true to her beliefs and not letting me pressure her into anything she wasn't with doing. She sure didn't mind me eating her pussy, but I was a hoe, so I did hoe things.

If I needed to feed my Big Cali ego, I would fuck with one of the rotation of bitches I had. The rotation was slowly going away because I would be with Meme all the time. So when those hoes were gone, I would go down to the pink light district and fuck with the prostitutes whenever the homies and I went out. It wasn't often, but it was often enough that I had a favorite hoe and that the other hoes knew who I was coming to see.

The pink light district was a huge brothel of women. They had them displayed in glass window cases like mannequins. They were posted in lingerie with pink lights flashing on them. It was an amazing sight to see, but you couldn't appreciate it like you wanted to because it was strictly off limits for soldiers. If you got caught, you could possibly get kicked out of the military. You had to run in there, find the one you wanted, and be in and out, all within fifteen minutes. Every thirty minutes the Military Police patrolled the area looking for soldiers. I'm sure they had to search the rooms every now and then to make sure all areas were secured for national safety, of course.

I was satisfied with dealing with Meme only. I didn't need any hoes if I had her. After a few weeks, I was able to take leave for two weeks' vacation. I told Meme I would be back and I was going home for a little bit. She was sad but happy that I left during the time that her company was going to be in the field training, so she wasn't going to see me anyway. At least she didn't have to go through two more weeks with me gone for vacation.

I took the long flight back home to L.A.X airport. When I arrived, Sharlean and my mom were there to pick me up. I hadn't talked to Sharlean since she confessed to using drugs. It wasn't by choice; it was forced because she would never pick up the phone and sometimes when she did call back, I would be childish and not answer because I was mad that she didn't pick up when I called. I would be lying if I didn't say that sometimes it was because I was lying in bed with Meme.

I was confused because they both drove separate cars. I had initially planned to get picked up by my mom and didn't know Sharlean would be there. I jumped in the car with my mother; this was my momma, why wouldn't I? I was still so angry and hurt that I stayed at my mom's house the first night. The next day, Sharlean explained to me that I was wrong and needed to be in our own home; the home her dad gave us. She was right; I didn't even consider that my son was there and that I should be spending time with him, even if I was mad at her. So, I made the right choice and went home. However, I could tell my mother had feelings about me doing this because she was aware of the situation that we were going through.

When I finally got home, Sharlean and I just appreciated junior and played with him all day. I decided to take a shower before I took my beautiful wife and son out to dinner. As I was getting out the shower, I had a towel wrapped around my body and was drying my hair with another one. I walked out the bathroom door and looked to my left. I saw Sharlean smoking out of a glass pipe. I prayed that I didn't see what I believed I saw. As I walked up to her, it was exactly as I had seen it; a glass pipe up to her lips.

I yelled at her, *WHAT THE FUCK ARE YOU DOING, NIGGA? Matthew, relax it's just a little bit of meth. Sharlean, are you fucking kidding me? Our son is right her crawling in the hallway! Kick back, fool, this doesn't even have a smell to it. Matthew will be alright. Here, do you want to try some?*

It took every little bit of good spirit I had left in my body to not body slam this woman. It was official, she was lost to the game, and I had to face it. I couldn't believe she had the muthafuckin audacity to do it in front of our son. She had no shame and the nerve to offer me some. I didn't want that shit, and I didn't want her if she was going to be on it. She really tried to finesse me into getting hooked on drugs with her and fucking my life up even more as well. I put my clothes on and got junior's things and tried to leave the house with him but, of course, that wasn't going to happen.

She began pulling on my clothes while yelling; *you're not taking my baby* and trying to pry him out my arms. I didn't want Matthew to get hurt, so I surrendered. I was smart enough to realize that when the cops got called I would go to jail for kidnapping, even if I was joint parenting with her. California is a state where women have all the rights for what the fuck ever is needed, and I knew that I wouldn't win. I couldn't go through that situation because I didn't know how I would have reacted toward the law and I wasn't going to snitch and say that she was on drugs or that she had some on her.

I did the wrong but smart thing. I took my loss in this battle to hopefully win the war. I left my son in the care of his high-on-drugs mother. It hurt, and I wished that I had taken him, but it wasn't smart. My heart turned cold, and this was the situation that put me in a deep dark place that would be hard to climb out of. I walked back to my mom's house and smoked a few blunts. I had to contemplate if I was going to go back to Korea or not.

During the remainder of my vacation, I stayed high, drunk, and linked up with my old clique.

Chapter 25: I Just Don't Give a Damn

I spent time with Robert, and he was still up to the same shit, nothing changed. Robert said Kris didn't come around much anymore after his dad died. Robert told me his dad was a crack head and died of an overdose. I wanted to reach out to him, but I had no way of finding him, I just had to catch him in the streets.

Robert had a kickback for me one night, and everything was going good. I was drunk and drinking everything that came my way. I felt myself starting to get into Big Cali mode. There were a few hoes around that I had never seen before. I whipped out a knot of money and started throwing twenties in the backyard. It was like putting cheese on a mousetrap; I just had to sit back and wait because the hood rats were going to come. Before long, just like I knew, a very short, kind of cute, white girl came and talked to me. Robert whispered in my ear; *hey, this is Mike's girlfriend.* Mike was a cool dude from high school, but he wasn't the muthafuckin homie. That meant his bitch was able to get fucked and dogged like the rest of them. She told me her name, but I didn't pay attention. I was calling her a different name all night on purpose to disrespect her. She found it funny and cute for some odd reason, but I didn't care, I was setting her up for the kill.

We sipped the rest of her Johnny Walker Whiskey bottle and got real flirtatious. The night was getting late, and a few people crashed at Robert's house. People were spread out throughout the house. I laid on the floor next to her, so I could have easy access when everyone was asleep.

I knocked out for about an hour then I woke up like I had an alarm clock set. I looked around, and everyone was asleep. I woke her up with my dick in her face. She opened her eyes, looked up, saw it was me and started getting busy. Once I was fully aroused, I told her to slide her shorts off, so I could hit her from the back. She was with it, so I got behind her and started stroking her. I was trying to be quiet, so no one would wake up. I put my right thumb in her ass as I simultaneously stroked and poked. She started to moan while being as quiet as she could. I thought I'd try something new, so I took my thumb out her ass and wrapped my arm underneath her chin then placed my thumb inside her left cheek while pulling it.

I was back on this pain and pleasure shit. Her pain was my pleasure. She's making an animal-like sound, a painful noise, but it wasn't that loud, at least I didn't think it was. Robert was lying on the floor next to me with his girlfriend Crystal. He popped his head up and looked at us. I gave him a wink with my right eye and smiled. He looked at me like, what the fuck kind of shit are you doing. I just kept smiling while nodding. He laid back down, and five minutes later I came in her. This was a fairly new, bad habit that I had started doing about three women before Meme. If I was going to be having sex with people with no condom, I could have at least pulled out and ejaculated on them. This was the only bitch I fucked on vacation that wasn't Sharlean. I wish I could say I took my leave when I did for just vacation but I didn't.

Joey's death was the main reason why I was here. He and my mom were going through a separation period that I wasn't aware of, and during their brief time apart from each other, Joey went back to Oakland to be around family and friends to help support him in his time of need. The story I got was that he got back on cocaine and his body wasn't able to handle it. On March 24th, 2004, his daughter found him face down with a bloody nose, stiff as a board. It was sad news to hear because nobody likes to hear someone has passed away. I didn't think it was going to affect me much, but it did. Sharlean, our son, and I attended his funeral as a family. I wasn't ready to share our problems, and it wasn't the time for it. I just wanted to be strong for my mother and my brother because they needed me.

That made my decision to go back to the Army a lot harder. Jared never showed any emotion about the death of his father, and it kind of scared me. I didn't know if it was because he didn't really know his father or because he knew what type of man he was. How could I leave at a time like this? My entire family was falling apart, and I had to leave them when they needed a man in the household. I couldn't protect them from anything while in Korea. I couldn't show my brother how to be a man, even though I was still learning myself. But, I had obligations, and it was in my best interest to report back to

Korea because I would have been on the run from the law for being absent without leave (AWOL) from the military. I rationalized my thoughts by telling myself at least I could financially help my family, but if I went to prison, I couldn't do that.

A day later, my wife drove me to the airport with my son. Even though we were going through some serious things, I still couldn't help the fact that when I was with Sharlean, I was still madly in love with her. I told her to pick up the phone when I called. I expressed to her that I loved her so much and I didn't want her using that bullshit anymore. *Sharlean, you need to think of your family. Matt needs you, and so do I, you're better than this.* We kissed, and she cried, but I couldn't let one single tear come down my face because I was all cried out.

An eighteen-hour flight was enough to make you reconsider if it was worth living in the United States. But I knew I had to take one more trip to get back home, and I really wasn't looking forward to it. I got to my duty station and arrived one day before Meme was to get back from training in the field. I had a key to her room, so I decided to stay in her room and wait until she got back. Meme had a roommate, and I always got a vibe from her, so that day was the day that I knew the vibe was real. I had a chance to appreciate her, and she had a chance to appreciate me. It was crazy that when I was with Sharlean, I was with her, but when I wasn't, I wasn't. She didn't run across my mind like she should have. It was like all I could think about was my next potential sex partner.

By this time, I had played NASCAR and had sped my way through about forty-five different sex partners. As night came, it was time to step out and get drunk with the homies. It was only me and Lil Will because everyone else was still training in the field. Normally, when we go out to the club, there's always the amazing story to tell in the morning after all the chaos. This time was different; this story was so unbelievable to me that I still can't believe what I witnessed.

The night was kind of lame because most people were gone training, so Will and I was headed to post early while taking the alleyway back. We got close to another familiar club, and some dude ran out the club into alley yelling, *Aye some bitch giving neck up to everyone in the club.* Lil Will and I looked at each other and took off running in disbelief. We had to see if it was true. We got to her after pushing and shoving through a line full of niggas waiting to get there Johnson cradled and hummed on. The line went from the men's restroom stall to damn near outside the club door. We got to the stall, and I saw my Korean lady friend that I tried to disrespect but ended up disrespecting myself. She had a cock in one hand stroking it and another cock in her mouth massaging her throat. I was in shock only because as soon as one distinguished gentleman would climax in her mouth then another gent would replace him. It was like clockwork, and she was clearly enjoying herself. We saw about six different dudes replace each other.

Will knew about my nasty, shameful night with her. He said, *damn nigga, you done turned this fine ass bitch that everyone wanted and couldn't get for a long ass time the fuck out. You probably scarred this girl. You a cold muthafucka, Big Cali.* I was the lucky, but not so lucky guy that had won the trophy of being the first person to have sex with her out of all the soldiers we knew of. But I got to thinking how unlucky I really was because there's no way I did this to her. I'm trying to reason with myself, but deep down, I believe all it took was someone nasty like me to bring her true self out. At least I hope that's what it was because if she was like this before me, then I was in deep shit.

This was the only time I thought that I could have a sexually transmitted disease. We headed to the barracks after we had seen enough. I got to Meme's room, and I laid down quietly, trying not to wake up her roommate. Her roommate walked over to my side of the room and told me that she wanted some more. I was tired and told her that she needed to take her ass to sleep, and she already had a taste, this was Meme's dick. *You weren't saying that earlier; that's our dick now.* I propped up like, *what do you mean our dick? Just what I said Mr. Man, ours now. If you don't give me some of that magic stick, then I'm going to tell your girl.* This dirty bitch was going to blackmail me for some cock. *You're a dirty ass bitch for this shit. And you a dirty nigga for fucking your girl's roommate, I want some more, and I want it now.*

That was the day I learned that women don't respect themselves or know their self-worth. I also learned that women could be very disloyal. She was going to be smiling in my girl's face and acting like they were best friends while fucking her man. As a man, it was expected to be sidetracked during a relationship. This didn't mean it was okay or right, but hey, I wasn't the one that came up with this double jeopardy. I sure wasn't helping it, but it had been this way of the land for a long time. I gave her what she demanded and called it a night.

Chapter 26: A New Road to My Dez' Ty' Nee

Meme got back the next morning, and I was excited to see her, and I needed a hug deep down inside. I helped her unpack, and we hung out for a few hours while I caught her up on my vacation, before she started to get sick. We were watching TV when she ran to the restroom, feeling like she was going to vomit out of nowhere. I asked her if she was ok, but she said for the past week that this had been happening to her. *Hmm, that's strange babe, maybe it's something you ate? No, I don't think it's that, babe. I think it's something else.* Not thinking about what she was telling me, I told her that I could go to the PX and get her some chicken noodle soup and come back. Every now and then she would call me by my middle name, Lamar. She kind of laughed and said, *yeah Lamar, go ahead and do that babe.*

I ran to the store and got back to her holding a pregnancy test in her hand. *Look babe, we're going to have a baby.* For some reason I was happy. I thought I would be upset, but I was happy. I was happy until the realization that I had a wife and kid at home kicked in. Holy fucking shit, what the hell was I going to do about this. There's no way to hide a child. I guess I'd figure it out somehow. I hugged Shametta and gave her a kiss. I told her that I knew what the name for a girl would be. She said, *what's that?* And I said, *Destiny.*

I always wanted a daughter named Destiny, and I have a chance to have her now. Meme said, *well since you have the girls name, then if it's a boy I get to pick the name.* I said, *cool, it sounds like square business to me.* I couldn't wait to tell the homies that I had a baby on the way. They saw how happy I was when I was with Meme and they knew the situation with my wife and her problems. They were happy for me and from time to time they would give me shit and make jokes.

A few months went by, and it's June 2004. I spend the majority of my time with Meme, and from time to time, I would get blackmailed to sleep with her roommate. I was afraid of getting caught because she would do silly shit. I believe she liked the rush of almost being caught. She would do things like pull my Johnson out and give me oral while Meme was in the shower or even using the restroom. I couldn't tell her no, especially now that Shametta was the mother of my unborn child. I couldn't fuck that up.

We never got caught, but I did get caught in a major way. Meme worked in the administration area that conducted paperwork for soldiers that had all their personal information. I can't remember exactly the reason my file got pulled, but it ran across her desk, and she found out that I was married with a kid. I was in her room like always, and she came storming in like a tornado. With paperwork in her hand she screams out, *you're married, Lamar, married really?* She threw the papers at me, and I couldn't deny it. I told her what she already knew, and she cried in my arms. I explained to her Sharlean's situation and what I saw her doing on my vacation. I told her the truth, that I hadn't talked to Sharlean since I had been back and no one could find her. She was lost in the game, and I didn't even know where my son was.

This sad, but true story helped soften the blow to her gut. Somehow, I smoothed talked her into seeing it my way, and I told her that I was getting a divorce. Shametta told me one thing that I would never forget which only made sense to me at this present time. *Lamar, I didn't ask for this life, this is what you gave me. It's now me, you, and our baby, but remember you gave us this life.* At the time I was just happy that she was still rocking with me and I was still able to keep playing my excited daddy part. It should have made sense, but it would all come back around.

I continued making late night store runs for her crazy cravings like pickles and peanut butter sandwiches or donuts with bacon on them. I liked the fact that I could be around since I couldn't when Sharlean was pregnant. I felt like I was trying to make it right with this go around because I wasn't able to experience all that came with it the last time. Time went on, and we were right back like we were before the drama came into our lives. Shametta's roommate got stationed somewhere else, so I had a chance at being faithful for as long as I could, and it actually was going well. Like anything else in my life, if things were too good to be true, then it probably was.

I got a phone call or two from more associates about my wife being on meth and strung out turning tricks for drugs. It put me in a deeper depression and in a darker place because even though I had all of the other things going on in my life, I still loved Sharlean and was concerned about where the hell my son was. My mom didn't help because she had no information for me and I felt like she didn't try enough to hold me down while I wasn't there. If I was able to hold her down and send money periodically, she should have been able to at least do that for me. I also stopped sending Sharlean the monthly money of fifteen to eighteen hundred dollars.

Worrying about Sharlean and my son drove me to alcoholism. I already was drinking four to five days a week, but now it was every day. I started drinking a fifth of liquor daily, and I would get mad and stare in the mirror, crying, then go punch on someone. Shametta didn't see me like this. She would usually see me during lunch break, then after I was done doing whatever I was doing until midnight. As long as my sex game didn't change, then I was normal to her. She knew I was a fighter and was always getting into trouble with the Army by the constant demotion of rank or extra duty. I had so much rage in me that it turned into running from my problems to running into danger. I stopped showing up to PT formations in the mornings because I would be too drunk or didn't give a fuck and showed up drunk. It got to the point that I would challenge my superiors when they would give me a direct order to do something. I would tell them flat out; *No, and you can't whoop me so what the fuck are you going to do?* Some were fearful and wrote me up, but some were brave and took their rank off and fought me in closet doors or office rooms where no one could see us. I would knock their dicks in the dirt easy because I was a warrior before I was a soldier.

Eventually, they would put me in the Army Substance Abuse Program (ASAP). I had to take three weeks of training, and I was told that I wasn't allowed to ever come back to ASAP courses while in the military or they would kick me out. I thought it was fucked up if someone truly had a problem and was dependent on a substance like mine that they couldn't receive help for taking shots of liquor. But it was fine if they were deployed two or three times and took shots for their country. I did what they asked and completed that bullshit program. I didn't believe I had a problem; I just enjoyed drinking. But obviously, no one else enjoyed me if they weren't getting fucked when I was drinking. I was reckless. I was basically a walking time bomb.

After all that, I got a call from another associate back home, and they told me that Sharlean overdosed. I let my chain of command know what was going on and they arranged for my tour to be cut a month short. It was only a week from August, and I was able to leave August 10th. I was so ready to go. I got all the time in with my niggas and Shametta, as much as I could. But I was not mentally there with them. I was there in a physical form but spiraling down in the mental aspect.

My leave date arrived fast, and it was time to say my goodbyes. It was a sad moment. Meme and I talked about her getting out of the Army and moving to Fort Irwin, California, which was my next duty station, and we were going to be a family. But, I still was unsure if this was going to happen. It just felt like a lie. I should have told her I loved her before I left in that cab because I didn't know if I was going to see her again. Fuck it, it was time to man up and go save my first family, and then I could worry about my secret family.

Chapter 27: People Are Unpredictable

The flight back wasn't long because my mind was drifting away on all the things that I needed to do and the questions that I had. I got to L.A.X airport, and my mom and brother picked me up. Jared had a strange energy coming from him, but I couldn't figure it out. He seemed more secluded and very quiet. Usually, he and I had high energy around each other, and since I played a significant part of him being raised his first seven years, I would have thought our bond would still be strong, but it appeared that he was not remembering a lot of things and was keeping me away from him. Maybe it was his way of dealing with his dad. But unfortunately, I didn't have time to look into it deeper because I had my own problems to deal with.
As I look back, I should have checked into it more. That's life though, mistakes are made, and lessons are learned.

I got right to it as soon as we touched down in Oxnard. I was on the hunt for her. I took my mom's car, even though she didn't want me to drive because I didn't have a license and she didn't have insurance. I had to make her understand that none of that mattered. The only thing that mattered was that I needed to find my family. After hours of roaming the streets and searching, I decided to call Sharlean's parents' house. I really didn't want to, but I had no choice. I talked to her mom and asked if Sharlean was there. She told me no and to come by as she should be back soon. Well damn, all this time in the streets, why didn't I try this first?

After going through top-flight security and getting approved to be in their luxury gated community, I knocked on their door. Her mother lets me in, but there were no words really spoken. The chemistry was all off, and I really didn't want to see her dad. He had a way of making me want to punch him in the face because he always talked like he was better than everyone. He also made sure to remind me, whenever he could, that I couldn't afford his daughter and shouldn't be with her. I carried on and had a fake conversation with them for about ten minutes. I saw their other daughter was there, which was rare, it was like they kept her in the basement or something. She was quiet and didn't have much personality, but she was a good person, I could tell. I guess timid would be best to describe her.

She walked into the kitchen, and I said, *what up?* She said, *greetings,* like a weirdo. I shrugged it off, and I was on my way to ask if they knew when Sharlean was going to be back, but her mom said, *come here.* She walked me to the kitchen, and then Sharlean's sister slammed a big envelope down on the kitchen counter like she was mad and said, *here.* I picked it up and opened it. It was paperwork saying that her parents had custody of my son. I was hurt, confused, and for the first time ever, I felt that I needed alcohol to deal with this problem.

It was so cold how they set me up. They knew damn well that their daughter was never there or on her way back. But they got me, and they got me good. I asked them how they had custody and I hadn't signed my rights away. They told me that when I gave Sharlean power of attorney, she signed for me. Ain't that about a bitch! I leave my family and try to set them up for success, and she does this to me. I guess I could appreciate that she was smart enough to place him in good care. I asked if I could have my son for the night and they told me no, it was best to go through the legal system like they did, and besides, he wasn't there right now.

After scrapping my heart and face up off the floor, I gathered what little bit of self-esteem and pride that remained in me, and I left. As they shut the door, I heard my son cry. He must have been upstairs sleeping and just woke up. Those fucking liars! It was a zoned-out drive home, and when I got there, I didn't feel like talking, just drinking and sobbing. The pain I felt, I didn't even want to inflict on someone else. I just had to sit down and let it soak in that I was fucked.

The next day, Robert comes by the house and we chop it up while getting drunk and high. He told me that Sharlean used to brag that I left them and was doing better without them and that I would never come back and associate with my brothers. He said she changed as soon as I left. It was strange for Robert to talk like this because the only emotion he knew was anger, but when he said the things he was saying, I knew it was true because he started to cry. He said he believed her and thought that she would make sure I wouldn't be around them anymore. I was in denial that my sweet Precious would act like that, I couldn't see why. But I guess I didn't know her like I thought I did because I had never seen her to be the one on drugs.

I opened up my feelings to Robert and started to cry. I asked him why she would do this to us? I couldn't wrap my head around the fact that I had no place to live, a strung-out wife, and no son. How did the best choice of my life lead to the worst outcome? This was too much for me to handle, I had to open up to my mom and tell her everything that was going wrong. Just being able to vent and to hear my mom say it was going to be alright was soothing. I knew what I needed to do to overcome this. I had to turn into a monster that didn't care, and that would block all the pain that I had and would have to come. That was exactly what I did, and I found a way to bury the problems so far away that I didn't think about them much.

Chapter 28: Bury the Pain So Far That You Almost Forget

It was time to report to Fort Irwin and see what they had to offer. Fort Irwin was hot as hell; it was almost one hundred and ten degrees every damn day. This was a post that trained soldiers to go to Iraq. We spent two weeks out of four each month in the training field. The muthafuckin Mojave Desert is no joke. When it's hot, it's scorching, but when it's cold at night, it's like a freezer box.

There's nothing good that comes out of Fort Irwin. I did meet a few new homies and developed a forever bond with some people. I had a homeboy named Orlando. We called him Juice or OJ. Juice looked and acted just like me according to the whole post, and I had to admit we were very similar. He loved to play basketball, he loved to drink, he had marriage issues, and most of all, he loved fucking with new hoes just like me.

We were a problem when we were together, and those hoes didn't stand a chance with us. We had another homie named Rodney. He was a quiet storm. Rodney was from the south, like everyone else in the military. Little Black America he would call it, Atlanta, Georgia. The passion he had talking about his state and how beautiful it was made me want to see it.

The three of us together were solid as a rock. It didn't take long for me to get active and start setting myself a team of females up to rotate as sex partners. Two months at this new post and I already had jumped in ten different bodies. Juice, Rodney, and I happened to be off post at the mall in Victorville one day. We spotted a herd of females, about six, to be exact. All of them were looking good and seemed to be free-spirited because they were loud, joking, and staring. We approached the ladies and introduced ourselves. After five minutes of talking, we had it set up to see them later on that night, and they were going to cook dinner for us. We told them we had a few cool dudes that we were going to bring so there would be an even playing field, and they were with it.

We headed back to post and got the homies, Wolfe, Burton, and Wallace. We didn't waste any time, we got dressed and headed right back out. The drive from post was about an hour and twenty-five minutes, but if you really have to be somewhere, you can get there in an hour. We showed up, and the ladies were looking good. The food was made, and a few adult beverages were poured up. Everyone was having a good time and was choosing who they wanted to fool around with. I wanted a different female, but Burton beat me to her, so I ended up with Ebony.

Ebony had a ridiculous amount of ass on her and wasn't too cute in the face, but she ended up being pretty cool people. A lot of the bros ended up sleeping with who they chose. I struck out and had to play the sidelines that night, but I knew eventually I would get a chance to break her in. We set it up to see each other again the very next night. I was thinking that we were going to have a super orgy, and everyone was going to get passed around, but it didn't play out that way. This new clique I was with weren't playboys like that, except Juice, that's why we linked how we did because we were pretty much the same person, the only difference was just that he was from Baltimore and had a gold tooth.

Ebony ended up giving me what I was there for, and she happened to be a conservative freak, she just needed a little push. This was what kept her in the rotation because she wasn't my normal cup of tea but she made up for it. The majority of the time, I didn't have to ask or instruct her as to what I liked or needed to be done. Ebony would give me money on demand with no question. She would hand it over without much game needed to be spit.

When the crew and I weren't in Victorville parlaying with those ladies, then we were in the field training. On October 11th, 2004, I was in the field, and I got a call from Meme. She told me that she just gave birth to our daughter Dez'ty'nee. Meme and I would talk all the time, and I knew it was going to happen soon, but it was still a shock. Meme was now stationed in Alabama, her home state, so her parents were able to support her through the birth of Dez'ty'nee.

Damn, another childbirth I missed. Meme gave me a website for the hospital so I could see her picture. When I searched and found my daughter's picture, I had chills and goosebumps on my arms. For one, this already felt different, knowing that I had a daughter, and two, this baby was ugly when she came out. She was as ugly as Meme spelled her name with her country ass. Shametta threatened to kick my ass for calling our baby ugly, but she knew I said what was on my mind and she laughed a little bit, so I didn't think she was too mad, but that baby was ugly. It didn't matter though, because it was my ugly baby and I was already in love with her.

Chapter 29: My Secret Family

As soon as I got out the field, I caught a plane to go meet my daughter and Meme's family. Ozark, Alabama was where they were and it looked just like it sounded. Ozark had a lot of open fields and no street lights. You better hope that you never run out of gas or get a flat tire on their streets. It was pitch black, and there's not much traffic in the middle of nowhere. I was a city slicker, so I wasn't too fond of this environment.

Shametta and her mother, Miss Elizabeth, picked me up from the airport. I sat in the back seat and played with Dez'ty'nee, Dez or Juicy is what we called her, until we got to her house. Miss Elizabeth was very country talking but polite. She was very excited to meet me and was always hugging me or kissing me. She would express how happy she was that her Meme found a good man, and not anyone from their area. I think she was happy because I had a career and made her daughter happy because if she really knew who I was and what I was about, she wouldn't want us to be together.

I played the good guy role like she assumed I was because according to all the people in Alabama that I had met over that week, I was very proper speaking and a good man. They had no idea that if any of her friends showed me a smidge of a sign that they wanted me, I would try and fuck them and whoever else. But, I kept my shit in my pants and enjoyed my future family, which had now moved up to my primary family.

My second day there, Shametta took me to her father's house to meet him, and I got praised up and down for being a good man. He seemed like a cool guy, but he was older and talked very slow, but all around, he was nice. He was nothing like Sharlean's dad; he didn't try to control every move or discourage people by using big fancy words just to say simple things. Jimmy spoke with knowledge and Meme's dad spoke with wisdom, so when Meme's dad spoke, I listened. He told me one thing that stood out and didn't make sense until a few years later. He said, *son, listen to me and listen real good. Her mom could be very conniving, and Meme is a younger version of her. I love all my kids, but this one I have to love differently. You keep doing right by my daughter, and she should do right by you. Son, I like you, and I can tell already that you're in love with my daughter and that you want to give her the world. She only has brought one other person around, and I didn't like him from the beginning but, you son, I like.*

I liked him too, mainly because he called me son and welcomed me with open arms, and it didn't sound bad to hear someone call me son. Meme, Juicy, and I enjoyed our time together. We even squeezed in family pictures during my short visit. But like every great thing that happens in life, our time had to come to an end.

The flight back home was hard, and I didn't want to leave, so I tricked myself into saying, I'm only four hours away. This made it easier for me and Shametta. I got back to my barracks room, and I tried to call my son, but nobody picked up, so I left a message like I always did. I figured if I flooded their voicemail with my voice then they would call back or at least get tired of hearing me and pick up. It never happened, and I didn't know why I kept putting myself through that torment. I tried to forget about him, but my heart wouldn't let my mind do it. I guess I was just going to have to deal with the pain and the only way I knew how was by drinking and fucking.

Chapter 30: Your Birthday Could Be the Worst Day

I wasn't home for two hours before Juice, Rodney, and I went on a road trip to Tijuana, Mexico. I had been there several times as a kid with my mom before she met Joey, but I was the tour guide for the homies since I was from California. Every month we would go somewhere, and Tijuana was on the list. Rodney loved that place, he loved how the food tasted, he loved how the tequila was served to you with flames and chanting, but most of all, and he loved traveling.

I believed Orlando and I loved the prostitution they had going on there. There would be between ten and fifteen hoes lined up on the wall looking delicious. How they grabbed your attention, besides having their entire ass hanging out those skirts, was by a whisper style type noise. "Chsssh, Chsssh" meant come get this pussy, and that pussy was at a much-discounted rate of twenty dollars.

It was easy for us to blow through a hundred dollars a piece on hoes. There was a sheet that covered you from the nigga five feet away in the same room. You would do your thing on a mattress that looked like it had been in a crime scene. There were condoms, lotions, lubricants, and sex toys, if you were into that type of shit. I was cool on everything they had to offer, I just needed her to slide the condom on so I could spit on that thang, and I was ready to go.

We had a good time, and I thought I was a good tour guide. If we weren't there, we would be in Las Vegas, Nevada or Los Angeles. I even took Rodney to my hometown of Oxnard because he helped me move my mom and Jared to Fort Irwin. I made my mom my legal dependent so she could save money and have a stable place to live. She and Jared were moving damn near every month and living with people sometimes. This is what other family members told me, so I had to go get my family. Joey's small income did help and was a valuable part of their stability. I think my mom was still grieving and needed help, but was too prideful to ask.

I liked the fact that I could live up to my promise that I told her when I was young. I told her that she would always live with me when I moved out of her house, and having my mom there was a help to me too. I went through the legal system like Jimmy told me to do if I wanted my son, but the legal system slapped me in the face once again. During the court hearing, which was conducted over the phone, the Judge told me that he couldn't grant me custody because of some bullshit ass reasons.

The first reason that he gave was that I was in the Army and didn't have a stable living situation. He said that when I did, someone from the courts would come out and inspect my home to see if I had everything that was needed for a child. Secondly, he stated that if I got deployed, who was going to take care of my son. He told me to get someone dependable for that concern. The third reason had nothing to do with anything if you ask me. He was bold only because it was on the phone. He said you're a young African American male!

What the fuck does that mean? I was beyond discouraged to continue to fight for my son, but I dug deep and completed all aspects of what he asked, except being a young nigger in his eyes. That was all he basically said, without actually saying it, because the call was recorded. We got Jared enrolled in school off post at a Barstow city elementary school. He qualified to ride the bus to Barstow with the rest of the Army brats. It was perfect timing when I moved my mom in because she needed it and I needed my mom. There was too much going on in life to go through it alone, plus I needed that motherly guidance when she would see me fucking up.

January 13th, 2005, it's my twenty-first birthday and the crew and I decided to hit the road to Tijuana, Mexico again. We had been there probably two more times since the first trip, but this was the last trip I would ever take to Mexico again. We got there at seven o'clock at night, and we had already been drinking on the ride up so by the time 1:00a.m. rolled around, we were beyond drunk. I was having the best birthday ever, by far. I knew I was going to go all out with the homies, so before we crossed the border I called my Uncle Richard and told him that if something happened to me, just know that I'm in Tijuana with the homies; Chris, Rodney, Orlando, and Wolfe.

He thought it was funny but smart that I called to tell someone. I said my drunken goodbyes and commenced to being all that I could be. Drinks, weed, and hoes is how the night goes. Rodney fucked around and fell in love with a stripper. He threw a good one hundred dollars at her within twenty minutes. To his defense, that bitch was finer than a muthafucka, but for twenty dollars he probably could have waited and fucked her when she got off.

Everyone was running low on funds because we were all fucking around with them "Chsssh Chsssh" girls. We had to make a stop at the ATM so that we could continue drinking and fucking prostitutes. During the midst of getting our money, we lose our homie Wolfe. I saw the Police, or Policia, walking down the street and we stopped them. There were three law enforcement officers, and I figured this should be something they could handle. Little did I know that they were going to handle more then I wanted them to handle. *Hey Sir, can you help me find my friend, Wolfe?* Of course, they didn't speak English. Why would they, we were in Mexico.

One greasy bearded, wild hair looking, tall officer repeated back, *Wolfe,* in his native tongue. I said, *yeah, Wolfe, we lost him.* I tried describing him with some "drunk" sign language, but it was a horrific fail. The greasy officer started to laugh and said, *Wolfe,* one more time and I said, *yeah.* Then, my intoxication was quickly sobered up.

The officer walked over to me and stood behind me, then forced my hands up in the air. The homies were laughing making jokes about me getting ready to go to jail in Mexico. I assumed the officer was going to do a pat-down search, which sounded like normal procedure when your black asking for help, so I didn't know why it would be any different in Mexico. Once he patted my upper torso down, he slid his right hand into my pants. This was when I started to get concerned and somewhat nervous. I had always heard or seen on TV about the corrupt police forces in Mexico. But that was and could be like that any and everywhere.

Big Greasy not only slid his hands down my pants, but he went skin to skin, fondling my scrotum and shaft, then he started to do semi strokes to my penis repeatedly. I loudly said, *Yo, this dude has his hand on my dick, and he's skin to skin stroking my junk with no gloves.* The crew looked in disbelief, and they stopped laughing about going to jail in Mexico because shit just got real.

I had to think fast, and life preservation kicked in. I said, *here, I'll give you some money,* and I slowly reached into my small hidden pocket and pulled out my emergency hundred dollar bill. I held it up, and one of the other two officers took the money. Big Greasy saw they had the money then he stopped groping on me after another minute or so. I wasn't going to dare say anything or resist because I'd be damned if I ended up in a Mexico jail with a burrito shoved up my ass.

We didn't have permission to be on a pass and cross the border, so the Army wouldn't even know where to find us. I was sure if one of us went down, we would all go down. I was shocked, and the worst part about this was, it wasn't good enough to be sexually assaulted, it was the fact that when I started to walk away slowly, he wanted to try and scar me mentally. When I got about ten feet from them, I looked back to make sure that they weren't following us and I saw Big Greasy sucking his fingertips like he had just eaten a bag of nacho cheese Doritos chips. He winked at me, and that was a definite sign that he did what I knew he did, which was he took advantage of me by using his position of authority. How the hell can I respect law enforcement and I've been physically, verbally, and now sexually assaulted by them and I was only twenty-one years old. I told you once before, they're just a big fucking gang that does what they want to, when they want to, and who they want to do it to.

I was done with Mexico and those hoes. It was time to head back to the car. They say never leave a fallen soldier behind in the military, but I could give two shits about where Wolfe was, it was time to go home. The clique made jokes to try and lighten the situation. Coincidently, it was all gay jokes. Chris said, *what if Wolfe is in the car with a dude drunk while Lamar is out here getting molested by cops and shit.* It struck a nerve with me, but I had to find it humorous, or at least pretend to because I was too prideful to let my homies know that I was shaken up by it and really felt dirty inside.

I'm the stature of a man with a six foot five body frame and two hundred and twenty-five pounds. I had to show my masculinity and not be weak or let them know that I was fucked up on the inside. So I laughed and let the jokes keep coming until we got to the car. I knew in some weird, strange guy code way that the homies were trying to support me and let me know it was alright and that I should have never gone through that bullshit. As men, we are not allowed to console or show emotions because in this society it discredits your role as a man. As a child, you're trained in your gender roles. As a boy, you are trained not to show when you're in pain because that makes you a sissy and weak, so the only emotion you're allowed to show is anger or laughter. So I laughed a lot because that's what I was trained to do. Laugh now and when by myself, cry later. This is my life, and this is my pain.

We arrived at the car and guess what we saw. Wolfe had already beaten us there and apparently knew his limit because he was drunk and passed out. The only problem was, he was passed out with a random dude in the car next to him. We all looked at each other and started laughing. *Damn, Chris, you called it, bro. Hey, Wolfe wake up and unlock the door.* It took ten minutes before the random drunk dude woke up and unlocked the car. *Hey, who the fuck are you, homie?* He mumbled enough for us to understand that he was a Marine and was clearly too drunk to get to his clique.

Wolfe woke up and we gave him some shit. *Wolfe, you're sleeping in the car with random dudes now?* Wolfe said he thought it was me because the Marine and I had green shirts on. *Ain't that about a bitch, Wolfe, all it takes is another nigga to wear green, and that's your homie now, huh? It's cool; I know you white people think we all look alike. Get your ass in the back. We got to go.* Rodney said, *wait a minute, what are we going to do with the Marine?* I said, *if he knew better, he would do better.*

It was time for us to get back to post. I was the most intoxicated person, hands down, but I had it made up in my mind if I was going to die in a drunk driving crash, it was going to be because I took my own life. I didn't trust these drunk motherfuckers. Twenty minutes down the freeway, I accepted the fact that I was beyond alcohol poisoned. I pulled over on the freeway and slept for five hours. There was no way in hell I was going to get us there, and nobody was awake to talk to me and keep me focused. I made a good decision, and we all got back safely to post later that day.

Chapter 31: Embracing My Sex Addiction

Since Dez was born, I traveled twice a month to Alabama to see my family. I maintained this while hiding them from Ebony, who was now my girlfriend. Over the months, Ebony showed me she was down to earth, and I had a really good time with her no matter what we did. Ebony was in love with me within the first four months, and like I shouldn't have, I told her that I loved her too. Which, indeed, I did love Ebony, but I wasn't in love with her.

She got serious and introduced me to her family. They were all nice people, and my best comparison would be the example of the TV show, Family Matters. Her Father was a skinnier Carl Winslow looking ass nigga, and he had retired with twenty years in the Air Force. He currently had a career as a firefighter chief or inspector, and her mom was a lead person at the church. She had two brothers, and they were cool. One brother played football at a D1 college and was pretty good on the field. The other one was inspired to be a music producer. It just seemed like the whole family was doing great for themselves and they had a strong foundation set up for them to be successful.

I took all that into consideration when I chose to be in a relationship with Ebony. In case Meme and I didn't work out, I had a backup plan. Meme was supposed to get out the Army and come live with me so that we could raise our child together, but it seemed like every month she had a new excuse. I was starting to get the feeling that she was seeing someone else. I couldn't blame her, because I sure had been fucking around with multiple women. Shit, I had two girlfriends, a secret baby, and a wife and child on the side with an alcohol and sex addiction. I couldn't knock her; I was all over the place in life. You know when you know, and I knew she had a side dude. At least I thought she did, but I came to find out that I was the side dude.

Shametta broke up with me in a Hotmail email. By this time, it would be Thanksgiving in a few weeks and I was supposed to stay with my secret family for five days. I received the email on October 28th, 2005. It read, "Hey Lamar, I don't know how to say this, but some things have changed for Juicy and I. You will need to find somewhere to stay while you're down here for the holidays because I'm in a relationship with someone now."

Deep down I couldn't blame her for moving on, and I wasn't mad, but it still hurt. It hurt so much because I thought, damn, I fucked up another family within a fourteen month period. I was a wreck, and I didn't know how to reply back to her email. It was embarrassing that I was dumped through an email. I replied back with some real feelings and took it like a man. I wrote, "I wish you would have told me that we weren't in a relationship anymore before you went and found someone. I admit that I haven't been giving you my time these past few months like I normally do and that could have helped push this. I'm sorry for not informing you about my wife and kid before we got involved so you could have made the choice to take part in this relationship or not. I thank you for blessing me with a beautiful daughter, and I will still be in her life as long as I breathe. I felt that you had met someone a while ago but I was scared of the outcome. I still plan on coming to spend Thanksgiving with our daughter, and I will find transportation and a hotel. Is this person you're with someone I know?"

I took my fate like a man and accepted it. The pain was deep though, and it was another slap in the face by life, reminding me how much of a loser and a failure I was. I released the pain the only way I knew how; I had sex with random people and drunk alcohol. I even incorporated taking drugs in the form of Ecstasy pills and doing Mushrooms a lot. My sex craving went from looking for the prettiest women in the room to any woman in the room. I didn't care if they weren't a ten out of ten. I would take five, twos, and put them in rotation to make a ten, and there were no standards. Fat, tall, short, cute, ugly, dark, pregnant, pale, ignorant, smart, old, young, aunt, mother, or daughter, it didn't matter, just whoever could give me what I needed.

It was similar to an alcoholic's method. I had a quantity of women so I could have sex all the time, fuck the quality. Alcoholics buy the cheapest liquor to drink all day for the feeling, not for the taste. I was having sex five days a week. Sometimes I would have sex with three different women within the same day and not wash up to see if they would say anything. They never did, like I knew they wouldn't because women didn't respect themselves and that was proven to me in Korea. I did whatever they allowed me to do. Obviously, I didn't have respect for myself either the way I was carrying on.

Some women would do anything for a man. There were a few occasions when I talked a woman into being sexually involved with another woman. Sometimes I would just watch and record them on my phone. I could only capture about thirty seconds at a time because this was when camera phones were just coming out and they didn't have all those gadgets like we have now.

Orlando was my homie, and when we were together, we would pull some bitches. There were times we would meet females and have sex with them within the first three hours of knowing them. We got caught one time in a park in Victorville. I was on the slide giving this rating scale of a four woman some good sex, and once we moved to the sidewalk area, we got surrounded by a gang of Mexicans. I hopped up and pulled up my pants as she was lying there with her pussy out and a shirt on. They told me they were from some gang and I was expecting to fight all six of them and take a good ass whopping. Orlando got out the car; I didn't know why he was butt naked making love to this woman. We were supposed to fuck them and leave them like always. I swear this dude was just naturally funny.

OJ put some pants on and one of the Cholo's said, *Damn fools, you guys disrespecting our hood by being here, fools.* I started to talk for us because I felt I knew how to handle the situation best, plus this was something of which I was familiar with. Juice sat back and let me do my thing. We got a pass, and we got it by leaving those hoes back for them. I didn't give a damn about these bitches and Juice didn't either, so it was settled. They got the hoes, and we got to go. I didn't feel bad at all at the time. I felt like if you were willing to fuck on the park floor at night with some dudes you don't even know, then you were probably willing to have a sex train ran on you by some gang members. I would like to think that's not what happened, but I'm sure it did. We didn't do anything wrong; we just told them hoes that they couldn't get in the car and get a ride with us and that wasn't illegal. This is what I told myself to make me feel better, I mean come on, I'm fucked up in the head, but I still had a heart at times.

Chapter 32: I Never Liked the Name Bill

Juice and I have many wild times and stories about how scandalous women can be. I never looked at myself as being scandalous, because I took sex as a sport. But I was just as nasty and scandalous as the women that let me do all that shit. The only time something made me think was when I took a bitch to her home after the club, and we got to the room to do the deed. I'm two minutes in her hitting it from the back, and I looked back at the corner of the room because I heard a noise. She had a son that was around six years old, and he was sitting up in his pallet of a bed looking me in the eyes. I stared at him, and I remembered that feeling because I knew that look. It was me thirteen years ago.

When I was around eight years old, and before my mother was married to Joey, she was a young woman and did what young women do. I had flashbacks of seeing her being sexually involved with men while I was in the bedroom with them. When I would get caught looking at them, they would tell me to roll over and look at the wall. If I was caught again, then she would stack pillows on the side of the bed, so I was only able to see their activity when I sat all the way up, like this young man I was staring at was doing.

I can remember there was a gentlemen name Bill. Bill is someone I will never forget, or should I say, never can forget. Bill stood about six foot tall and weighed approximately two hundred pounds. He was a bald or very short-haired man with a light skin complexion. I assumed he was older than my mom by the crinkling of his face. He was an extremely nice, polite, and handsome man. He and my mother complimented each other. Bill carried a brown paper bag around every time he came over. In this bag, Bill kept candy suckers. He always gave me a sucker when he got there and when he left. I hated Bill for this because I always felt that Bill was trying to pay me off to shut the fuck up and let him fuck my mom. Bill thought I was stupid and that I didn't know what was going on and that insulted my intelligence. Bill made me feel small, like I was less than dirt when he would do this. Bill may have genuinely been being nice and meant no harm. He might have just been trying to impress my mother by showing that he accepted her and her child. This was not how I perceived it. I took it as disrespect and it felt very hurtful.

I hated myself when I took the candy because I felt like I shouldn't have taken it if I knew it was pay off money for my feelings. Even to this very day, it's stomach-turning to hear someone say the name Bill. I automatically still feel small and less than dirt, just like that child who was disrespected and taken advantage of, even though I now stand massively at six foot five, two hundred and twenty five pounds.

I snapped out of the flashback and removed myself from the woman. She asked, *what's wrong, do you want me to switch up positions?* I told her no, as I put my pants on. I explained to her that we could do this all day, but not while her child is in the room as I looked back at the kid. She yelled, *turn around and look at the wall, boy. He's fine now, come back to bed. No, he's not fine. Look, if you want to disrespect yourself that's all good, but I can't disrespect that little boy.* I gathered my things and left. I never spoke to her again; besides, I didn't have her number or even remember her name. When I got home, I was mad at myself for caring about that kid. Nobody gave a damn about me, why the fuck did I have to care about him. I ended up falling asleep counting and replaying every sex episode I had. Man, I sure reached one hundred sex partners fast.

Chapter 33: Europe It Is

I figured I had nothing left but the Army since I had lost both families. I kept hearing that Germany was the best place to travel and that they had some of the prettiest women in the world there. I reenlisted in the Army for four more years and picked Germany as my next duty station. I was to report to Hanau, Germany on January 12th, 2006. I offered to make my brother my dependent, so my mom and Jared could come with me overseas. My mom didn't want to sign him away to me for whatever reasons. If I was to guess, it was the fact that she didn't like that she legally wouldn't have rights to her own child. I didn't know if it was because of Sharlean's situation of being adopted by her uncle, whom she called dad, and never given back to her mother that scared my mom or what. But I set her and Jared up with an apartment in Barstow before I took the ten-hour flight to my new duty station.

I contacted my son as much as I could, and I saw him twice throughout the sixteen months I was stationed in Fort Irwin. But ninety-five percent of the time, I was unsuccessful, and it was heartbreaking. I got a chance to visit him on his birthday, and it meant the world to me. I took Jared with me so he would get a chance to meet his nephew and, plus, I wasn't strong enough to face Sharlean's dad by myself.

He had a way of discouraging me, and I knew they blamed me for the wrong choices that their daughter made. They never said it, but everything they did and showed said enough. They felt like she turned her back on her family when she moved in with me and she would have never been in that situation if she would have never met me. I did get a chance to see Sharlean that time that I was out there, and I couldn't help but to make love to my wife. I said it before; when I was with Sharlean, I was with her and nothing else in the world mattered. I was madly in love with her, even if she was in bad shape and strung out. I took her to breakfast at her favorite restaurant called Henry's, on the corner of a five-point intersection in Oxnard.

Sharlean looked like she was badly on drugs and she was not how I remembered this beautiful, smart woman. I remember her feeling embarrassed and ashamed of herself. I didn't judge her, and I never looked down on her. I wanted to be there for her, but she didn't want the help, so I had no choice but to support her while at the distance she kept me.

While the food was being made, she walked into the restroom and stayed there for about twenty minutes. I mean it was so long of a wait that the food was cooked, served, and cold already. I got scared because I thought she was so embarrassed that she went and had a fix to deal with being around me. I almost left because I didn't want to add more to her plate by seeing her like this. She finally came out as I was getting ready to take off. She came back with a big ass red poinsettia in her hair. I thought that she was embarrassed because her hair was in distress and she had no make-up on her face and had what they called, the tweeker craters. Tweeker craters are when your skin gets bad and there appears to be small craters all over the face. I thought it was nice that she went to fix herself up, but she was upset and must have felt like I had to see her spruced up to love her. She was wrong because she was still precious to me regardless.

When we made love, we went to a motel that was run down. I could have never seen her staying in a place like that. I knew it was one of her spots and she was obviously familiar with the place. It was her go-to place where she got a room for two hours at twenty dollars. First off, I had no idea that motels would let you get a room for two hours and, two, the only reason you would need a motel room for two hours is to turn tricks. I'm not saying that she did turn tricks, because I honestly didn't know, but it was enough to make me believe she was prostituting for money or drugs. I felt that verified every dirty, nasty, painful rumor that I was told by friends and family.

No one took it into consideration that maybe I didn't want to hear that the person who I would have died for and loved so much was doing this bad and going through it all by herself. Some of the most painful rumors that turned out to be true came from my mom, and I knew she didn't mean anything by it; she was just trying to inform me of her condition. But at some point, I felt she got excited to tell me that hurtful stuff whenever she heard it.

Even knowing all the things Sharlean was into, I was still willing to put my life at risk by sleeping with her. I was already living reckless and if anyone was to give me AIDS or HIV, I would rather it be from the person I was in love with. Till death do us apart was what we said, and I meant it. After we made love, I thought it sparked an old feeling that she was trying to block out because she had to go back to her life and I had to go back to mine. She started telling me everything she was feeling and that she was ready to move home with me in Barstow. I told her she couldn't if she was still going to use those drugs. I had clear indications that she was and she never said that she wasn't; she just kept saying that she wanted to come with me.

When she did give up trying to come with me, it was because she knew that she wanted the drugs more than our son or me. Then she kept asking me to stay with her. How was I supposed to stay with her and not report back to the military? Lord knows I wanted to, but the outcome would have hurt us more in the long run. I remember driving to drop her off wherever she wanted to go, and while she was expressing herself, she slapped the right side of my jaw. She really got into it, and her pain turned to anger. I pulled the car over and walked around to the passenger side and pulled her out the car. I didn't hit her, but I did a far more hurtful thing than any fist could do to someone. I told her to get out, as she was pulling, kicking, and scratching to stay in the car.

I eventually got her out and I locked the door on her side so she couldn't get back in. When I walked to my side, Sharlean dropped to the floor and grabbed my leg like a child that didn't want their parent to leave for work. I was trying to walk, but I was also dragging Sharlean down the sidewalk as I tried to get to the car. I felt like a villain. I felt cruel. I felt that moment was surreal because I could only visualize that scene from the Tyler Perry movie "Diary of a Mad Black Woman." It was at the beginning of the movie when the mean, cold-hearted and downright ugly human being of a man left his wife and kicked her out of the house. She cried, begged, and pleaded for him not to leave her and even got down on the floor and grasped his legs as he tried to walk away. Was I that ugly person for not staying with my wife and reporting back to my duty station? Was I that cruel and cold-hearted man that hurts the ones that love you the most? When I looked through my rear view mirror as I drove away, I saw her on the road sitting on the ground crying. It wasn't just her I left, but a part of me was left there too.

Chapter 34: Fuck Bitches and Burn Bridges

It was my first day in Hanau, Germany. I arrived about five in the evening. I went to set up my room and meet my roommate, but he was gone in the field training, according to a dude name Frison. Frison was a cool down to earth guy from Georgia. He reminded me of a pretty boy type thug that didn't know what he wanted to be yet. We can say that he was half of a thug. He showed me around the post and told me we were going out that night so to get dressed and be ready by ten. I went to sleep and got ready by that time frame.

Frison got me and we took a taxi to the club. I thought Germany's freeway, which was called the Autobahn, was crazy because it was normal to see a car speed pass you doing over one hundred miles per hour. I had a chance to see a few cars do that on our short trip to the club. We got to a night spot called The Black Sounds, and there were beautiful women everywhere. I asked why we went so early and he told me because they had one euro night drinks until midnight. He said that we had to order at least ten drinks each trip to the bar, that was the standard for partying out here. Grey Goose and Red Bull energy drinks was the drink of choice in Germany. They lived and died by this mixture and so would I eventually.

Frison said, *you're going to trip when you see people fucking on the dance floor*. I didn't believe him, and there was no way people were that bold to have sex in the club or, should I say, on the dance floor. He explained to me sex was different out here and that they didn't try to hide it. As soon as he finished his sentence, a short, beautiful woman walked up to me and didn't say anything. She looked at the both of us, then handed me her keys. I looked at Frison confused. *Oh shit, don't worry about it, put the keys in your pocket, bruh.* I didn't understand, but he said, *you'll find out later.*

It was my birthday once the clock struck twelve and I was drunk by that time. I didn't realize it was my birthday until I looked at my watch at three in the morning. By this time I had already seen two people fucking in the middle of the dance floor and someone getting head in the booth area. I asked, *what time does this place close?* He said, *not until five in the morning.* That was dangerous if you asked me, but I could dig it.

An hour went by, and the club started to thin out. That short, beautiful woman, who I hadn't seen all night, now walked back to me and said, *are you ready?* She hardly spoke any English, but I did make out those words. Frison had told me that I would see what she wanted later and I knew what that was now. Frison said *you got chose my nigga. Bitches out here are like men, they will be on the hunt, and we are their prey.* I could get used to this real quick. Germany was the shit, brah, they told me stories about this place, and I had to find out for myself, and I was about to.

She took my hand and we walked out of the club and down the street to what I assumed was her house. She didn't waste any time. She stripped me out of my clothes in an aggressive manner. Once she got to my pants, she reached into her cleavage area and took out a small baggy that was filled with white powder. I was pretty sure it was cocaine, and she confirmed it when she put a line out and snorted it off my rock hard Johnson. That was something new to me; I never thought that people did these types of things. I've had women do drugs before we got down, but not off my body. It took less than five seconds for my dick to go numb and have a tingling sensation. After she was done enjoying herself down there, it was my time to perform.

I put on a show and performed like I never had before. That cocaine had to be in my system because no matter how long and hard I tried, I couldn't make myself climax. She got a good work out because the coke had me fucking in an aggressive way. With a little more than an hour into our shenanigans, I ended up breaking her bed. We had already fucked the mattress almost all the way onto the floor. I guess it couldn't stand the punishment I was giving her and collapsed completely. She didn't care about it collapsing. She kept saying *nine don't stop.* I didn't know that nine meant no, so once I heard stop that was all I needed to hear to climb out of her. Once I got up, she started yelling repeatedly *come you* and was pointing to her vagina. I wasn't big on eating pussy at this time, but with that shit in my system and it being my birthday, I said why not. I even took it a step further and ate her ass too.

After that shit wore off, I finally had a chance to climax. There was a massive amount of sperm that I projected on her face. I didn't care about sleeping over at women's houses, so I stayed the rest of the night there. I woke up three hours later to what sounded like a video game. I went to go to the restroom, and her bedroom door was cracked open. That's when I saw him, a young man like myself that was playing a football game on the X-box game system. I thought, fuck, I have to find a way out of this house because her husband was here and I didn't know how he didn't see us in the bedroom. I put my clothes on and whispered to her; *hey, your husband is here, where can I get out of here without him seeing me?* She looked confused and said in broke up English, *my son.*

I was really confused because she didn't look one day older than twenty-five years old. I asked, *that's your son?* She said again, *my son.* Her phone ringed, and she answered it and then handed it to me. With a lost voice, I said, *hello.* It was Frison. *Hey nigga, get up I'm coming to get you. Ok, how do you know where I'm at because I don't even know, brah? Man, you went home with Anna, everyone knows where she stays, plus, I'm at her home girl's house, we're coming to get you.* I asked, *how old is Anna? Oh, that bitch is old bruh. She's thirty-eight, and her son is nineteen. Man, I thought that was her husband or something, I was scared shitless, man. Man, I broke this bitches bed, homie. Well, you are a big ass nigga, bruh. True that you're right. How long is it going to take for you to get here? We are in the car already, it shouldn't take any longer than three or four minutes. Hey real quick before you hang up, let me tell you what this bitch did. What she do, bruh? Homie, she snorted a line off my dick and then I went crazy in that shit. My dick was numb for damn near two hours.* Frison laughed, and said, *damn bruh, you ain't hip to that? That's shits called "Dope Dick" it will have you out here punishing hoes. Yeah, I like that shit, that might be my new shit for now on. Alright man, I'll see you in a few minutes.*

I was glad I wasn't jammed up in any bullshit with someone's crazy spouse. Frison finally got me, and we went back to post so I could get some good sleep. This was another birthday that I could never forget and it damn sure was better than last year's memory.

Two weeks went by, and I finally get to meet my roommate. Jeezy was a white boy with the heart and soul of a nigga. Sometimes in the hood, you met white boys like that. A lot of the time you met people who tried to portray something they're not, and it's clear as day that they're fronting to kick it; but not Jeezy. Jeezy was smooth, had street knowledge, dressed clean, and fucked with sistas. We got along instantly, and we didn't waste any time processing hoes in and out the room.

One week Jeezy would find a few hoes and bring them back to the barracks room that we nicked named the "Boom Boom Room," and the next week it was my turn. After he would break them in, he would send them my way and vice versa. There were times we would be in competition with each other. He would be fucking one on his side of the room and trying to make her moan louder than my bitch. Or we would see who smacked whose girl's ass the hardest by snickering at the pop that was louder. We were childish and didn't care about fucking in front of each other because the hoes never cared anyway. Sometimes we just swapped them out in mid stroke and asked *are you ready for this one yet?*

We were ignorant. We put a world map up on the wall and we used different color thumb tacks to see who was in the lead for the friendly competition we made up. The game was to see how many different races we could fuck. The map was so colorful after the first three months of being there. I had already fucked someone from Argentina, Spain, Italy, France, Yugoslavia, Ukraine, Czechoslovakia, Dutch, Turkey, Bulgarian, Eritrean, Columbia, Costa Rico, Sweden, and of course, Germany. I didn't know that some of these human races existed. This actually, in a twisted kind of way, helped me with my geography because I was able to study the map and find out what we were missing.

We would give a certain amount of points for some races. A prime example was a New Zealand hoe; they were worth five points because they were rare to find in this beautiful country of Germany.

When we got bored and started filling up the countries, then we'd incorporate silly shit like fuck a midget or sisters. It was ten points if you fucked a mother and the daughter and if you were bold enough to try and pull the hat trick of fucking them both at the same time, then you won the game. We were never able to achieve that, but it was sure fun trying. I pulled a couple of impressive moves, like fucking the mother then the daughter. Sisters would always fuck; it was so common that I would ask them in the beginning if they had a sister. If they didn't, I knew their best friend would fuck. I never understood how people could call each other best friends and sleep with their homies sex partner behind their back.

Dope Dick was used almost all the time for the first three months. If a bitch said she never tried coke, I would put it on my dick and face plant her on my shaft. Most of the time women were easy to talk into doing this. They just wanted the wild, fun experience with a soldier to run and tell their friends. It was very easy to reach one hundred and thirty sex partners. I had already been in thirty plus bodies during my first three months. The only thing that slowed me up was that I met a Turkish woman named Nellie. Nellie was five foot flat with a spicy attitude and a bold figure. She took no shit but the shit I gave her.

Nellie chose me at the club Black Sounds, and it was a night to remember. I was just coming from the bar ordering the standard amount of drinks for the little clique that I was with. It was Hov, a nigga from Long Beach, CA. Hov had money that wasn't coming from the Army obviously because I was with him when he bought his BMW with twenty-five thousand cash. BMW's were cheap in Germany because that's where they're made. Hov would always make big purchases in cash, but I never asked about it because I was taught never to count another man's pocket and it simply wasn't my business. Charlie was there, and he was a real man. Charlie wasn't with the bullshit we were on, but he would fuck some hoes too. He was from South Carolina and had a good head on his shoulders, just an all-around solid dude. Boom was from North Carolina and was married to a thick, fine ass, white girl. He didn't give a damn about her though, and if he did, he had a funny way of showing it. I think this nigga got caught cheating at least five times in a few months span. Beast was a short Puerto Rican nigga who had Obsessive Compulsive Disorder (OCD). He would have everything in his room at a certain angle and was super clean. It wasn't a bad thing, but he would go too far and have to have things like the volume on even numbers. We were actually just finishing a debate before I went to the bar about what he thought the volume in the club was on. He wanted to go and ask the DJ to show him and to make sure it was on even numbers. The nigga was crazy, and he was a lot older, he never really gave his age, but if I was to guess, he was at least twenty eight.

I happened to see Jeezy start to get into it with some clown nigga. I was already due for a fight, so I was itching for one. I only got into eight fights at Fort Irwin, so I was ready for this moment. I put the drinks down and took my shirt off because I wasn't playing any games. This was the perfect stress relief besides drugs, alcohol, and sex. I handed my shirt to Nellie before I even knew her. She looked at me with the, who the fuck do you think you are look, and I winked at her and said, *watch this gorgeous.* I grabbed a Bud light bottle out some niggas hand and cracked it over that clown's head who Jeezy was arguing with. That shit sounded like a firework went off in the club. He was bent over holding his head with a little bit of blood leaking. The dude whose bottle I snatched decided he felt bad. We got to tussling on the dance floor, and his homies jumped in, as did mine. I fucked around and shut the club down early that night.

While outside waiting on a taxi, Nellie pulled up to me and gave me my shirt. She said *here dummkopf* and handed me my shirt while continuing to say more things in the German language. I asked her what dummkopf meant, and she said *dumbass. Damn, why do I have to be all that, beautiful? Because it was my girlfriend's birthday and you ruined it.* I told her I would make it up to them and she said, *oh yeah, how are you going to do that? Just tell me what you want me to do?* She said, *give me your number,* so I did, and she told me she would call me in two days and not to miss her call. I was turned on by what she was saying and how she was talking to me, so I made sure not to miss her call.

While waiting on her call for the next day or two, I kept attempting to call my kids, but I was always sent to the voice mail. I knew with my son they would never pick up, but with my daughter, I didn't understand why Shametta would act like this. I kept my relationship going with Ebony while being stationed in Germany. Ebony was a rider, and I couldn't just get rid of her. She fucked around and worked her way in with me. I let her meet my family and all. They loved her, but I knew deep down that she wasn't going to be more than what she was. I couldn't respect a woman who was extremely naïve that lets me do whatever I wanted to do. The dividing factor that kept Ebony in her title of girlfriend and nothing more was when she told me a secret. Her secret was that she was out of town one day and she was staying at a hotel. While being there, she ran into her father and his mistress. She told me that she blackmailed her dad into buying her things and doing pretty much whatever she wanted him to do for years. In exchange, she wouldn't tell her mother that she caught her father cheating on her.

In my mind that was some downright cold-hearted shit to do. I always wondered why her dad would constantly buy her shit or why she was so quick to call her dad if anything had to do with finances. Most of the damn time, Ebony had the money and would ask him to pay for it. I knew something fishy was going on. I thought maybe he molested her when she was young or something and this was his way of keeping her quiet. A father's love for his daughter runs deep but this shit wasn't adding up, and now I knew why.

I told you women were the most non-loyal creatures on earth. There was no way in hell that I could be with someone that allowed their mother to be disrespected and cheated on. Let alone she was blackmailing her father in the process. This told me the one and only thing I needed to know about her. If she would do her own mother like that, what the hell would she do to me? But I kept her around for financial purposes, and like I said, she was very easy to get along with, she was a rider.

I think deep down inside I just didn't want to be alone and needed a companion to vent to, and when sex was involved, it was more than fucking or feeding my addiction. There would be meaning behind it and conversation. While waiting on the phone call, I found myself in trouble once again with the Army. My nickname amongst most of my military family through my career was (UCMJ), which stood for Uniform Code of Military Justice. They also called me Private ED which stood for extra duty. I got in trouble for the fight at the club because there was a super Hooah soldier in the club.

A Hooah soldier is similar to the teacher's pet. They come in all shapes and forms with disguises. There happened to be one in the club that I wasn't aware of, and it was the Command Sergeant Major of the post's driver. When it comes to rank in the military this was the tip top on the enlisted side; they're the ones that really ran shit and got it done. I was served a UCMJ for fighting and, once again, I was sentenced to fifteen days of extra duty. This extra duty consisted of pretty much stripping and waxing tile floors with buffers and other janitorial equipment. I became really familiar with buffers in Korea because I was always in trouble for fighting, drinking underage, or not reporting to formation. I was demoted twice in rank in Korea and once in California. Now after I just earned my rank of E-4 Specialist back, it was taken again.

I finally received that call from Nellie on my first day of extra duty. *Hello, who's this? This is Nellie, and you owe me. Oh, hey beautiful how you doing? I'm okay, so I figured out what you can do to make that day up to me and my girlfriend. Oh yeah, what's that sexy? You can take us out to dinner. Okay cool, but I won't be able to do it until about two weeks because I got in trouble over that fight. That's fine, but now you owe us three dinners. Ok, you got it sexy.* I finally got a chance to tell her my name because she had just asked. *My name is Lamar, but they call me Boogie.*

Boogie was a name given to me by Hov. I introduced myself as Lamar when I met everyone in Germany because I felt Matthew was dead with all the shit he had going on, so I thought my middle name would be a fresh start to a different life. Hov took Lamar to L-Boogie because I was dancing to the old school song by rapper Mack 10, Back Yard Boogie, in my room one day. Since he was from California, he knew that was a hood classic, so he started calling me L-Boogie, then it caught on with the rest of the clique and went to Boogie only sometimes.

Nellie repeated my name, Lamar, and said that she liked it. She told me to call her when I got out of trouble, so we could link up. I gave her that call in less than two weeks because I snuck off post to go on our first date to a Chinese restaurant. Nellie and her girlfriend, Sara, picked me up and we enjoyed each other's company over a meal. I found out that Nellie had a kid and her and her girlfriend had only been together for a year. This was a new challenge to me, one that I was excited to take on. Not only will I be able to fuck two bitches at the same time, but that they were in a relationship, that was beautiful. The first dinner date went well, but I didn't get a chance to enjoy them like I wanted to. But within that same week I took them out all three times, and on that last date, it went down.

We got to Sara's house which was a decent drive away from post. We got there, and a porno film was already playing. They whipped out some ecstasy pills and put two in my mouth. I tried it before, but these pills were going to be needed to really enjoy this experience. They had several sex toys that they brought out. Whiplashes, nipple pincher, anal beads, hot lotions, and candles. I was in for something new and a hell of a night. I would be fucking Nellie from the back while she ate Sara's pussy. Then they would switch positions, so I could enjoy the other one. I got rode while one was sitting on my face, I didn't mind eating the pussy that day. The drugs put me in a euphoria, and everything felt like heaven. I was eating ass while getting my ass ate. Toes were getting sucked, and butts were getting fucked.

One time I snapped out of the unreal moment and reality kicked in when Sara took the candle and a lighter and melted the wax on my chest. That shit hurt and there wasn't any pleasure in it. They laughed at me and continued to do it to each other. It was an amazing night, and I didn't want it to end, but it did. The pills that they gave me made everything feel so much better. After a good night's rest, we woke up and they made me breakfast. All I could do was have flashbacks of last night and the things that occurred. Germany was hands down the best place on earth. The nerve of Adolf Hitler giving this place a bad name; he almost fucked up the world's best-kept secret.

I got dropped off at the barracks, but before I did, I got a few of those pills off the ladies. Nellie said her cousin could get me any amount I needed for three dollars a pill. I thought to myself, I just got linked up with the plug, and I'm going to make me some money. I told Jeezy about the wild ass night I had and that I could get some X whenever we wanted. Nellie, Sara, and I planned on having another episode again, but Nellie told me otherwise shortly when she called. Apparently, her girlfriend said Nellie was enjoying my sex too much, and she didn't like to see someone else pleasing her like I did. I tried everything to get this episode to occur again, but it was a no go. I thought maybe Sara didn't like my sex, which would be a first for me, but Nellie said she loved it but she just hated seeing me make her feel like that.

Time went by, and I made Nellie my girlfriend within a month. Sex was great, she didn't take any shit, and she was fine as hell. Nellie knew how to treat a man; she would always have food prepared whenever I came over, and she was submissive. Not weak, but she knew her role as a woman and like I said, she didn't take any shit. We could be in the club and, of course, I'm trying to do my thing, but she would stop all that silly shit I was doing immediately. If she had to punch a bitch for trying to dance on me or even looking at me, it didn't matter. I was hers, and she made sure those hoes knew it. That shit turned me on, and it felt good to be wanted like that.

Nellie still had a girlfriend for the first two months we were together. My girlfriend had a girlfriend, and I loved the sound of that. Every now and then I would be able to have sex with Sara when Nellie was at the store or something. I didn't understand Sara, she didn't like to watch me please her girlfriend, but she was fine with her being in a relationship with me in front of her. She was confusing, but it didn't really matter to me because she still wanted me to fuck her. One day Sara and I got caught having sex, if that makes sense. Nellie walks through the door, and I'm giving Sara back shots on the couch. Nellie dropped the take-out food we ordered and started whooping Sara's ass. *This is my man you bitch, you don't touch him. This is my dick. You fucking cheater, Lamar, I'll beat your ass and your ass too if I ever catch you cheating again.* "SLAP" to the face. I was just as confused as you are. How was I cheating if we both fucked the same person at the same time? But in some weird way, I guess I was because we had to sneak and do it.

Nellie was flat out crazy, but I had to respect it because that's what she demanded. The excitement was settled, and I changed the topic once the smoke cleared. *Hey babe, I need to get a large amount of X pills. Are you able to get me around five hundred? Lamar, I told you I could get you whatever you want. When do you want it by? The sooner you can get them the better babe. Ok, I'll have it in two days.*

I was ready to make a power play for my son. I had to get my money up, so I could attempt to get custody again with a good lawyer. I knew if I went through with it I was going to need the best lawyer I could afford. The name of the game was if you have money you can purchase the lawyer to either get you out of trouble or win you the best judgment for whatever your situation is. Sharlean's parents had the upper hand, and I wanted to at least compete with them. I was tired of going back and forth with my emotions when I tried to communicate with him. To always talk to the voicemail and hardly ever get a chance to talk to him was crushing me. The same shit went with Dez. It wasn't as bad when I called, but it did seem like I was bothering Meme because she would always cut the conversation short and make something up that she had to do. *Lamar, I have to take my mom to the doctor, I'll have Juicy call you later* or *Lamar, Juicy is sleepy, I'm going to lay her down.* My conversation had to happen within sixty seconds. It was fine though because I was going to get my shit together sooner or later.

Ebony would still send me money and before I was using it to drink and bullshit, but now I planned on stashing it for the great cause. Nellie informed me about their bank systems and how they worked. She told me that once you open a bank account, they automatically give you a three-thousand-dollar, or should I say Euro, overdraft. I thought I could use that when I needed to re-up or right before I left to a different duty station. There's nothing wrong with having a backup plan, and if that was true, it was a free three thousand dollars, why wouldn't I go get that money.

During my waiting period of those forty-eight hours, I went to enjoy the great Red-Light District. Nellie was holding me down sexually, so I didn't want to take the chance of finding new pussy in the club because the odds were Nellie knew them. As big as this country was, it seemed like all those hoes knew each other. So, until I was able to get my hands on those pills, I wasn't going to fuck that up. I shopped for pussy at the most famous fucking brothel on earth. Just like Korea, there were gorgeous women everywhere, but now there were so many different races to choose from.

I had to have sex with at least three hoes the first time there. To me, there was nothing better than pussy but new pussy. In this brothel, I was unaware of the hat rule. If you wore a hat while walking and shopping for your hoe, other bitches would snatch your hat off your head. They would all stand by their door as you chose one but if they didn't have enough clients for the day, they would snatch your hat and run into their room and jump onto the bed. The only way to get your hat back was to fuck them. They were cheap like Korea, but maybe ten dollars more. As you can imagine, I wore about three hats the next time I went.

The first time I went by myself, the next day I went with the homies. This addiction was really getting the best of me because I still would have sex with Nellie six days a week. The day was finally here to get my shit and Nellie told me we had to go pick it up in Wurzburg and that was about two hours away. Nellie said we had to rent a car because hers wouldn't make it up there and back. That was cool with me because I always heard you could rent a brand new BMW for twenty-six dollars. The homies always said to get the extra five dollars insurance because you can literally demolish the car and, as long as you had that, you were covered.

We get the car, and the homies weren't lying, a brand spanking new luxury car in the states, but treated like a Honda Civic in Germany. Once we got to the destination, she walked me into this home with about five Turkish men inside smoking like a train while bagging up what appeared to be at least thirty thousand pills. The house was run down and looked like a homeless shelter. They talked in their Turkish language for a few minutes. Then I heard my name being called. *Lamar this is my cousin Zoltan.* I extended my hand, and he pulled me in by grabbing the back of my neck. We were about the same height and size, which was odd for a Turkish man because they were usually small and rowdy. He leaned his forehead on mine and spoke words I didn't understand. His breath smelled like the mixture of dog shit and motor oil. I couldn't wait for him to stop talking.

Once he was done speaking, Nellie told me what he said. Zoltan said he only agreed to meet me because she was his favorite cousin and people didn't get to walk into his operation and meet him. She told me that he knew how excited and happy she was when talking to him about me, so he had to lay eyes on me. He said he wanted to make it personal if he had to kill me for breaking her heart if I didn't treat his favorite cousin right. I told her to tell him that I wouldn't dare.

He spoke some more bullshit, and I felt like he was already killing me slowly because I could damn near see the words coming out his stank ass mouth. Nellie handed him the money, and we get the pills. She said that Zoltan told me that was the last time I would see him and when I needed more to go through her. It didn't matter to me; I just couldn't wait to get this money. What's the odds that I would come to Germany and fuck the favorite cousin of the connection to the pill game? I'm sure he wasn't the big dog, but he damn sure wasn't a corner guy.

I got right to it and started selling to almost everyone in the barracks. I had two hundred and fifty blue dolphin pills and the other half in pink panther pills. They both sold quick as fuck, and within two weeks I had to re-up already. I rented a car for Nellie, and she would get on the Freeway to grab some more. It would go like that for three more rotations before I had to start going weekly. During those two months, I was spending money like a damn fool. It was easy to spend five hundred a night in the clubs. We kept a rental car for so long that people thought I bought Nellie a car. I didn't have my license, so I couldn't bring the car on post, but I sure did experience all of the no speed limit driving on the freeway. I almost wiped out at one hundred and forty miles per hour one day. But I blame it on being drunk because that car wasn't hard to handle.

Nellie was becoming overly aggressive with females in the club. It wasn't me fighting a lot anymore, it was her. I was focused on getting money and once my mind is set on something I obsess over it and can't stop thinking about it. Nellie said all I did was talk about making more money. She didn't know it was because I wanted to get a great lawyer so I could have my son. She thought I just wanted to be the man, as she would say. I didn't treat Nellie like just any woman, she was my woman, and eventually, we fell in love and expressed it to each other. I didn't know if it was lust or love, but I thought it was love. I could've been easily influenced by what we had going on and just loved the lifestyle.

During this time, I was introduced to a few different substances. I didn't mind trying new shit because I was still in pain and if I kept myself medicated I never had to feel the hurt or deal with it. So, I stayed heavily on a controlled substance in all the forms that they came in. I would have to say besides the eye drop form of LSD, shrooms were the worst. I was introduced to laced mushrooms by a woman named Shawna. Shawna was a soldier and was married. Normally soldiers didn't get any love overseas because why would we want something we could always have. But occasionally I would knock off soldiers. For some reason, Shawna had my attention, and she received a lot more than that.

One time I stayed the weekend with her, and while she was making dinner, she whipped out some laced mushrooms, better known as shrooms. I never saw her as the type to be into that kind of thing, but people are unpredictable, so I just rolled with it and took a side note. I told her that I had never had it before, but I had tried regular shrooms before, I just wanted to see what her angle was. This hallucinate was to the extreme and I didn't know how anyone could enjoy this trip. I had things popping out the TV on me. I thought a lamp was melting on me. This was the worst high ever. I guess I should have asked what it was laced with. I tried to sleep it off, but it followed me in my dreams. I was so high that I was riding the dog Falkor from the movie, The Never-Ending Story. I never tried that shit again. I couldn't appreciate what it had to offer. I'll just stick with my normal alcohol, promethazine, ecstasy, marijuana, oxycodone, and any other pill thrown to me.

Also, little did I know, Dope Dick wasn't just numbing my dick, it was all in and through my system. I was on coke and didn't even know it. I was almost a damn coke head. I'm glad I only associated that with sex because I'm sure it would have been hard to kick that shit. I tell you God is good all the time. I think I was so willing to try different drugs because I still had suicidal thoughts and I would fall back into a deep depression but was too much of a coward to actually kill myself. I figured if I drunk enough and stayed medicated it would catch up to me and I could go out with some respect from my family. People overdose all the time being young and dumb. If I took my own life that action couldn't be respected by anyone where I'm from.

One day Nellie told me that she was pregnant and wanted to keep the baby. She already had a daughter named Elise that was nine and she wanted another child. Nellie's daughter stayed with her dad half the time. When Nellie would go to work, I would watch Elise. It was kind of weird. I didn't speak Dutch, and she didn't speak English. Elise's dad was a prick, and I thought about whooping his ass, but I didn't because Nellie had gone through enough already. She almost lost custody because she didn't have a provider for her while she was at work until I came into the picture. Nellie explained to me that she doesn't have family because she was ostracized by them for marring a Gypsy. I guess it's a big thing for the Turkish to be with Gypsies. All her brothers, sister, and her father had turned their back on her. Her mom would sneak and go see her once every month, but if she got caught, she would get beat with a stick no bigger than Nellie's father's thumb. She would beg her mom to stay away because she said she caused too much pain and shame to her already. She would never listen, but that's a mother's love for you.

I didn't have a happy or sad feeling about her being pregnant; it was just another day to me. Besides, she told me that the child wasn't allowed to have my last name in Europe unless we were married. That would seize the momma's baby, daddy's maybe shit. I've always felt if the child wasn't given my last name, then that was not only disrespectful, but a sign telling me the child wasn't mine. It didn't matter like I said, I knew I would come out here and probably make what we joked about in the Army, a war baby. War babies are just that, you're on deployment or overseas and you knock a bitch up. Every now and then you will be somewhere and see a little-mixed child and you knew it was a military person that made that kid. The great benefit of war babies are you didn't have to claim or take responsibility for them. You can finish your tour and leave them right where they were at and forget about them. I know I have a few out there somewhere.

It only took two months to have the post booming with X pills. I was selling to First Sergeants, Captains, Privates, Lieutenant's; it really didn't matter. Everyone did drugs. I saw that it wasn't a poor black or white thing, it was just a part of life. Everyone had problems and needed a quick cure to run away from them. My door would be cranking non-stop all day. It got to the point that I had to stay at Nellie's house every night because I couldn't get any sleep. These niggas were disrespectful.

Jeezy had moved in a woman by this time, and I was trying to respect his relationship, plus I was doing my own thing. Jewel was his girlfriend's name, and for a short while, we were all roommates. Jeezy was one of the reasons that motivated me to want to try and get a lawyer and get my son. I literally saw him go from being a dirty whore, fighting and living life fast with me to being in love and getting engaged with a child on the way all within six months. Learning and observing from him showed me that you never know what life has planned for you and it could all change quickly. Jeezy gave me a little bit of spirit and hope to attempt this shit again. Week after week it was the same shit; get money, fuck bitches, and burn bridges was the motto. By the end of November, I had made about thirty thousand dollars in four or five months, but I was also spending like a muthafucka.

I had two X-box game systems, two laptops, two phones, two everything. I kept one set or pair at the barracks room and the other at Nellie's house. I was young and never had money, I had to show people I had some now. I would buy Don Perignon champagne bottles for around a hundred dollars to eat with my Chinese food takeout. I didn't even like champagne. It made me burp too much and was pointless to me. But I had to show people I was getting money and live the full experience of having it. Besides, I might not get this chance again.

December 1ˢᵗ Nellie went to re up and when she arrived there; she said she saw Interpol surrounding her cousin's house. That fucked up all the money and my plans. I was on the verge of getting kicked out the Army because I wouldn't show up to work and when I did, I would get into it with someone. I messed around and got into it with the tip-top of rank, Command Sergeant Major of the post. It was over something small, petty, and stupid. I was getting money and feeling myself, kind of like when I first turned eighteen and made that terrible choice with the principal. The issue was so small that I really can't remember it. But I had already made my mind up that I was going to force them to kick me out because I had to be home and try to fix this shit that I called my life. If I would stay in the Army, I was going to die because I had no respect for my own life, let alone anyone else's. I had too much drugs, sex, and now money.

I was secretly happy that I wasn't going to sell anymore because I didn't like that everywhere I went someone was trying to buy and muthafuckas would steady knock on my door. I wasn't cut out for drug dealing, but I sure could slang some shit. I had the post and the clubs going crazy for them blue dolphins and pink panther pills.

Nellie was three months pregnant when she lost the baby, and she took it very hard. I think she thought I was going to marry her and take them to the United States. She might have thought that because I might have led her on a little bit. She definitely was a woman I could marry and would have loved to have in my life for life, but it was wrong timing, and I had too much going on. She was the first woman that I felt I did wrong and sincerely wished I could apologize to her and make her understand that I was in a bad place in life. She will always have a special spot in my heart, and for what it's worth, I'm sorry Nellie.

I got to California on February 18ᵗʰ, 2007 with a general discharge from the Army under honorable conditions. I was kicked out according to Chapter 14 paragraph 12b, Pattern of Misconduct in the Uniformed Code of Military Justice. I didn't care, I got out a month early from the original date I enlisted for, and I didn't have to do the Army Reserves. I still got all my benefits and the G.I bill for education, so I manipulated the system. I think the Army still won because they got my wife, my son, and my secret family.

My rider, Ebony, picked me up from L.A.X airport, and we stayed at her homies house a few nights before we could move into our apartment. I had only seven thousand dollars left out of that money I had racked up. I continued living the lifestyle I created after the plug went to prison. I had blown so much money that I had to open up that bank account Nellie was telling me about.

We got our apartment in Victorville, and the first thing I did was buy a car. I don't know how they let me buy a car with no license, but they did. I put some rims on it and a stereo system inside. I thought I was in the ball game doing it big. The first night I had it, someone broke into it and didn't steal anything. I guess the alarm scared them off, but that small window they broke cost me four hundred dollars.

Ebony and I got our relationship back on better terms. It was hard because the first two months back home I wasn't trying to be intimate with her after seeing and being with all those fine women in Europe. I was now acting snooty. I did shock myself and not fuck any different women except two the whole short time we were back together. I think I burned myself out. I suppose when you have one hundred and eighty sex partners within a four-year span it will happen.

Camilo got out the Army too, and I invited him to stay with us until he could figure out what his best move was. I needed my homie around anyway to try and figure out what the fuck I was going to do also. Before he got back, I had gained about thirty pounds since I got out the Army. When he came, it was easy to pack on another thirty because all we did was drink, smoke, and eat. Oh yeah, I can't forget watching the classic television show, Maury. You ain't the daddy was the best thing on TV, especially since I hadn't watched TV like that in about four years. I could only imagine that this was how a nigga felt who just got out of prison. Sometimes we would go to the worst mall this country had to offer in Victorville and just sit down. We would sit and watch people; it was mind-blowing seeing individuality. We were used to seeing nothing but people in green, blue, or brown and everyone talking alike and thinking alike. There weren't fat people or many options of being an individual in the Army. It was a culture shock coming back home, and it took time to get adjusted.

Time was flying by since I had gotten out the Army and it was now, June 7th, 2007. This was the worst day of my life and when I actually had the courage to try and kill myself. It was a normal day that consisted of drinking and eating. That night Camilo and I decided to go out to a bar named Shooters. We walked in and grabbed a drink. We had been here before, so it was nothing new to us. Usually, we played pool and talked shit. Camilo had met a woman a few weeks back and said he was going to run to her house really quick to go beat it up and then he'd be right back. He told me to try and find some new hoes. That was a game plan, and it sounded like a normal task.

Chapter 35: Pay What You Owe

After he left, I saw a nigga that looked familiar in the bar. Oh shit, it's my homie and childhood friend, Shannon. We talked and caught up on old times. I asked what the hell was he doing out here in the boring ass dessert? I knew the answer, and it was usually because you're on the run from them people or you are selling drugs in a major way. Shannon said he was doing a little bit of this and that, which meant selling drugs. No more than five minutes of talking and Shannon saw a nigga that supposedly had gotten over on him for about twenty-five hundred. I already knew where that was going, and I didn't forget that I owed him one, so that was going to be me paying my debt to the hood.

Shannon said, *come with me outside real quick, so I can get something.* We went outside and loaded up some guns that he had in the car like I figured we would. *Look, nigga, I'm going to get my money from him, and you just watch my back for his niggas. If they act up you know what to do, you from the 805. I gotcha dog.* Shannon gave me an old ass six-shooter revolver pistol, but I'm cool with it because my bullet shells don't leave my possession, unlike the semi-automatic pistol that he had. We got inside and he approached buddy. No more than ten seconds later he pulled out his pistol and whipped him across the head. Buddy's three homeboys pulled their guns out, and I didn't waste any time, it was a natural reaction to start firing at them.

I hit one person in the leg, and Shannon shot the dude he was arguing with. Shannon got grazed with a bullet on his ear, and I was okay. I couldn't shoot as much as I wanted to because I didn't panic and remembered that I only had six shots. I shot three more rounds as we made our exit out the bar to the car. When I got dropped off at home, I saw he had three bullet holes on the side of the car. I asked Shannon if we were even and he said we were good. We exchanged numbers, and I went into the house to have a drink and calm my nerves.

Chapter 36: It Magically Disappeared

All the real excitement didn't kick in until I got home. After a drink, I tried calling Dez because it was too late to call Matt's grandparents' house. It was about eleven o'clock when I called. I wasn't expecting for Meme to pick up but she shocked me and did. *Hello. Hey, what's up Meme, how are you doing? Why are you calling? What are you talking about? I'm trying to check on my daughter and let you know I'm back in the states now and can come out there in a week or two. Well, Dez is sleep. Shametta why are you acting like I'm bothering you?* She took a few seconds and said, *man, this is what's going on and why I'm speaking to you like this. I don't know how to tell you this, but my mother has been telling me to tell you for the past few years.* What could Shametta have to tell me for some years that her mom had to force her to say?

I don't know how I didn't see what was coming and when she said it, I immediately wanted to die. *Lamar, Dez'tyn'ee is not your baby. What are you talking about? How is she not? Lamar, I knew she wasn't your child when I was pregnant, what I felt at that time, was that you would be the best man to raise her.* The feeling of a thousand swords through my body was what those words felt like. I couldn't make sense of the situation, and I didn't want to believe it. *Shametta, why did you let me name this child and give her my last name? I know. I'm sorry, Lamar. Shametta, no, don't do this to me. I love that little girl, and you know what I've been through with my son's mother. Why would you do this to me? You said you loved me and then you took that away from me, now you want to take my daughter away from me too? Your dirty, this isn't right, you let me build a relationship with this beautiful child, and now you want to take it back. Shametta you made a clear decision when you chose to give this child my last name and let me name her. I told you I always wanted my daughter to have this name since I was thirteen. You let my mother think she had a granddaughter. You're not a woman. A real woman would have taken this to the grave or told me upfront.*

She started crying and saying that she was sorry. *I made a mistake.* I yelled, *No, this is not a spilled glass of milk, bitch! That's a mistake. You just fucked my world up even more than it was already, and I thought that you would understand out of all people what I'm going through. Bitch, I was writing your brother in prison trying to show you that I loved you because I knew how much that fucking rapist meant to you. Yeah, that's right, the fucking rapist, that's why he doesn't want to tell you what he did because he doesn't want you to take your love from him like you did me and now you're taking my soul. You dirty little country Auburn, Alabama fucking hoe!*

She hung the phone up and I couldn't or wouldn't dare give her the pleasure of hearing me sob like a big broken hearted, lost, confused baby. I finally let out the most painful cry that I had ever engaged in. I did this for twenty minutes while drinking. My pain turned into rage and rage turned into a deadly, suicidal thought and game. I still had the six-shooter pistol revolver on me, and there was one shot left. I was going to play a game of Russian Roulette. I took a big swig of the Crown Royal Whiskey that I had and sparked a cigarette. As I'm smoking, I challenged and questioned GOD. I was yelling, *Why the fuck do you keep doing this to me, muthafucka? You like seeing me in pain and don't give two shits about me you fucking fraud. If you exist, then you're going to watch me blow my fucking brains out since you like me in pain so much.*

I opened the cylinder, saw the bullet, and spun it around a few times. I let out one last gruesome cry; then I yelled to amp myself up while I put the gun to my head. I was ready to be done with this world. I was ready to end the pain, and I had the balls to take myself out this day and this moment. I squeezed the trigger "BANG." The cigarette drops out my mouth onto my chest. The only reason I knew I was alive was because the cigarette burned a hole through my shirt and I felt the cherry of it burning my chest. I dropped the gun and broke down to my knees from sitting at the table. Something whispered, *look in the cylinder.* After being heavily shaken up, I was able to calm down and get my nerves under control. I opened the cylinder, and there was no bullet. The bullet had up and disappeared. It was GOD telling me that he wasn't ready for me yet and not to question his existence.

I heard a whisper again, and it said, *this pain will make you great.* I was able to gather myself and walk to the dumpster and throw the gun away, along with all the pictures that I had of Dez. While doing this, Camilo arrived, and I updated him with all the events that happened that night, except for the suicidal incident. I didn't want to be perceived as weak and not respected by him anymore.

I never told anyone of the break down that I had. I vented to him and cried until I was able to go to sleep. Camilo was there for me in a very dark time in my life, and if he wasn't there that night, I don't know what I would have done to myself. I still couldn't believe I cried in front of him and expressed so much. The next day I got a call from my dad, which was random. I didn't even know that he had my number, but he told me his heart was not doing too good and a bunch of other shit. All I heard was his heart wasn't doing well, and I could possibly get a check out of this nigga. I needed to get the fuck out of California after that bullshit shootout last night.

While on the phone with my dad, I was watching the news and they were talking about the shooting and one man was in critical condition. I would be the one to shoot a nigga in the leg and hit his artery. I was shook, so I told him I would be out there next Friday after I got my last unemployment check. Camilo already had plans to go back to Oxnard, and I had to disappear. Ebony was originally from Columbus, Ohio and my dad stayed in Lima, Ohio. I thought this was something she would be on board with. I explained to her what was going on and updated her about Dez as well. She understood that it was best for me to leave the state. She was going to stay back and continue working on my divorce, for free might I add, since she was a paralegal and eventually she would come out when I was set up.

Friday came, and I didn't get the check. My unemployment ran out. I had to file for an extension which would take another month and a half to get my checks flowing again. Ebony was holding me down financially until it was time to go. Summer was almost over, and it was August. I got that first extension check, and then I drove thirty-one hours straight from Victorville, California to Lima, Ohio. I drank Red Bull energy drinks and smoked cigarettes while enjoying the open roads. I really needed that time to reflect and think to myself.

It was beautiful seeing and driving through all the states. Texas was extremely long to drive through, but after that, it was all downhill. I had $736.44 to my name and a duffle bag full of clothes. I think I was excited and scared. This had to be the reason why I couldn't sleep and drove thirty-one hours straight. I was ready for a new beginning, and I came to the conclusion that I couldn't keep living life like I was if I was choosing to live. I tried it my way, and it didn't work. I needed to try it GOD'S way. It didn't mean I had to be super religious, just do my best to abide by the Ten Commandments and, as of right now, the only thing I hadn't done was rape and murder. For about seventy-two hours I thought I was a murderer. Boy was my mind playing tricks on me during this time. When I normally heard critical condition on the news, it usually led to death, so I had to deal with the thought that I may have possibly killed a person for a few days until I got an update.

Buddy and his homies were fine and lived, but they did have to amputate from around the middle of his thigh down for some medical reason. I was fine with that. I had so much going through my head on that drive. It was a beautiful memory, but I wished I were driving across the country on different terms.

Chapter 37: Best Choice I Ever Made

The first day I arrived in Lima, Ohio I couldn't sleep at all. I was emotional, and I didn't know what to expect. It was as if something came over me during that drive and I wanted to live better. This was the perfect chance to start fresh because I didn't know anyone, and I figured I couldn't get into trouble unless I was looking for it. I still was out here for a check, but maybe with that check, I would have more opportunity.

I stayed with my pops in a rundown apartment complex on Fourth Street, which was on the south side of the city. You know like I know, nothing is ever good on the south side of any city, so I was ready for whatever. My pops actually knew a decent amount of people, and they had somewhat of a level of respect for him. This eased my mind and made it easier to transition. It was a weird but easy transition. Pops was excited to have me in his town and in his life. He tried to show me off to everybody he knew the first day. I was tired of meeting people and him acting like we had a great relationship. I let him get his front on because I knew the reason why I was down here, and I would get the last laugh, so I could play that role.

The funny thing was that I felt more comfortable around his family than with him because I kind of knew them better than him. Those times that I would visit, I was around my aunts, cousins, and grandmother more than him. I was really happy that I could spend time with my grandmother, Harriet. That woman was the only reason that I considered even allowing a chance to build a relationship with my pops. Grandma Harriet once came and visited me in California when I was about seven or eight years old. She had won a trip to Las Vegas, Nevada for a NASCAR racing event. She drove to Oxnard and surprised me. I didn't even know she existed, but I did know that I could never forget the love she showed and how she made me feel wanted.

She bought me clothes when it was extremely needed, and she just loved me. I didn't understand how you could love someone you didn't know, but it made an impact on my life. I had a chance to know something about my other side of the family, and most importantly, I'll say it again, she made me feel wanted and loved even if my pops didn't want me.

I call him pops because I can't just give him the title of father or dad. But I do know that he is my biological parent, I couldn't deny that, so I give him his respect by just calling him, pops. My grandma and I built a stronger bond over the next few months. I enjoyed talking to her and listening to her wisdom. She speaks with so much passion, and she is the funniest, most serious person I had ever met in my life. Since I was trying to do better, I believe the Lord was talking through her to tell me what I needed to hear. Lord knows there wasn't much that I was going to pay attention to, but he knew I loved and respected this woman, so he used her to reach me.

We would talk about everything from politics to family members. My pops would normally be the main topic. I think she was trying to warn me to guard my heart in her strange way. Grandma loves her kids, but she doesn't mind telling you the truth, even if it does hurt you. She told me my pops would like to lie and trick off with women. She said he was a damn fool for women and he would give all his money to them. Sounded to me that pops and I had one thing in common, we both loved hoes but had different experiences with them. I wasn't ready to talk to my pops about the whole where the fuck have you been my whole life spill yet. I still needed to see what this town had to offer, and I wasn't trying to fuck up the blessing that I was waiting on.

I had a few bumps in the road adjusting to the culture. The first thing I realized was that Lima didn't have any gangs out here. I never thought a place without gangs existed. Everyone was friendly and spoke to you, even if they didn't know you. I had a gentleman walk up to my car at the stop light, knock on my window, and tell me I had a tail light out. This was an uncommon and terrible decision back home. In some areas, you didn't stop at stop signs because people would get snatched out their windows and carjacked. I could be sitting on the porch, and a random guy would walk by and start talking to me or waving. This was unbelievable to me. If I didn't know you, then I didn't speak because you could find yourself in a deep situation trying to be friendly back home. Friendly meant you were an easy mark and probably would get robbed. I eventually settled in and met some homies. I spent too much time with my female cousins and grandma.

Chapter 38: A Familiar Difference

The first homie I met was a nigga named, Bubby. Bubby was a person who just lived life and played it one day at a time. We met at his pops house, who lived a few doors down from my pops. I didn't know how, but the first time we met, he had some pretty young thang butt naked in a room full of niggas playing some drinking game. The crazy part was he said, *watch this nigga,* and sent her in his dad's room. I knew we were going to be cool by how he got down.

The next homie I met was a nigga named, Josh. This nigga was different. He was young but had an old man vibe to him. He was way past his years of age, and his wisdom showed. Josh introduced me to his clique, and I started to hang with them. These niggas were not what I was used to, but they were everything different that I needed in my life. I would get a call from Josh on a Friday or Saturday night asking if I wanted to come over and play Monopoly. I couldn't believe these niggas were literally playing the board game Monopoly with a house full of dudes arguing about some silly shit: not one bitch in sight and they were having a good ass time doing it.

I couldn't wrap my mind around it, but I said I wanted to change so this meant doing different things. We played basketball three or four days a week, so that was cool because I thought they were lame. This was the first time I heard people say they knew their fathers and that their fathers lived with them. This clique would talk about going to college and church. The only time college was brought up where I was from was because someone got a scholarship in sports to go play. They were talking about going because they wanted to learn and get good jobs and careers.

My mind was blown, but I just sat back and soaked up all the knowledge they were giving me for free by observing their behavior and conversations. The only thing I knew about church was that they were usually corrupt or had a lot of drama going on. I used to go to Saint Paul's Baptist Church when I was young. Once during a sermon, the preacher's daughter came busting through the door running and screaming frantically. Behind her was a pimp chasing her up the aisle demanding his money. I guess she was short on her daily tricks and thought if she ran into the church he wouldn't do anything to her. Boy was she wrong because he started pimp slapping her in the church yelling for the rest of his money.

That was my first bad experience. The second experience was at a church called, New Hope Baptist Church. Apparently, the congregation had enough of their pastor and on one holy Sunday morning decided to lock the pastor out of his own church for sleeping with several women within the church. But those guys that I was hanging around were going to praise the man upstairs and going because they wanted to. This was amazing to me, I had no idea there were black people like this in real life. I mean, I would see them on TV shows like "The Cosby's" or "The Fresh Prince of Bel-Air," but not in real life.

It was so weird to me, but it was interesting at the same time. When I wasn't around them, I would be with my pops drinking and talking shit. We would try to build our bond stronger, but he would always say something that was so far from the truth that I would get turned off and angry. He would lie all the time in front of people to hide that he wasn't in my life. It could be from him saying that he showed me how to work on cars or he took me fishing etc... I had never been fishing a day in my life, and I'm not mechanically inclined.

One day I couldn't hold it in anymore, and I didn't give a damn about a check while I'm waiting on this nigga to die. It seemed like his heart was getting stronger and stronger every day, so I had to say what was on my mind. *Pops, you're always talking to me about fucking hoes or lying about what you didn't do with me. I call you pops because I can't fix my lips to say dad, but I try to give you some respect, but you make it damn hard. You're not giving me any fatherly advice or wisdom. I can talk about fucking bitches with my homeboys, give me something I could use in life nigga. You need to stop lying to make yourself feel better, deal with the facts or we can never grow. Why the fuck weren't you there for me? The only reason I considered having you in my life is because of your mother. She showed me love and welcomed me, not you. She let me find out who I was. I'm a Sanders, and I didn't know anything about them, thanks to you. I have to carry a last name around that I know nothing about from a man I don't know. Matt, I'm sorry and if you want to punch me, then punch me.* I teared up and said; *I don't want to punch you, I want to know you and know why you weren't there.*

He told me that my granddaddy tried to give him a shotgun wedding. He was going to force my pops to marry my mom and that he was scared and didn't know what to do, so he left. *I was a young man, Matt, and I made a bad choice. I can understand what you're saying but why didn't you make things right and be in my life? I needed you, and I had to learn to be what I thought was a man on my own by watching other people's mistakes. An uncle, coach, or any other type of father figure can only teach me so much, pops, why weren't you there?*

He told me a little bit about his life and how he grew up before I got my answer. I wished I never had that conversation with him, but it was needed, and I had to know. They say don't ask questions if you don't want to know the answers. I found out what that expression meant. My pops told me that his ex-wife didn't want me around and that he basically listened to her. I was supposedly the topic of the last argument they had before they got a divorce.

I tried to come to his town with an open mind and for the reasons that I made up in my head why he wasn't around like he should have been. I always thought it was because he was a Navy guy and was unable to be around because of his career. I thought he was the type of man that I had seen on TV shows and had a good square life with a good head on his shoulders.

When he explained his life and the things he went through, it made me angry. I was angry because I fooled myself and made a perception up about him to bury the pain of not having my pops around. It made me feel good to have the thought that he wasn't like all the rest of the niggas in my neighborhood that I had seen growing up. But he was exactly like them. He used drugs, cheated on his wife, and abused alcohol too.

I didn't judge him for anything he told me about himself, but it was an eye-opener that I had the same stereotypical type father that a lot of people had. I wanted him to be different and I never once thought he was the average person from the street corner. It crushed me, and he let me down once again. Yes, he hurt me again even though this was by my own doing from painting that picture of him. I guess if I didn't know much about him, I was praying and hoping that he had a good explanation for all the lost time. I decided to be the bigger person and forgive him, so we could start a relationship. It's never too late, and even though I was in Ohio because of my own reasons, I also felt like the Lord kept him and me alive so we could have a new start.

The first year in Lima went by fast. I was still adjusting to the culture and how things were. Racism was at an all-time high in the mid-east. You were either black or white, they didn't have much diversity, and most of the racism that I had seen came from black people and white people. I didn't think black people could be racist, but it was nothing for someone to call a white person a cracker. But I didn't really understand how much black people still went through racist bullshit here because back home, white folks weren't as blunt as they were here. Over time I would find out slowly but surely just how crazy they would be.

The first year I met a few ladies and tried to treat them right, but none had anything to offer me, so I toyed with them. I did meet a woman name Tamarah while working at the local Y.M.C.A. Tamarah and I got serious within the first six months of being with each other. She had a son who was the same age as my son. You never know who, why, or how long someone's going to be in your life. I believe we came into each other's life at the right time for specific reasons. Her purpose in my life was giving me a chance to be a father, even if it was to her son, and helping me stay balanced while realizing my worth.

She accepted all the baggage that I brought to the table. I believe she saw the good in my heart, so she gave me a chance like I gave her. I learned what it was like to be a father and I took pride in doing it. I probably never would have gotten my divorce finalized if she didn't push to see the paperwork in order for us to stay together. I strung Ebony along until it was completed because I didn't have the thousands of dollars to make that happen, but when it did, I had to let her go gradually because she was really into me still. At one point in time, she came out and visited and I fucked around and got her pregnant while being with Tamarah. The gradual break up was well needed, and she deserved to be weaned off since she just had an abortion for me.

Tamarah let me move into her house when my pops did me wrong and moved somebody else into my room over the weekend. I guess he figured since I was spending so much time at her house that I wouldn't notice a person living in my room where I paid rent at. He would periodically do silly things like that. This would make me feel like he still didn't want to have a good relationship with me. He must have figured since I was out here and I had forgiven him, that he could continue not stepping up to the plate. Maybe he was just trying to figure out how to do that, but it didn't matter to me, I wasn't stunting him, I was working on myself and trying to be a better person.

Tamarah and I were going strong in our relationship for a good three years before real problems would arrive. During those years together, I cheated a few times, but I was respectful enough not to get caught. I would relapse and fuck around with hoes, but to me, it was only two or three times a year, so I was doing well. This was an extreme improvement from my past. I worked several types of jobs trying to find out what fit me best, but I could never stay with one longer than six months, except the Y.M.C.A.

I refereed kid's soccer, basketball, and flag football games. To me, it was peaceful and meaningful because a lot of the time I would daydream that I was one of the parents in the crowd cheering for my son. Every now and then I would miss a call by zoning out and seeing myself playing with my son. I knew Tamarah's son wasn't mine, but I did develop a love for him as if he was. But I found myself being angry with myself for being a father to another nigga's kid when I should be doing this with my own.

I would start arguments with Tamarah so she would break up with me because I didn't have the heart to hurt another woman like I had done several times before. She wouldn't do it, so I started telling her she didn't appreciate me, and to some extent, she didn't. My prime example was that I got inspired by her going to college, so I started to go myself. At first it was to keep her from finding a better man who had more to offer than I could. I never thought about a woman enough to try and change or, let alone, felt that I could lose her to another man. It wasn't going to happen before because I never gave anyone a chance, but Sharlean. I would say Meme too, but I didn't give her a chance either. And, as far as Nellie, it was just the wrong place and the wrong time.

I let Tamarah get to know me, and she was getting the version that plenty of my women in the past wished they could have had. I cooked, cleaned, nurtured her child, and made her feel special. This was also the type of stuff you have to do when you don't own anything in the house where you live at but the clothes on your back. But, that's beside the point.

I had nothing to bring to the table but unneeded stress. I figured if I went to college I had an equal playing field with these cornball ass dudes out here. It's strange how one reaction or feeling led me to be a full-time student that was passing all my classes in the criminal justice field. I was putting my best foot forth, and I was doing it for a woman, at first. A woman who became lazy and made me feel as if I was caring for her child more than her.

I started taking my classes seriously and kept myself surrounded with good people, like Josh and his crew. Come to find out Josh was my cousin, so it made our friendship turn into somewhat like brothers. Bubby was already like my brother over the past few years that I've been in Lima, so my family kept growing. Their words of encouragement and Tamarah's beautiful and kind personality was able to keep me balanced and provide the opportunity to see what I could have if I got my shit together and was motivated.

I started studying for me and then I saw how close I was getting to earning a college degree all by myself. Wow, that was empowering to know that I was smart, and I could be part of a productive society when in the right environment. I got that A.A.S degree in

Corrections over a twenty-four-month span at James A. Rhodes State College. That was by far the best feeling and accomplishment that I had yet to ever have. I was going to have to wait and walk the graduation line about eight months later in June 2012, but I didn't care. It gave me time to save up and hopefully get my mom out here to see me do something with my life.

Everything was coming together. I started hanging around a good crowd of people and doing things out the kindness of my heart, and I was getting blessed back. I changed the way I talked and the way I walked by learning from some positive people. I might have learned even more by making my previous mistakes. Tamarah and I had to separate for the best of us. I taught Tamarah how to love a man and trust again. She went through some difficult thing's before we met, but haven't we all. I helped build her confidence back up and showed her that there are good men out in the world. By taking that leap of faith and falling in love again, she was able to find that out. It just didn't work out for us, and I kind of knew it wasn't going to, but I needed her around to keep balancing me out because I wasn't able to be on my own yet. I used her, but she used me too, this wasn't a bad thing because we both benefitted from our time with each other.

Chapter 39: Humble, Blessed and Focused

Shortly after our break up, I met another woman on January 6th, 2012. I decided to go and have a drink at the bar with one of the homies, and while sitting there, this bold, beautiful, gorgeous, short woman walked in the door. I had never seen this woman before, and I knew when I saw her that she was going to be mine. I thought I had worked a game plan out to buy her a drink then take it from there, but I lost her in the midst of the crowd. I looked through the bar, but couldn't find her so, I thought, oh well, I'll have to catch her the next time. As I was leaving the bar getting ready to pull off in my car, another vehicle pulls up to me. I see it's her on the passenger side with a mutual friend that we had. They were trying to go to another bar, but I was thinking that I was going to lose her to the game if I let them do that.

I thought quick and got clever by offering to buy them some breakfast food. It was like shooting fish in a barrel. They went for it, and we ended up at The Waffle House at three in the morning. The mutual friend knew me as Cali because for some reason everyone was fascinated that I was from there no matter where I was at in the world. I always introduced myself as Matthew when I came to Ohio, but once people found out that I was from California my name went out the window, and Cali was all they knew.

Our mutual friend introduced us, and before she would say her real name which was Kayla, she said her name was Sparkle. I saw where she was going with that, so I thought I would match her with my name being Shine. I told her that sounded nice because we could Sparkle and Shine together. It was just wordplay to me, but in that moment, she ate it up and was interested from there on.

We ate and talked a little bit after exchanging numbers. I never met a woman like that before. I had been all around the world and seen a lot of different faces in a lot of different places, but I never met a woman like her. She was young, really young to me. She had just turned twenty years old and had her own place, her own car, no kids, and she was in college to be a nurse. She had nothing in common with any woman that I had ever met in my life. I seemed to have a pattern of the type of women that I met. They always had three things in common and one of them you couldn't fault them for. The first common thing was they always had been with another woman, even as little as kissing another woman. Secondly, they never knew who the father of their child was. It was either this guy or that guy, and usually, it was the wrong person who they thought. And, the third thing was not to their fault, but the woman had been either raped or molested. I don't know how on earth I kept meeting women that had all three things in common. It was like it never failed.

Not her though, she was different. I got to find all this out the next day after she came to see me before she went back to college at The Ohio State University in Columbus. Columbus was only two hours away if you're driving slowly and I liked to drive, so it wouldn't be a problem for me to make a road trip to see her. We talked on the phone for the next few days, and I get her real name out of her, so I could stop calling her Sparkle. We finally set up a date to enjoy each other's company. On our first date, I was polite and respectful just like the gentleman I knew I could be. I did the gentleman thing when we walked on the sidewalk; I was closest to the curb. She told me that I was corny for always making her walk on the inside of me. I was baffled that she thought that me respecting her was corny because I was taught if you let your woman walk on the curbside then you're telling the public this is your hoe and she's being pimped.

She kept making little comments that made me aware that she never had a real man like the one I was now becoming. This was obviously going to be something new to her and to me because I never really tried to respect a woman or give them a chance. I did have my test run with Tamarah, which helped me put things in play for this new, pretty young thang.

We continued to go on dates for about three weeks, and I was getting fed up with her because she still hadn't put out yet. I had never waited longer than a week, so I thought, who the fuck does she think she is? She had me mentally fucked up in the head already. I was talking to my homies about her and bragging on her, but all they kept asking me was, did I hit it yet? I would try to put myself in the position to get it, but it never worked. I went from being angry the first three weeks to being curious the next three weeks, to us falling in love within two months.

It was crazy to me because our phone conversations were amazing every time and it was the same when we saw each other. We talked on the phone like junior high school kids for hours at a time. How in the world did this woman get me to fall in love with her without even having sex yet? Everything was so fast-paced, but it seemed to click. I wasn't scared or didn't second guess my feelings. I remember one time I was working at the Y.M.C.A and an old white man told me to come here because he wanted to tell me something. I almost didn't go because I figured, what the hell could this old white dude have to tell me. He said, *listen, son, there are only two things that matter in this world.* He caught my attention, so I asked, *what's that sir?* He told me, *what you want to do and who you want to do it with.*

All I could say was every time I saw Kayla, that's exactly what was going through my head. That's wisdom, and I wish that wisdom could have come from my father or at least someone who meant something to me in my life. It didn't matter though, because you never know why, who, or how long someone is in your life. That old man served his purpose, and I will always remember him for that short but powerful advice. Thank you sir!

Kayla finally gave in three months later, and it was well worth the wait. I never met a woman who knew her worth and respected herself. It was something different, and I had to respect that. By this time, we were madly in love and had already thought of our children's names for the family we planned on having. This shit was the easiest, non-scariest, fast roller-coaster love journey that we were on. I said roller coaster because our love kept elevating by the day. Even though they do come down, it didn't seem like our love would. We just kept rising. Usually, the higher you go, the scarier it gets, but that wasn't the case with us. By six months, I moved into her apartment in Columbus, and we had each other's name tattooed on our bodies. This was a love that I could never imagine or have dreamed of.

I had always heard that when you know you have a good person, you will just know. I went through so many bad people in my life that

I knew she was the one for me. I thought I would have messed it up by cheating on her, but I didn't. I guess I never had anyone that I wanted to be faithful too. Don't get me wrong, it is a struggle and every day is a challenge. The flesh can be weak and having a sex addiction didn't mean that I wasn't addicted anymore because I had done better and stopped cold turkey. It means that any day I could relapse, but I just take it one day at a time.

We had sex on the regular, but I still needed to masturbate twice a day to control that urge. The secret is trying not to put myself in situations for the flesh to be weak. Falling in love with someone is easy but loving someone the right way is hard to learn. I never had a healthy example to learn from. My mom, uncle, and aunts relationships only displayed domestic violence or cheating. My grandparents had been married for all my life, but I wasn't around them enough to pick up how a man or a woman should treat and love one another. But I figured it out on my own like everything else in my life.

Things were so good with us and I was excited to bring her around my family. I wanted any and everyone to know who I was in love with and who kept me happy. It was time that a piece of my heart met another piece of my heart, which was my grandma Harriet. Once I got the approval from the matriarch on this side of the family, it was easy for everyone to love Kayla.

My pops was even acting right. He was at the point that I could bring her around him. It took some time for us to get closer and it still is a work in progress, but we can never really have that bond that I need and want so badly until he comes to terms with himself and accepts the choices he's made in life. His lying hasn't stopped, but it has slowed down and is not as extreme. I don't say anything to him because that's what makes him sleep better at night. I understand how it can be to make lies up about your kids because you don't know much about them or you're not in their lives. It makes you feel better as a parent because the truth hurts.

I caught myself making lies up about my son saying crazy things like he was skipped up three grades in school because he was so smart. It made me feel like I was a part of his life and that I had a good relationship with him. When people would ask if I had kids it was embarrassing when you can't answer some of the questions they have for you, so you lie. You lie just to make it seem like you know something about them and you really know nothing. Even if you try to explain the reasons, which I shouldn't have to, they look at you and judge you like you're a piece of shit deadbeat, no matter what. It still hurts to think I've never spent more than a full month's time with my son, even if it wasn't by choice like some.

I was excited for Kayla to meet my mom because she was supposed to come down for my graduation and watch me receive my college degree. That never happened. She had some excuse again, so I cancelled walking down the line and received my degree in the mail. All I wanted was my mother to see me finally do something right in life and be proud of me. I know she counted me out and thought I would be a statistic because I even did at times. Regardless of anything, I love my mother, and the crazy thing is now that I'm older she tells me that she loves me and she's proud of me.

I was selfish for cancelling my ceremony because there were other people that wanted to celebrate that milestone with me. I was so caught up on not sharing that moment with my pops because he wasn't there to see the struggle, the pain, or the journey to becoming who I am now. He only knew the man in front of him, and I felt that he didn't deserve to be a part of that if my mother couldn't or wouldn't.

It didn't matter because I now knew who I wanted to cherish my life with. All I have to do is find out what it is I want to do. The first five months in Columbus I couldn't find a job. I would have interviews four days out the week, but no results. I had no luck. I kept hearing I had the education, but not the experience. I couldn't understand why the hell I went to college if I was going to keep getting turned down on jobs. I was blessed not to have a felony but more blessed to have a military background and a degree. But somehow, that was my curse too.

It didn't make any sense to me. I started feeling myself getting discouraged and disappointed, but I tried to keep my head up. I had some money saved up, so I was alright, but for how long, I didn't know. I got everything going right for me, and now I had trouble finding work. I had changed my thought process and was doing the good things out the kindness of my heart. I was living and walking how I always wanted to and within the Lord's Ten Commandments, to my best ability. It didn't make sense to me, this wasn't fair, and I couldn't let this woman think that I wasn't a man. I wasn't a bum dude, and I didn't want her to look at me differently.

I applied to everything, and nothing was coming around for me. I felt pressure to revert back to my old ways and go rob someone. I knew how to get money if needed to but was it worth it. I felt it was because if I didn't get a job, then I would probably lose one of the best things to ever happen to me. But, if I reverted back to the old me, then I could still possibly lose one of the best things that could have happened to me.

My mind was playing tricks on me. I would talk to myself and say encouraging words like, *be strong Matt. You can do this; you're doing everything right it will all come together.* Then here comes the inner demons, better known as the devil speaking to me; *fuck that shit, go take your respect and let this woman know you're a man and you can protect and provide for her.* Back and forth, all day every day until it happened. I made a choice that landed me in the Allen Oakwood Correctional Institution.

It's been five years, four months, and some odd days in the system. Every day I walk the yard with muthafuckas that have murdered, raped, and human sex trafficked people. I have to deal with over sixteen hundred different attitudes daily. The cells are freezing in the winter and scorching hot in the summer. The pain I feel while in the cells talk to me. There's a story in each one. The fact that I'm around walking time bombs that will crash out at the smallest purpose every day is my reality. The racist, false sense of authority that some staff will use to abuse their power day in and day out is now part of my world. Men who've been raped, beaten, stabbed, or suicidal are around the corner from me. I see people at their breaking point, cutting their intestines out because they can't take the realism of where we are and want to die. If you are black, then you hang with black gangs. If you are white, then vice versa. Race is how prison is divided up, and if your numbers are low, you're going to get rolled over. Predator or Prey is how you're labeled, so you better chose fast which one you're going to be. I always knew I was going to be in prison someday. At times I even looked forward to it. I just didn't think I was going to be in prison like this.

By the grace of GOD, I currently have a career as a Correctional Lieutenant. I guess going to college and doing the right thing from the goodness of your heart does pay off. I get asked all the time by staff and inmates, what am I doing here? They say you're so big; you should be playing in the National Football League for the Cleveland Browns. I tell them that this is where GOD wants me. I like to think by building a rapport with inmates and giving them equality like they deserve is part of my purpose. By my actions and words of encouragement while placing structure in their lives, is me doing my part. I can relate to what they were into before prison, and I'm proof that if you really want to live a square life and change, it's on you.

GOD will give his strongest soldiers the hardest battles for a reason. All my pain and struggle was used to touch some else's soul and get a fellow brother or sister through their adversity when they felt like giving up. I provide hope and show that if you don't have GOD, things are not going to go the way you planned. Living life righteously and doing things out the goodness of your heart is what I learned through my journey.

I used to chase money and everything else that didn't matter. Now I have a family with Kayla, and we're married with kids. We have a daughter, Sanaii, who is four years old, and our unborn son, Messiah, will be here December 2018 lord willing.

My relationship with my son Matt has improved, and we're able to see each other more. Facetime on the phone and periodic visits have been blessings. From time to time there are bumps in the road, but I have to accept whatever time I'm given and on their terms. I'm just grateful that it's even being given, even though I deserve more.

Kayla played a tremendous part in helping me find my way to building a bond with this fifteen-year-old young man. Did I forget to mention, I'm a proud small business owner of a commercial and residential cleaning company in my community. I'm now chasing my happiness because, with that, I'm forever truly rich.

I'm just a man who played his cards the way it was dealt by the way I felt. I ask for no judgment, but rather understand my journey and what caused me to take certain actions. I know right from wrong, and there's no excuse. I've opened up my most inner and darkest secrets, so I can finally release these demons.

It's okay to be emotional and express myself; this doesn't make me less of a person if I do so. I can never truly let my pain go or deal with my issues if I've never been allowed to let it out.

I will be strong and courageous, I will not be terrified nor discouraged for the lord, my GOD is with me wherever I go. This is the Truth of a Lost Soul.

Dedication

First and foremost, all praises go to the almighty GOD for giving me breath to walk this precious green earth. I would like to recognize the pain because it gave me growth for structure and understanding. I would never be able to appreciate joy without knowing pain.

I want to thank my granddaddy, Mr. Lee for being the spark that created this thought to write a book about myself. I don't know much about him, but I plan on building a better bond while the good Lord has still blessed him to be alive at the age of 70 plus years old.

The thought of my children or grandchildren not knowing anything about me was enough motivation to leave my legacy behind. If I'm not able to be around in the physical form, the connection could still be made through my words. Think about how many people are in our lives and mean something to us and we really know nothing about them.

I want to thank my beautiful wife, Kayla, for all her support during this process as well as balancing my life and showing me something I never knew existed or that I could have. A strong Black Nubian Queen who's an amazing mother to our children and what I would say, is the definition of perfection as a person.

To my mother, Sherry, I respect you, love you, and I'm grateful for everything you have done through the journey of an innocent boy in your eyes to the development of the man I've become. There's no manual on how to be a parent, and I know you did the best you could do with Jared and I. From the bottom of my heart, I want to say thank you. Thank you for loving me, thank you for disciplining me, thank you for working late nights so we could have shelter and food, thank you for always telling me to speak my mind, thank you for nourishing me when I was sick, thank you for being my mother and my father, simply, just thank you.

TRUTH OF A LOST SOUL

If I consider you as my friend, then I consider you as my family, and if I consider you my family, then you're a valuable piece that is a part of my life. I need you, and you know who you are, thank you.

Stay Connected

The author, Matthew Sanders, would love to connect with you and help you find your truth. Reach out and share your story.

On the web: www.matthewlsanders.com

On Facebook: www.facebook.com/lostsoul805

Instagram @truthofalostsoul

Twitter @matthews_truth

Contact #: (567) 242-8055

Made in the USA
Monee, IL
27 December 2021